BLACK COTTON

CREATED BY / STORY BY:
Patrick D. Foreman & Brian Hawkins

ART:
Marco Perugini

LETTERS:
Francisco Zamora

EDITING:
Erica Shultz

COVER/CREDITS ART:
Marcelo Henrique Santana

GRAPHIC DESIGN:
Jerpa Nilsson

LOGO DESIGN:
Brant Fowler

SCOUT EDITOR:
Andrea Lorenzo Molinari

PRODUCTION:
Marcus Guillory

Brendan Deneen, CEO
James Haick III, President
Tennessee Edwards, CSO
Don Handfield, CMO

James Pruett, CCO
David Byrne, Co-Publisher
Charlie Stickney, Co-Publisher
Nate Johnson, Head of Design

@SCOUTCOMICS

LEARN MORE AT:
WWW.SCOUTCOMICS.COM

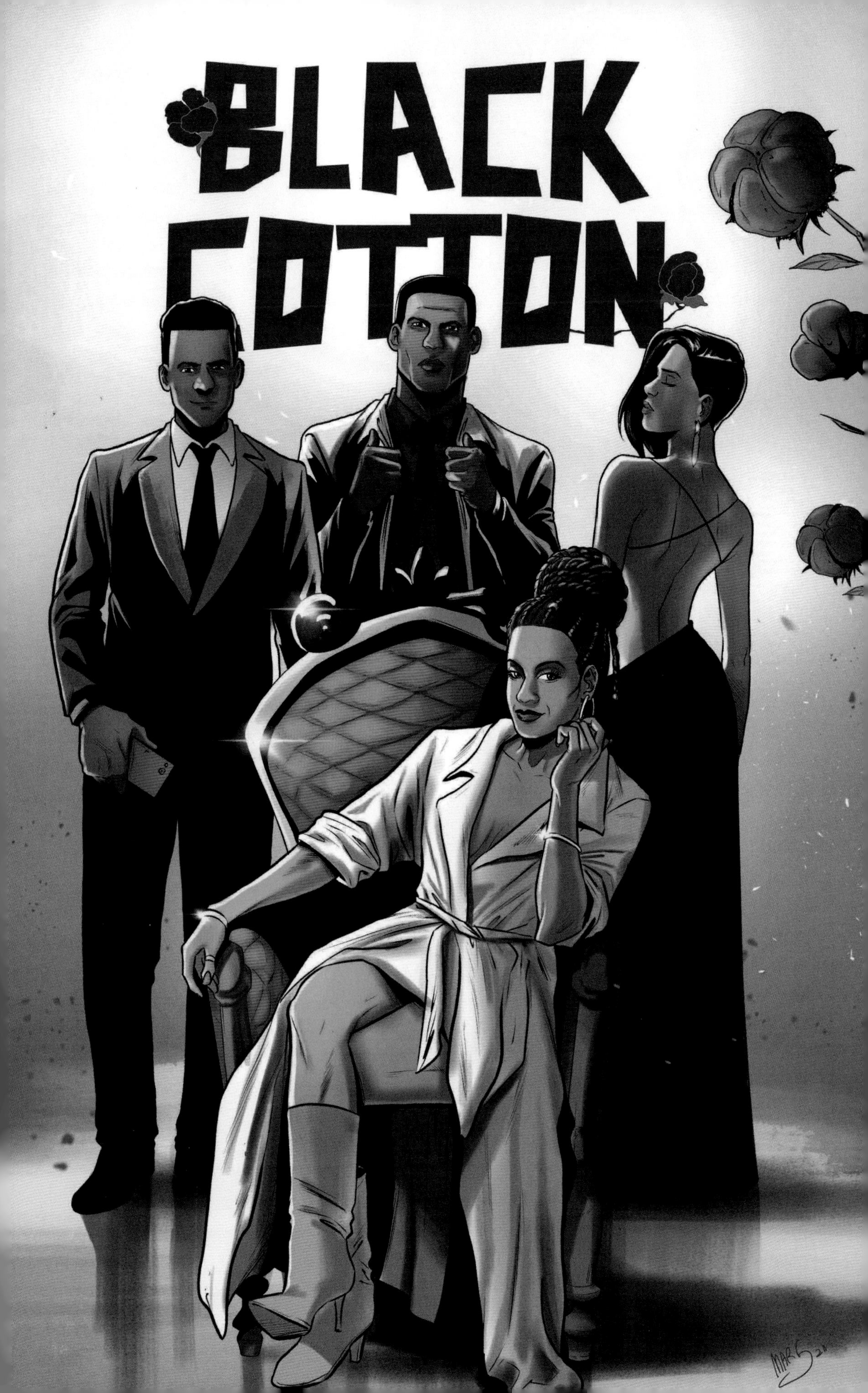
BLACK
COTTON

CHAPTER
1

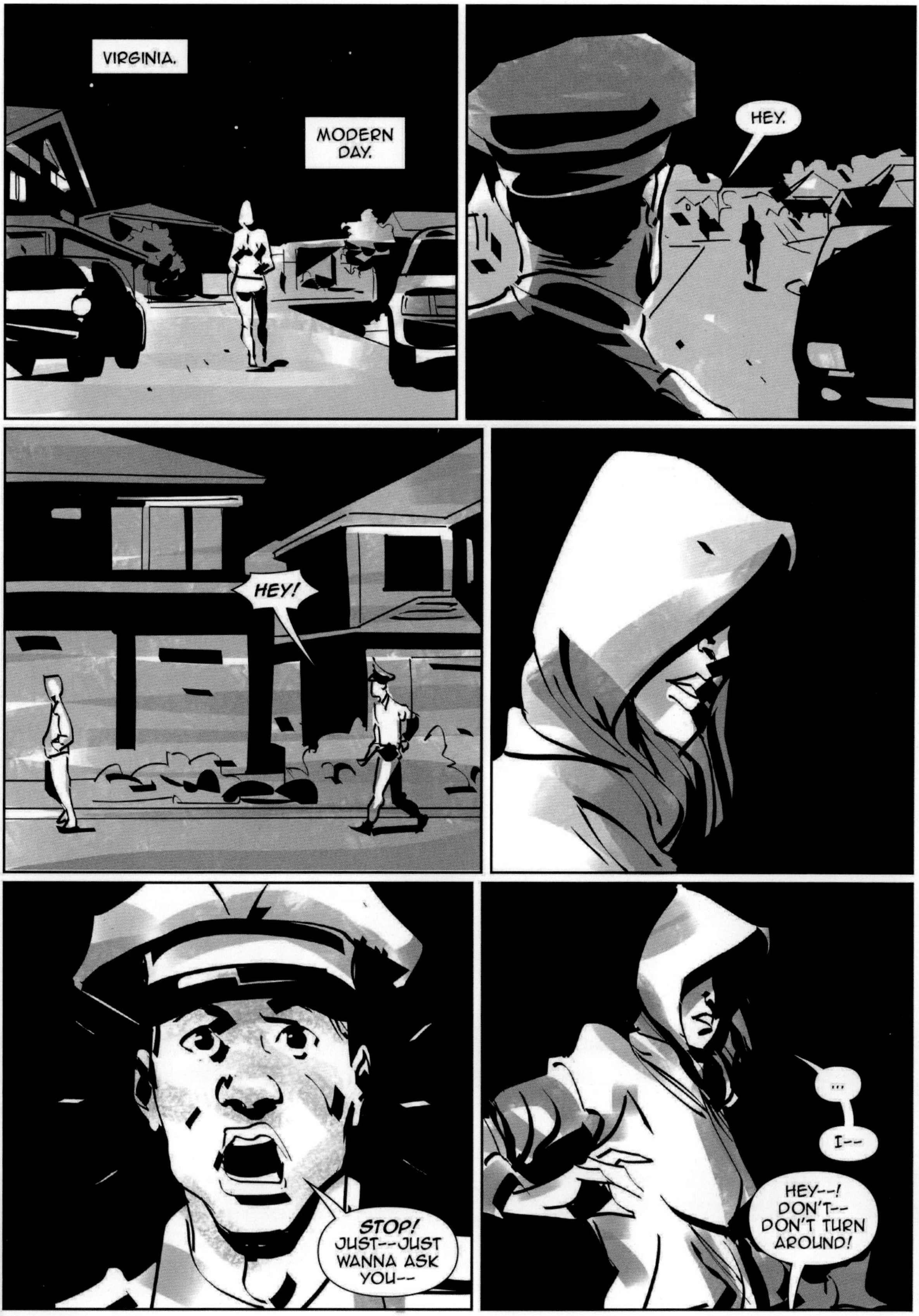
VIRGINIA.
MODERN DAY.
HEY.
HEY!
STOP! JUST--JUST WANNA ASK YOU--
...
I--
HEY--! DON'T-- DON'T TURN AROUND!

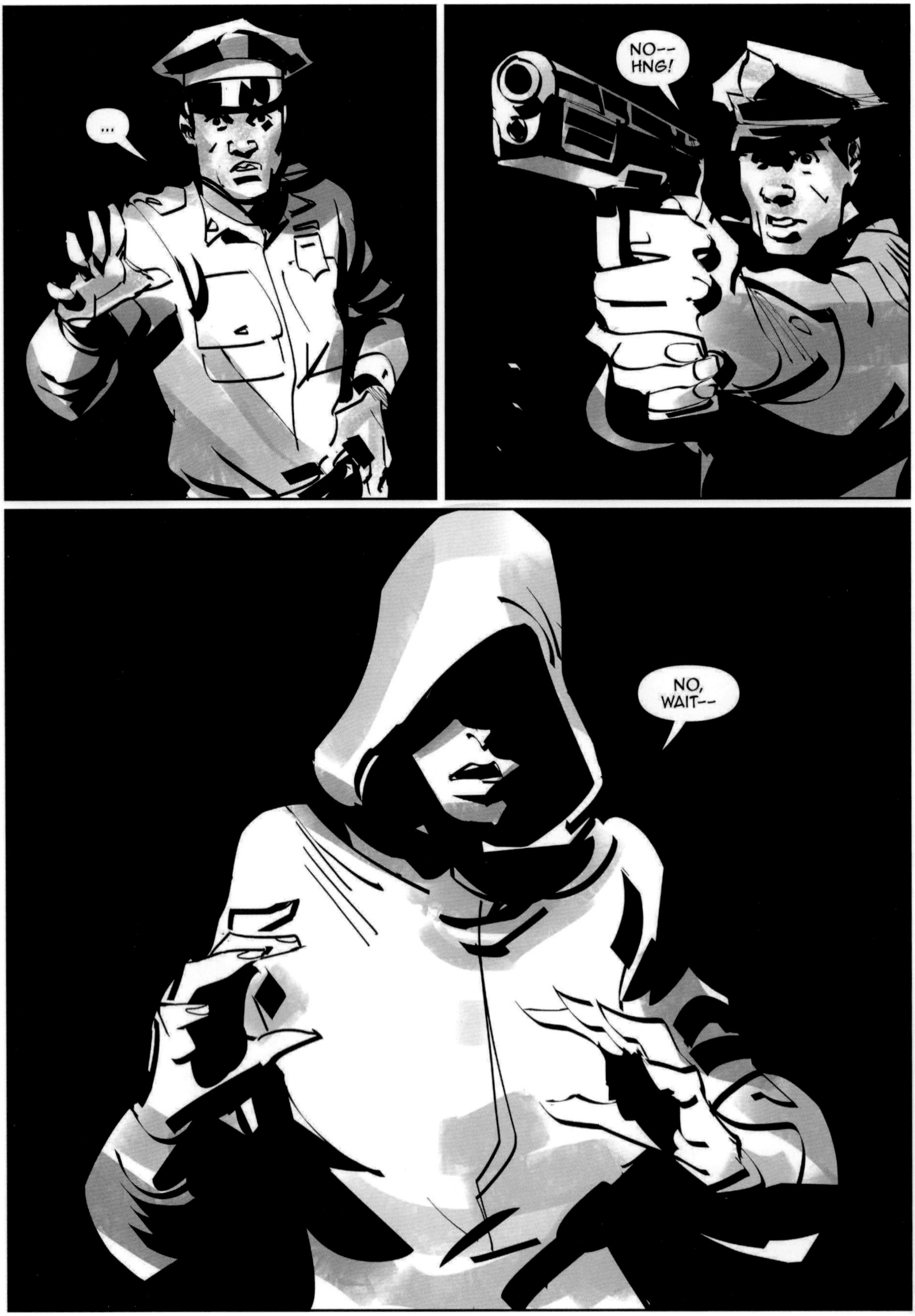
...
NO-- HNG!
NO, WAIT--

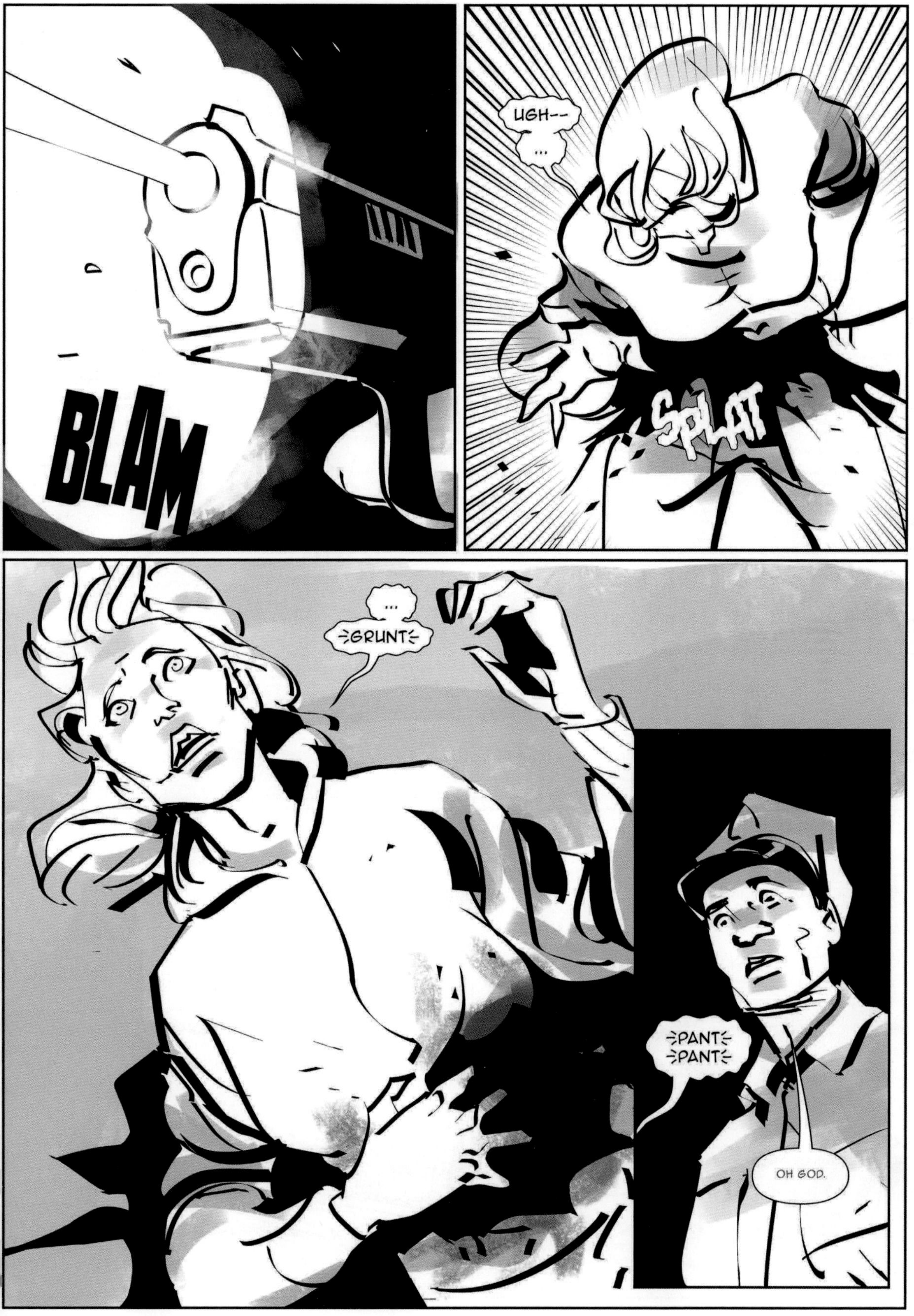
BLAM
UGH--
...
SPLAT
...
GRUNT
PANT
PANT
OH GOD.

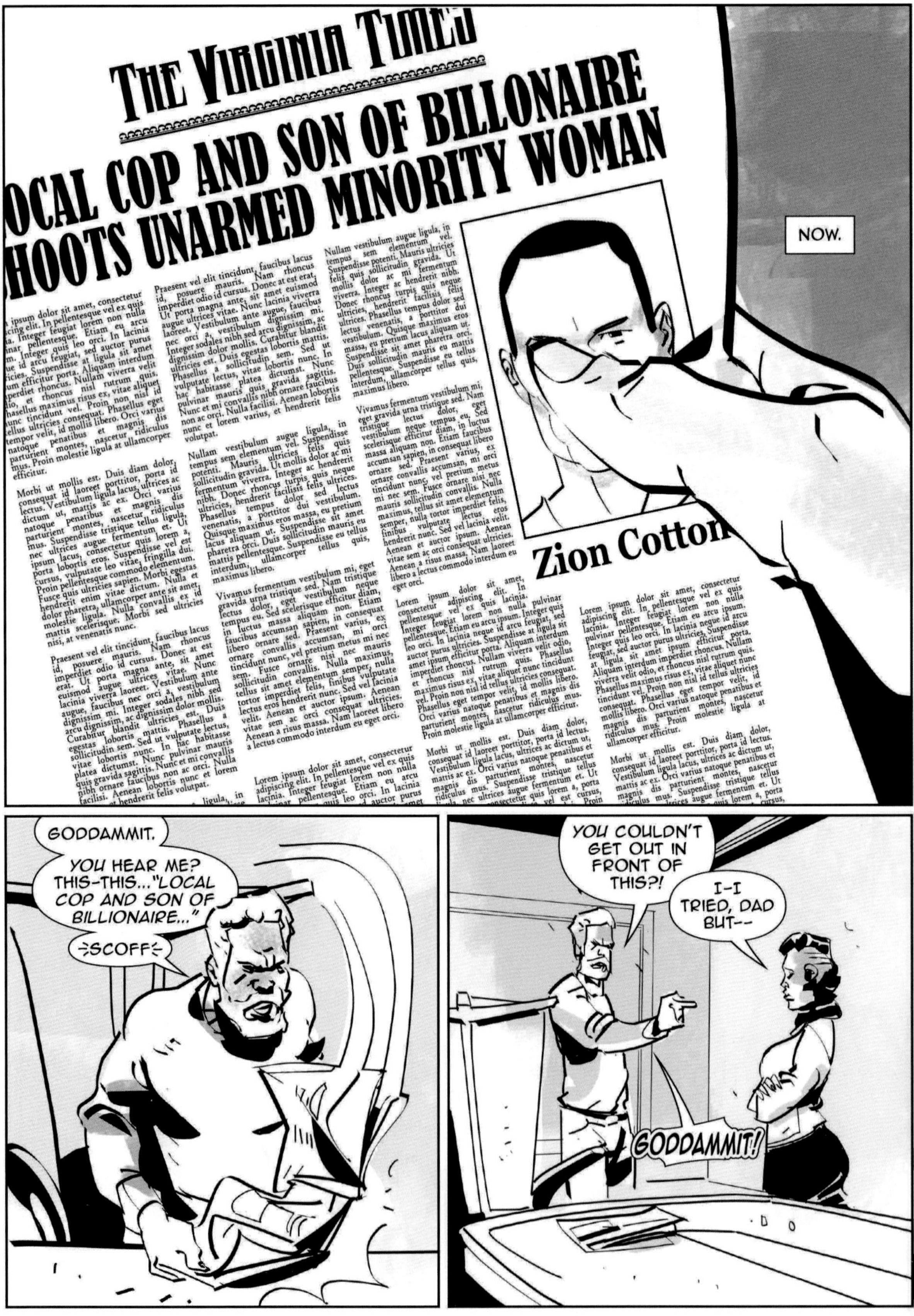
THE VIRGINIA TIMES
OCAL COP AND SON OF BILLONAIRE
HOOTS UNARMED MINORITY WOMAN
Zion Cotton
NOW.
GODDAMMIT.
YOU HEAR ME? THIS-THIS..."LOCAL COP AND SON OF BILLIONAIRE..."
SCOFF
YOU COULDN'T GET OUT IN FRONT OF THIS?!
I-I TRIED, DAD BUT--
GODDAMMIT!

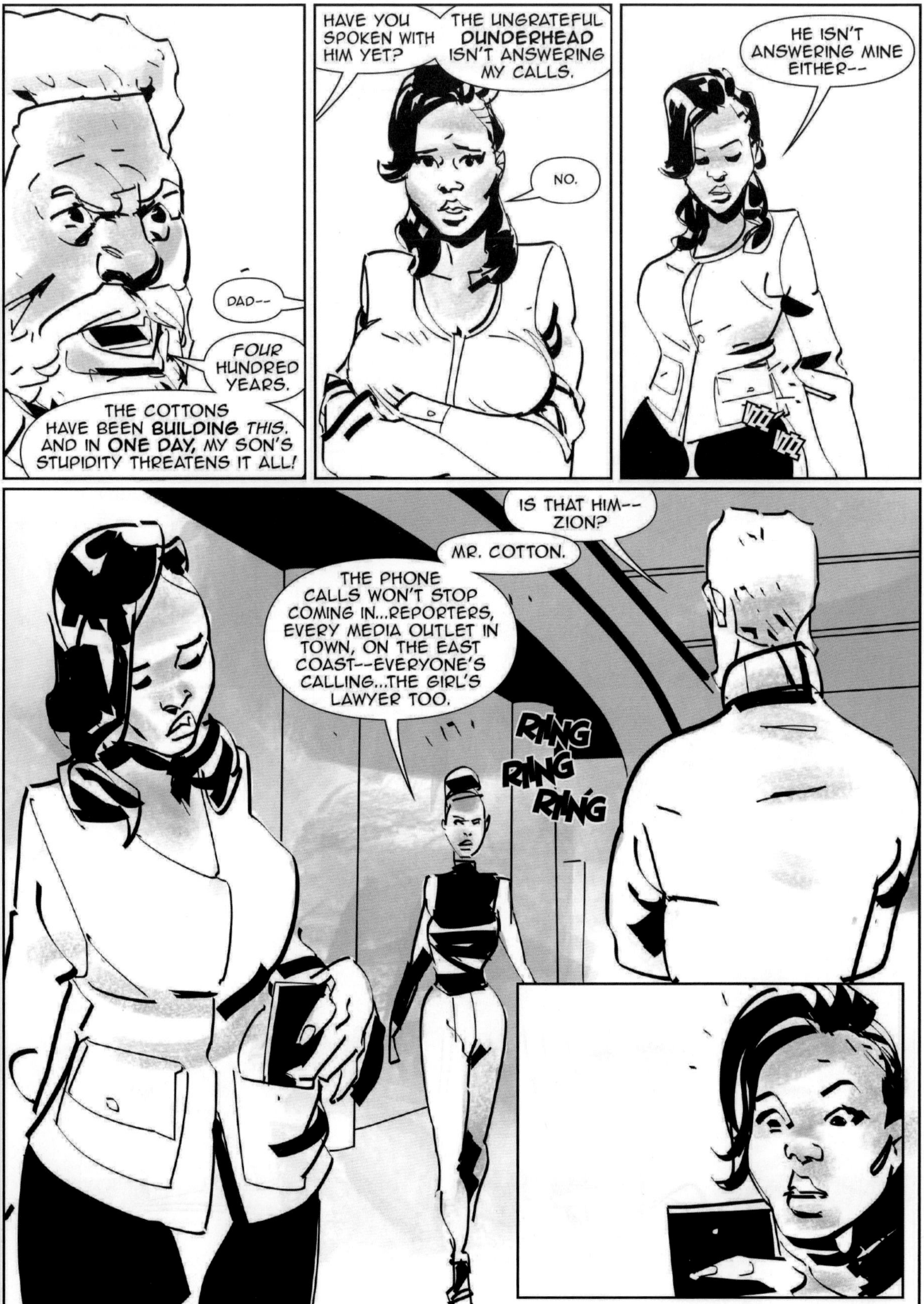
DAD--
FOUR HUNDRED YEARS.
THE COTTONS HAVE BEEN **BUILDING** *THIS*. AND IN **ONE DAY,** MY SON'S STUPIDITY THREATENS IT ALL!
HAVE YOU SPOKEN WITH HIM YET?
THE UNGRATEFUL **DUNDERHEAD** ISN'T ANSWERING MY CALLS.
NO.
HE ISN'T ANSWERING MINE EITHER--
IS THAT HIM-- ZION?
MR. COTTON.
THE PHONE CALLS WON'T STOP COMING IN...REPORTERS, EVERY MEDIA OUTLET IN TOWN, ON THE EAST COAST--EVERYONE'S CALLING...THE GIRL'S LAWYER TOO.
RING RING RING

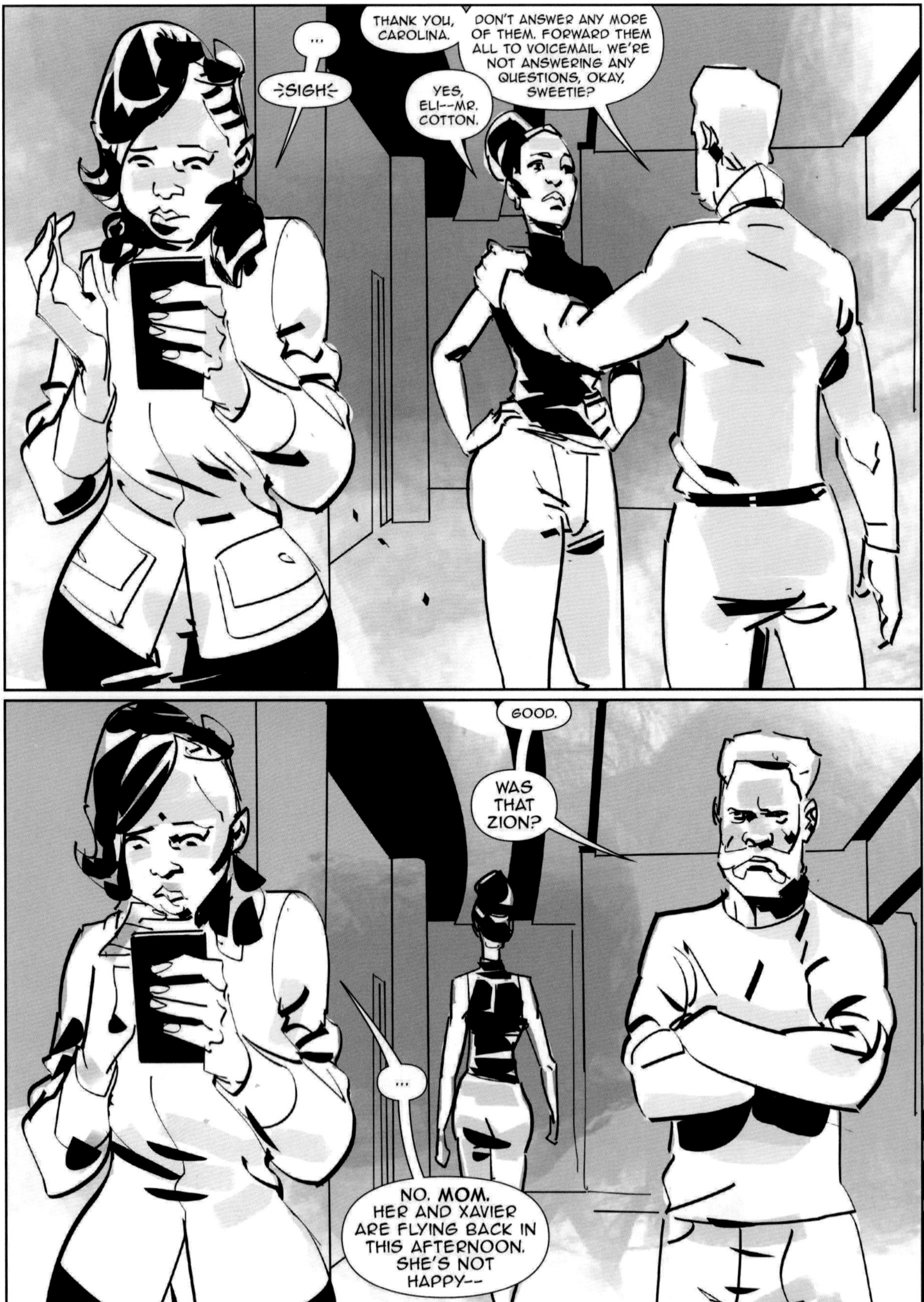
...
-SIGH-
THANK YOU, CAROLINA.
DON'T ANSWER ANY MORE OF THEM. FORWARD THEM ALL TO VOICEMAIL. WE'RE NOT ANSWERING ANY QUESTIONS, OKAY, SWEETIE?
YES, ELI--MR. COTTON.
GOOD.
WAS THAT ZION?
...
NO. MOM. HER AND XAVIER ARE FLYING BACK IN THIS AFTERNOON. SHE'S NOT HAPPY--

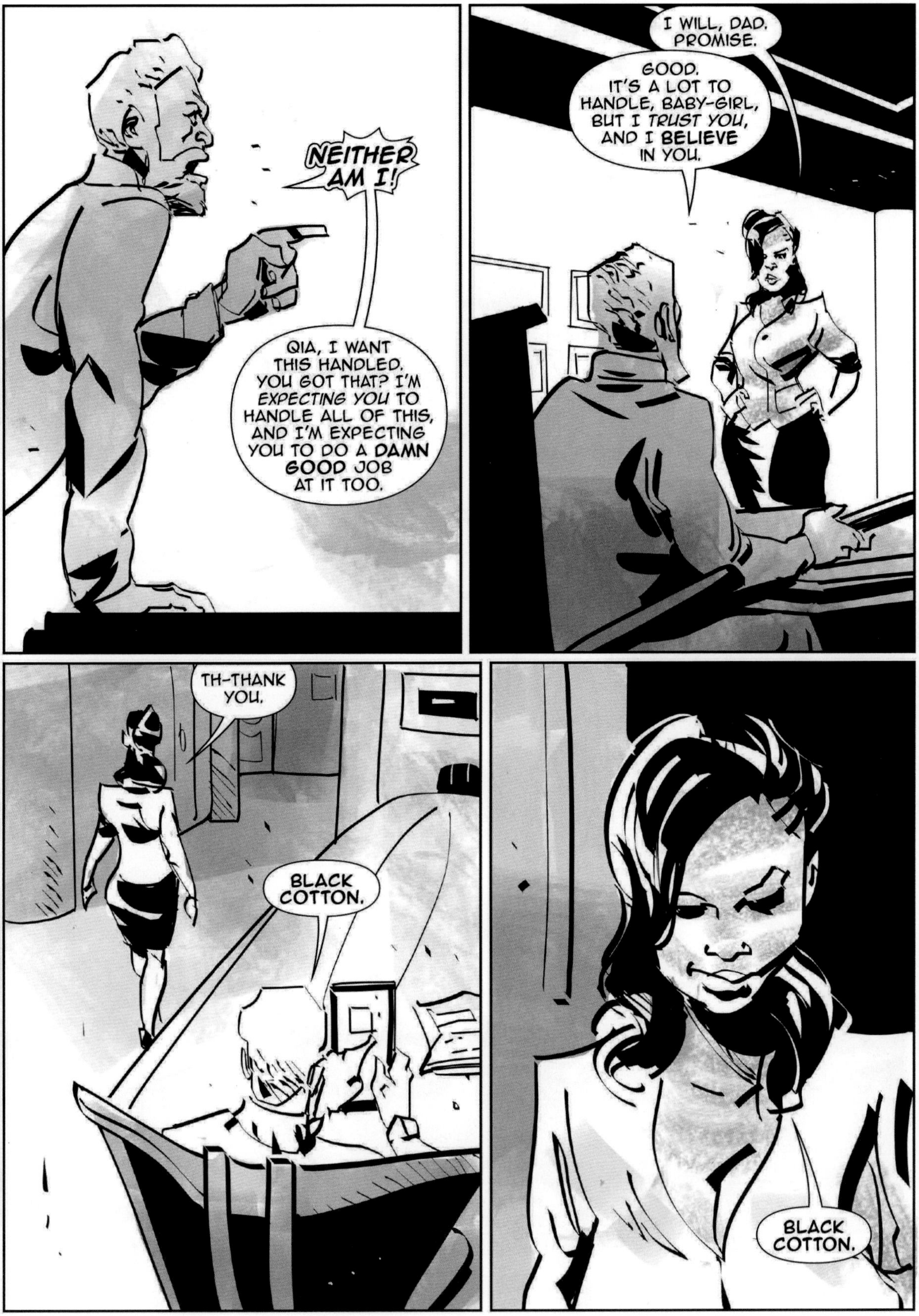
NEITHER AM I!
QIA, I WANT THIS HANDLED. YOU GOT THAT? I'M *EXPECTING YOU* TO HANDLE ALL OF THIS, AND I'M EXPECTING YOU TO DO A **DAMN GOOD** JOB AT IT TOO.
I WILL, DAD. PROMISE.
GOOD. IT'S A LOT TO HANDLE, BABY-GIRL, BUT I *TRUST YOU*, AND I **BELIEVE** IN YOU.
TH-THANK YOU.
BLACK COTTON.
BLACK COTTON.

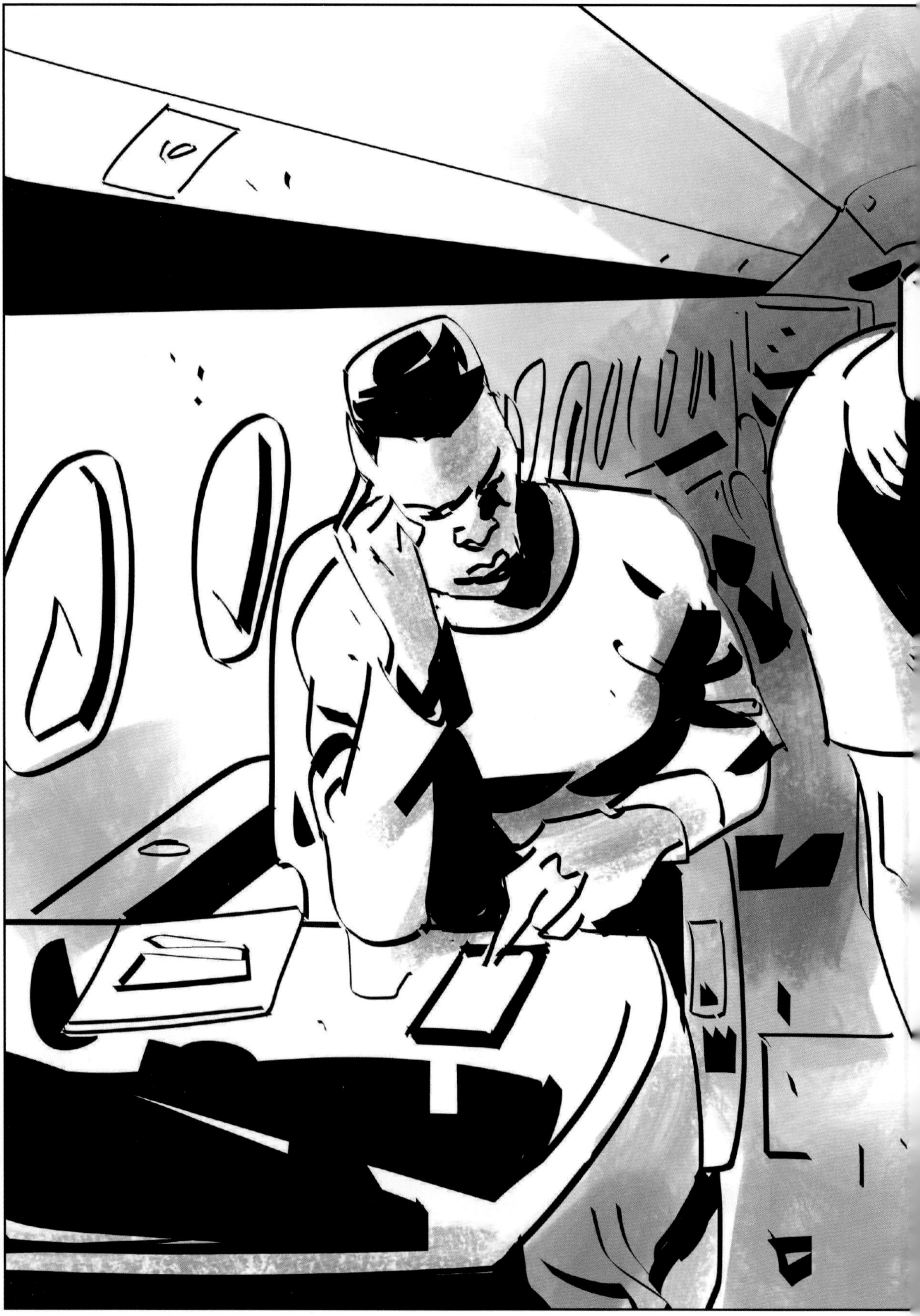

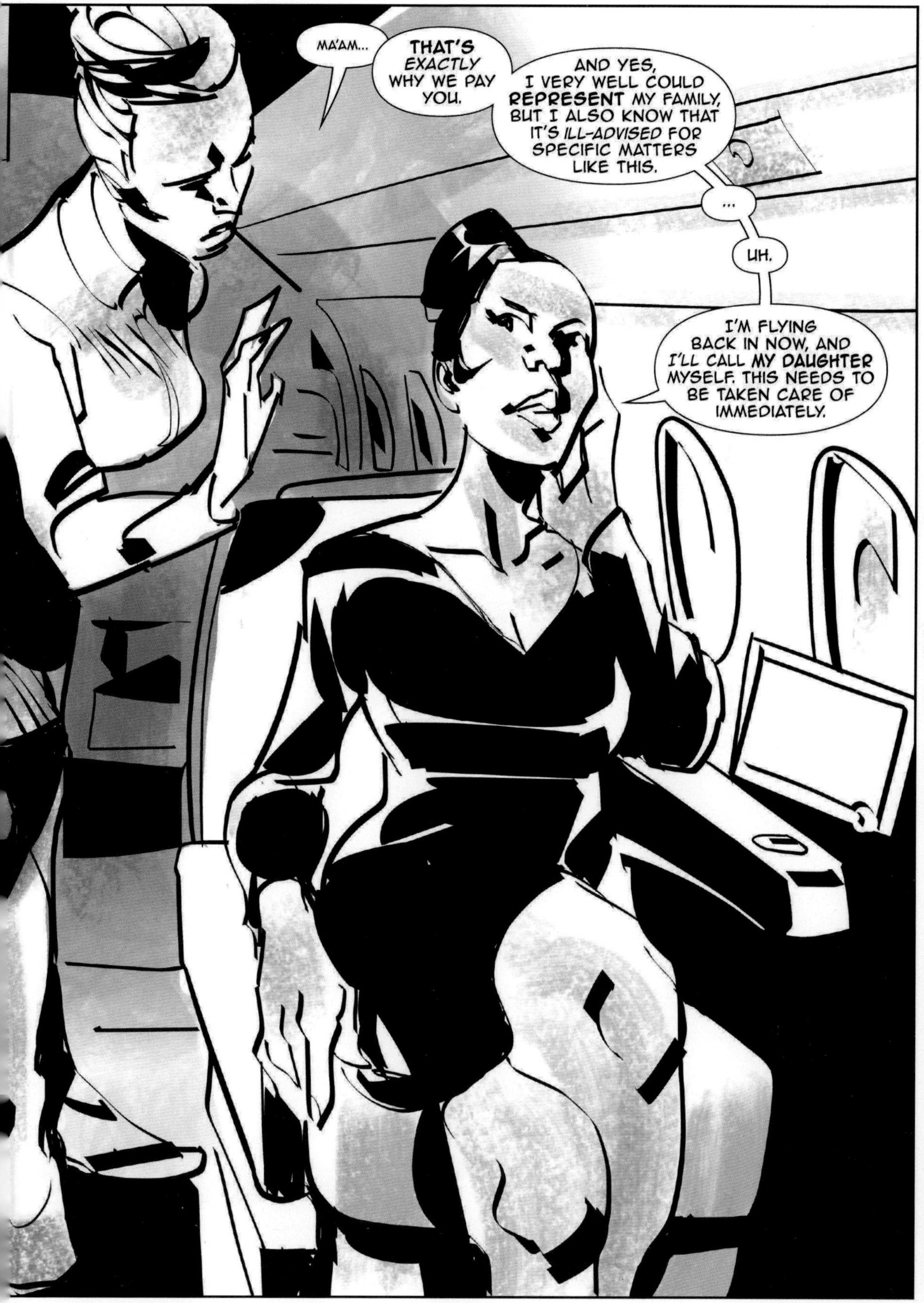
MA'AM...
THAT'S EXACTLY WHY WE PAY YOU.
AND YES, I VERY WELL COULD REPRESENT MY FAMILY, BUT I ALSO KNOW THAT IT'S ILL-ADVISED FOR SPECIFIC MATTERS LIKE THIS.
...
UH.
I'M FLYING BACK IN NOW, AND I'LL CALL MY DAUGHTER MYSELF. THIS NEEDS TO BE TAKEN CARE OF IMMEDIATELY.

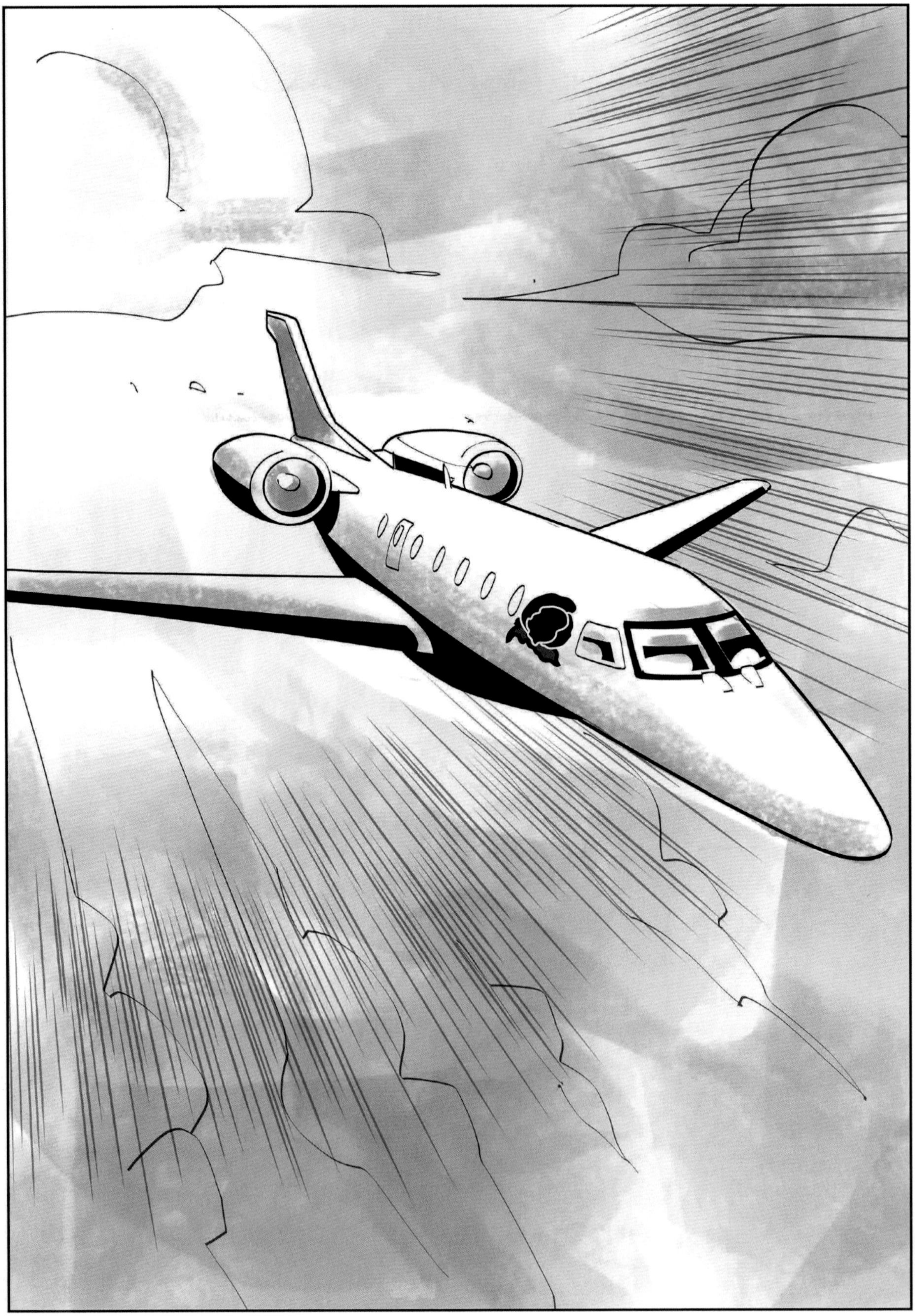

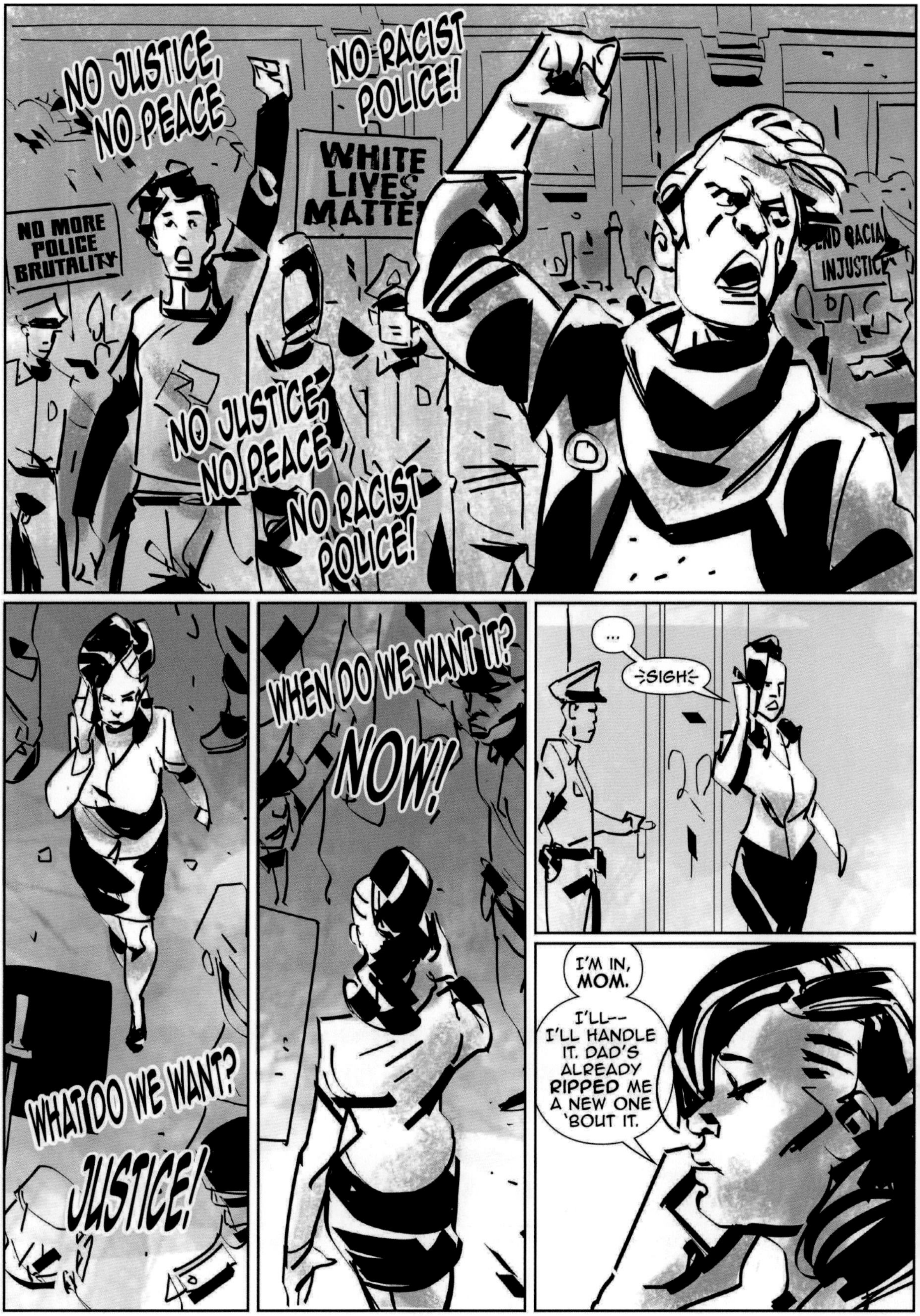
NO JUSTICE, NO PEACE
NO RACIST POLICE!
WHITE LIVES MATTE
NO MORE POLICE BRUTALITY
END RACIA INJUSTICE
NO JUSTICE, NO PEACE
NO RACIST POLICE!
WHAT DO WE WANT?
JUSTICE!
WHEN DO WE WANT IT?
NOW!
...
SIGH
I'M IN, MOM.
I'LL-- I'LL HANDLE IT. DAD'S ALREADY RIPPED ME A NEW ONE 'BOUT IT.

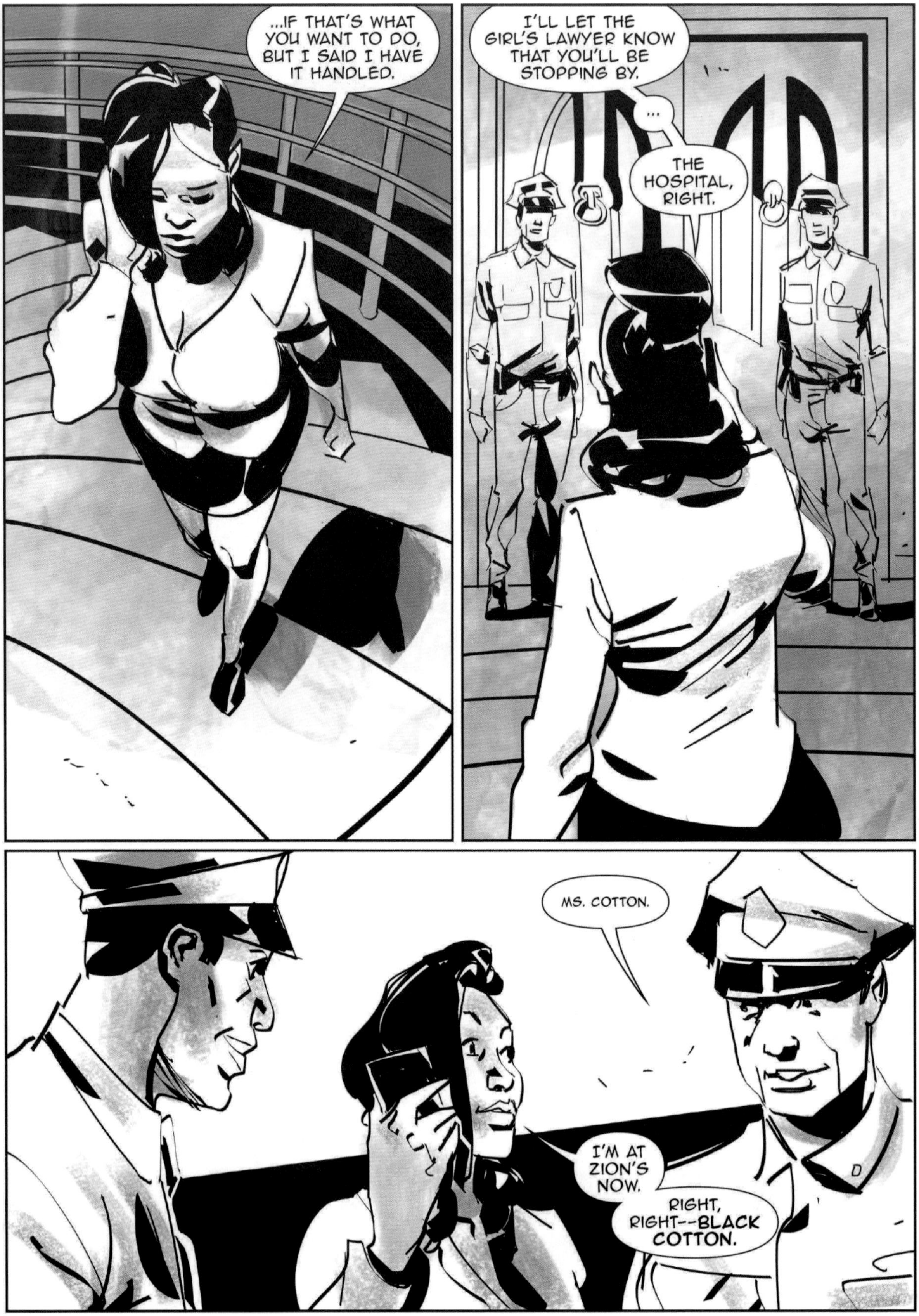

...IF THAT'S WHAT YOU WANT TO DO, BUT I SAID I HAVE IT HANDLED.
I'LL LET THE GIRL'S LAWYER KNOW THAT YOU'LL BE STOPPING BY.
...
THE HOSPITAL, RIGHT.
MS. COTTON.
I'M AT ZION'S NOW.
RIGHT, RIGHT--BLACK COTTON.

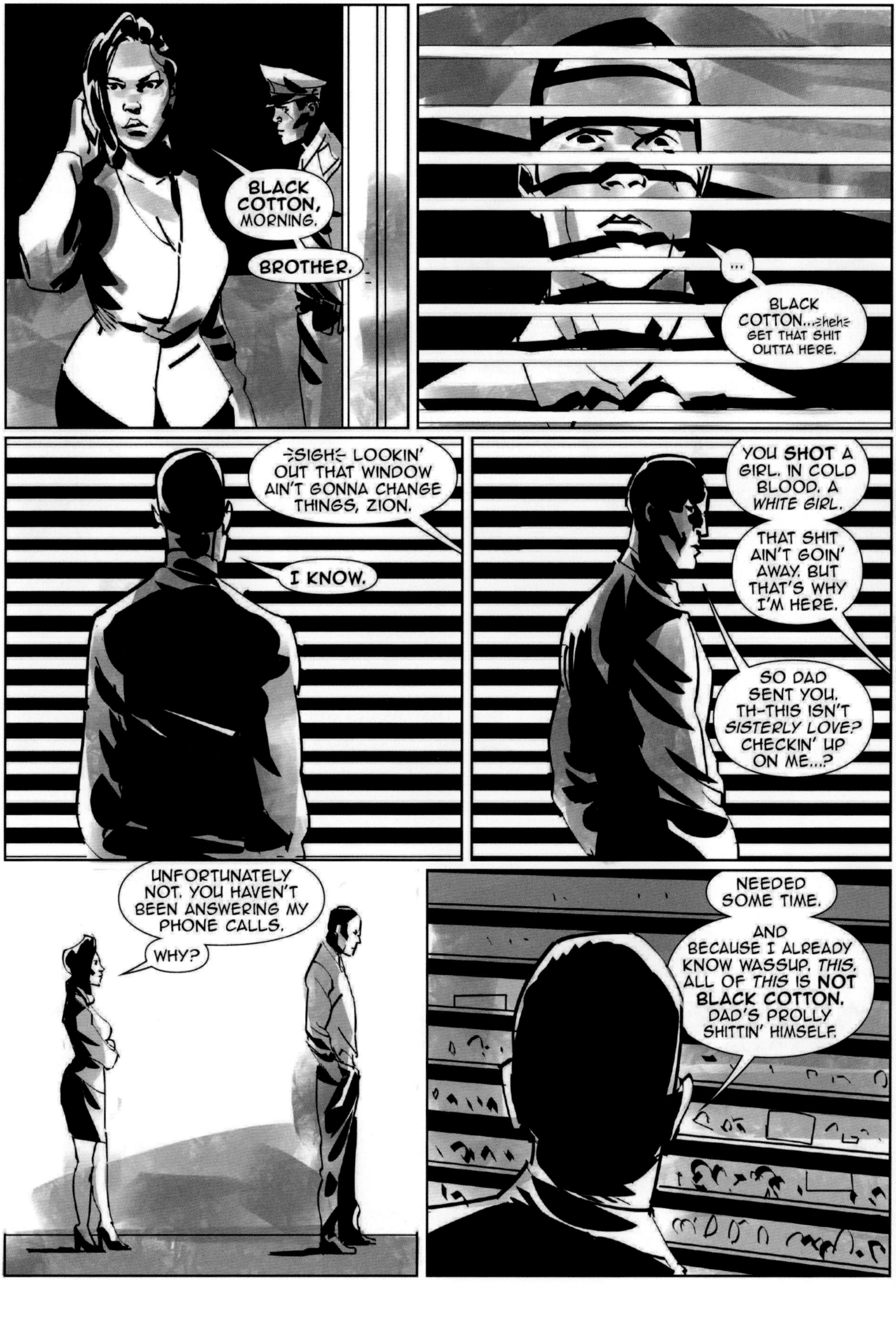
BLACK COTTON, MORNING.
BROTHER.
...
BLACK COTTON... =heh= GET THAT SHIT OUTTA HERE.
=SIGH= LOOKIN' OUT THAT WINDOW AIN'T GONNA CHANGE THINGS, ZION.
I KNOW.
YOU SHOT A GIRL. IN COLD BLOOD. A WHITE GIRL.
THAT SHIT AIN'T GOIN' AWAY. BUT THAT'S WHY I'M HERE.
SO DAD SENT YOU. TH-THIS ISN'T SISTERLY LOVE? CHECKIN' UP ON ME...?
UNFORTUNATELY NOT. YOU HAVEN'T BEEN ANSWERING MY PHONE CALLS.
WHY?
NEEDED SOME TIME.
AND BECAUSE I ALREADY KNOW WASSUP. THIS. ALL OF THIS IS NOT BLACK COTTON. DAD'S PROLLY SHITTIN' HIMSELF.

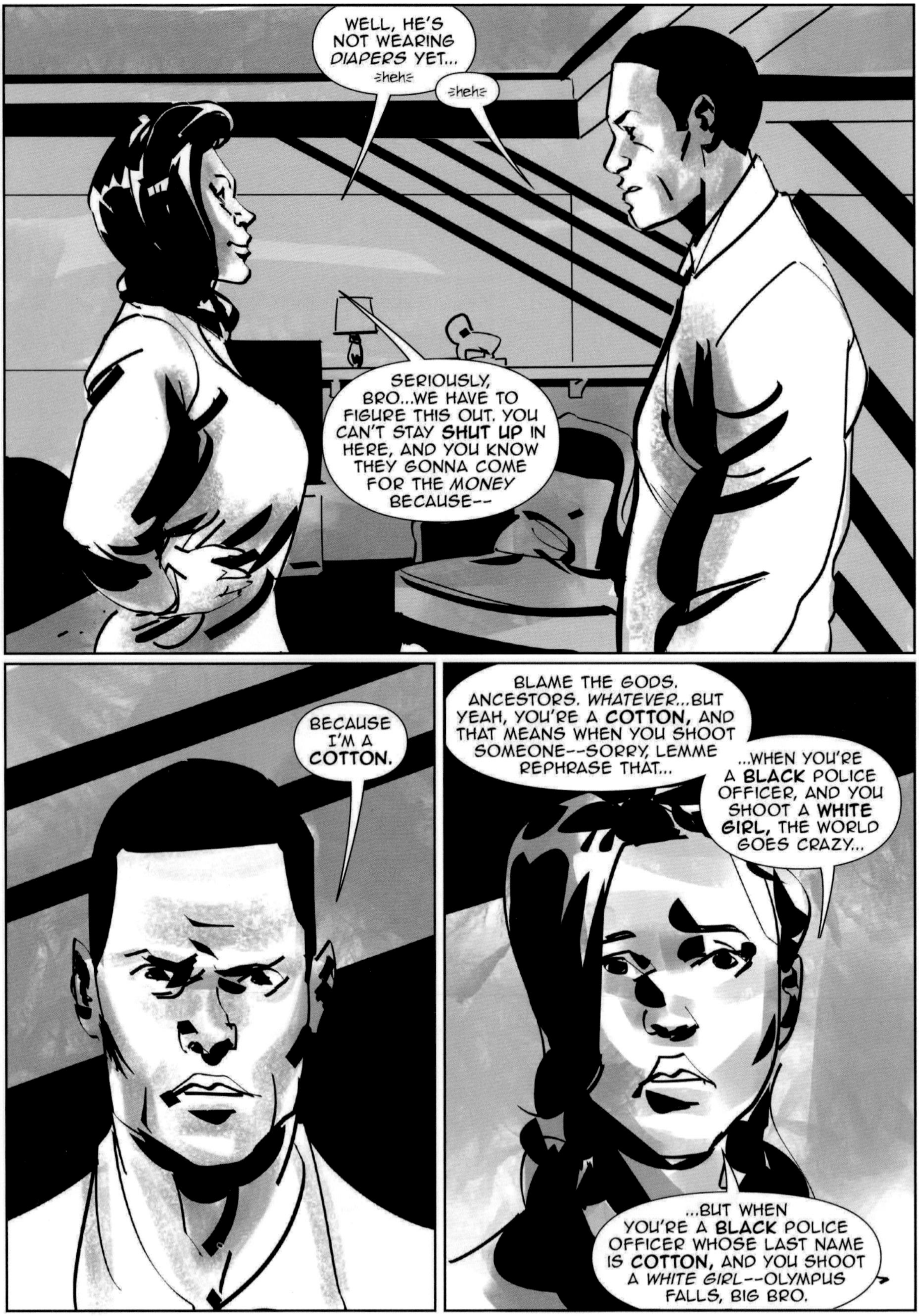
WELL, HE'S NOT WEARING DIAPERS YET...
heh
heh
SERIOUSLY, BRO...WE HAVE TO FIGURE THIS OUT. YOU CAN'T STAY SHUT UP IN HERE, AND YOU KNOW THEY GONNA COME FOR THE MONEY BECAUSE--
BECAUSE I'M A COTTON.
BLAME THE GODS. ANCESTORS. WHATEVER...BUT YEAH, YOU'RE A COTTON, AND THAT MEANS WHEN YOU SHOOT SOMEONE--SORRY, LEMME REPHRASE THAT...
...WHEN YOU'RE A BLACK POLICE OFFICER, AND YOU SHOOT A WHITE GIRL, THE WORLD GOES CRAZY...
...BUT WHEN YOU'RE A BLACK POLICE OFFICER WHOSE LAST NAME IS COTTON, AND YOU SHOOT A WHITE GIRL--OLYMPUS FALLS, BIG BRO.

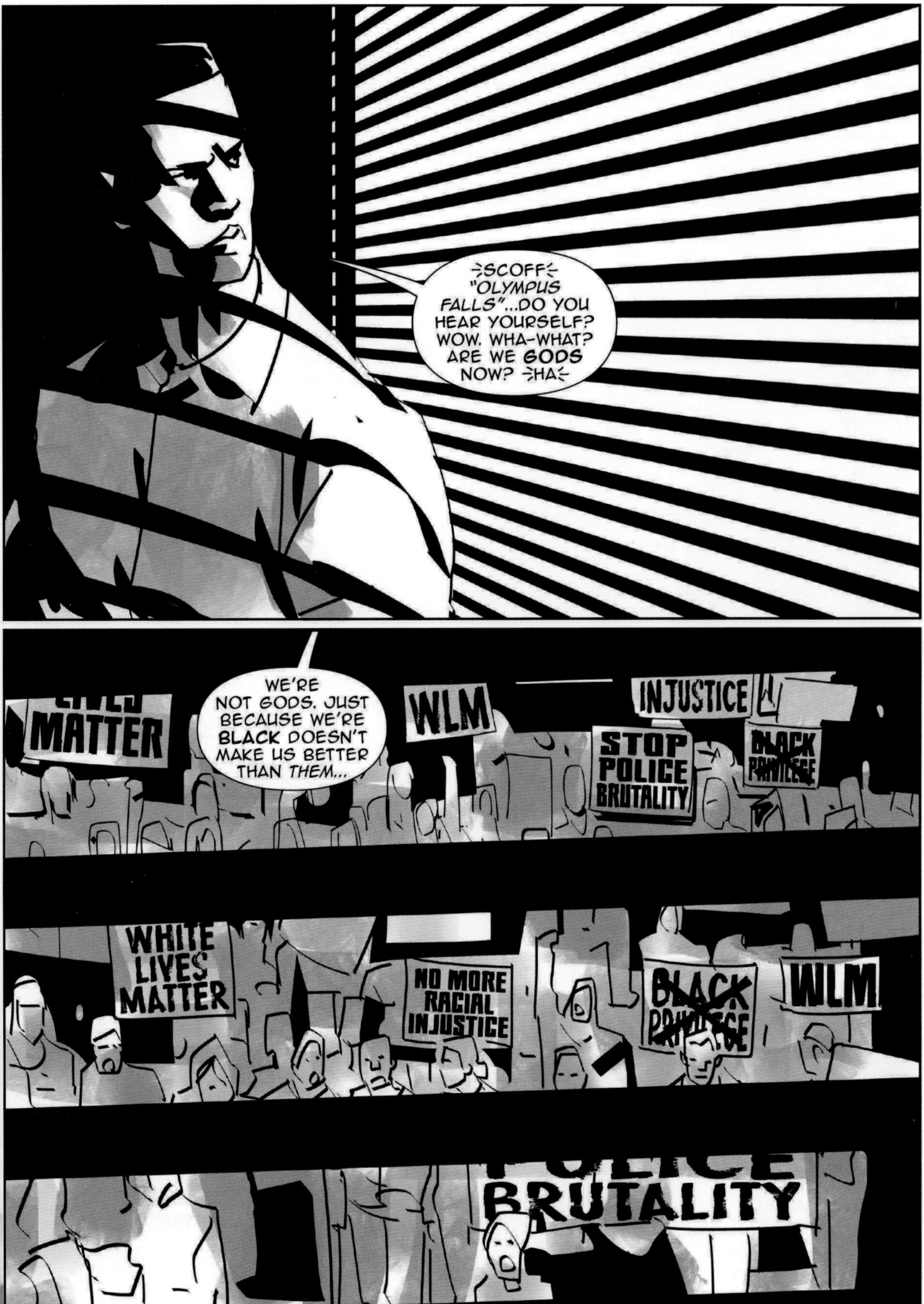

-SCOFF- "OLYMPUS FALLS"...DO YOU HEAR YOURSELF? WOW. WHA-WHAT? ARE WE GODS NOW? -HA-
WE'RE NOT GODS. JUST BECAUSE WE'RE BLACK DOESN'T MAKE US BETTER THAN THEM...
MATTER
WLM
INJUSTICE
STOP POLICE BRUTALITY
WHITE LIVES MATTER
NO MORE RACIAL INJUSTICE
WLM
BRUTALITY

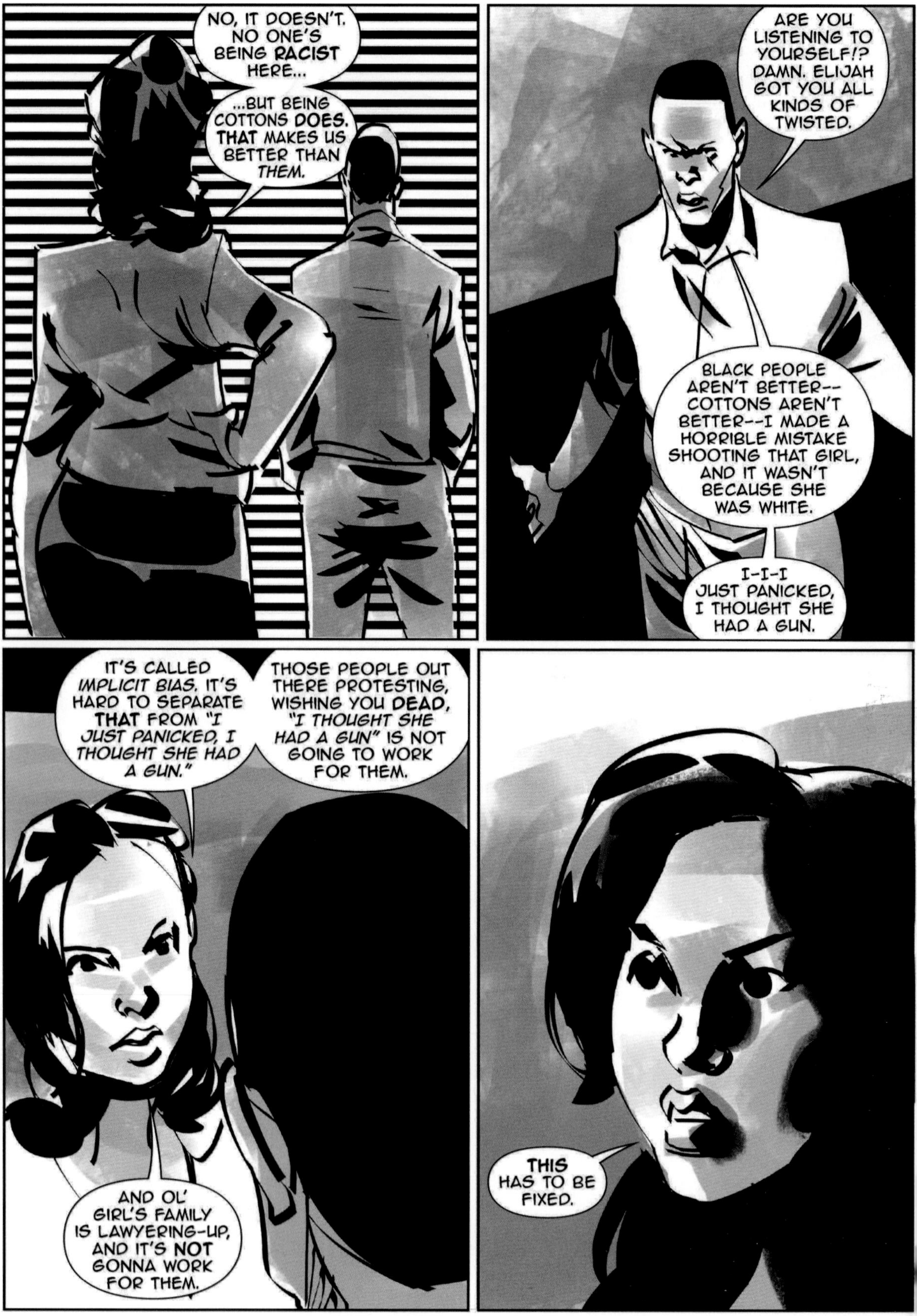
NO, IT DOESN'T. NO ONE'S BEING **RACIST** HERE...
...BUT BEING COTTONS **DOES**. **THAT** MAKES US BETTER THAN *THEM*.
ARE YOU LISTENING TO YOURSELF!? DAMN. ELIJAH GOT YOU ALL KINDS OF TWISTED.
BLACK PEOPLE AREN'T BETTER-- COTTONS AREN'T BETTER--I MADE A HORRIBLE MISTAKE SHOOTING THAT GIRL, AND IT WASN'T BECAUSE SHE WAS WHITE.
I-I-I JUST PANICKED, I THOUGHT SHE HAD A GUN.
IT'S CALLED *IMPLICIT BIAS*. IT'S HARD TO SEPARATE **THAT** FROM *"I JUST PANICKED, I THOUGHT SHE HAD A GUN."*
THOSE PEOPLE OUT THERE PROTESTING, WISHING YOU **DEAD**, *"I THOUGHT SHE HAD A GUN"* IS NOT GOING TO WORK FOR THEM.
AND OL' GIRL'S FAMILY IS LAWYERING-UP, AND IT'S **NOT** GONNA WORK FOR THEM.
THIS HAS TO BE FIXED.

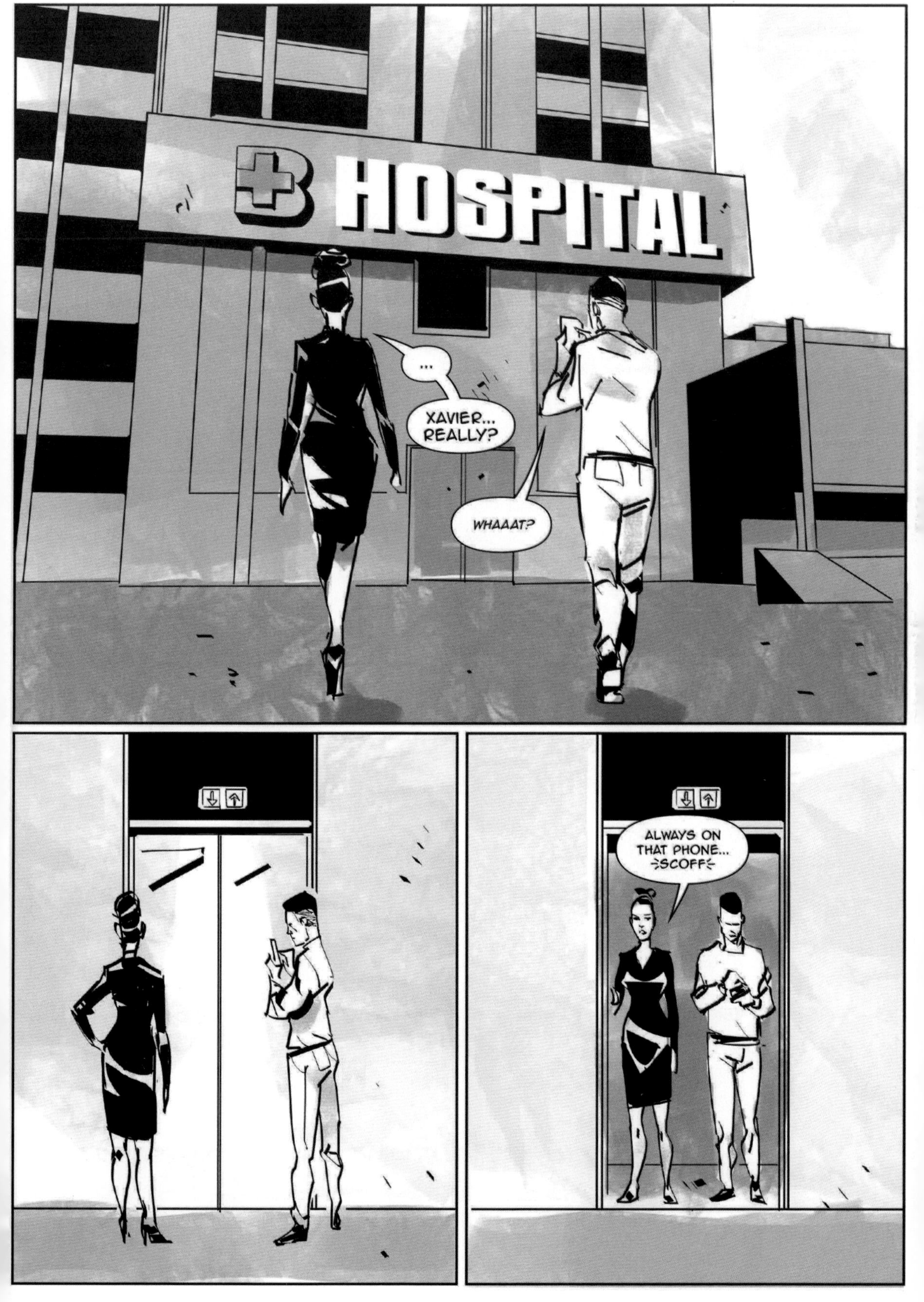
HOSPITAL
...
XAVIER... REALLY?
WHAAAT?
ALWAYS ON THAT PHONE... *SCOFF*

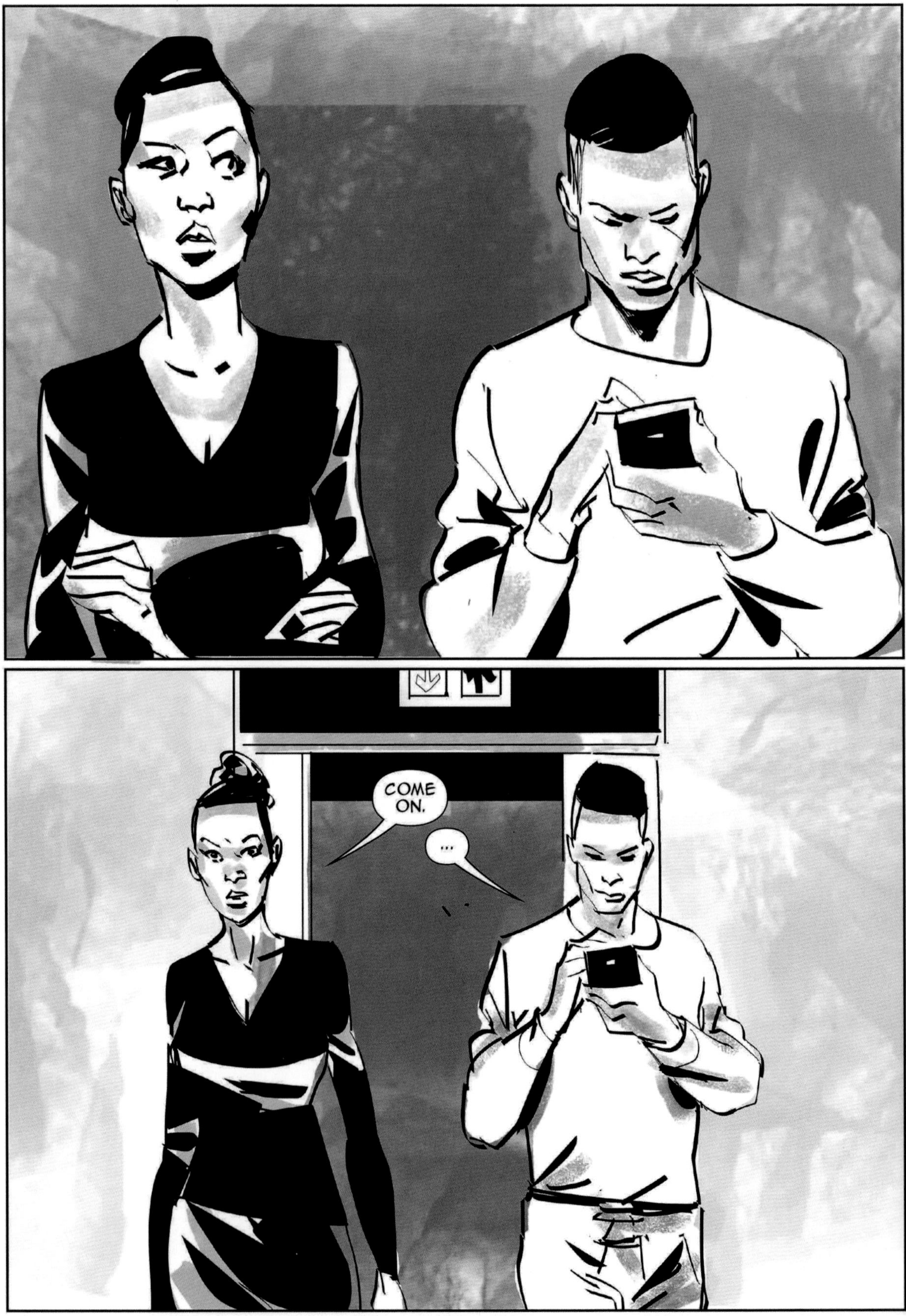
COME ON.
...

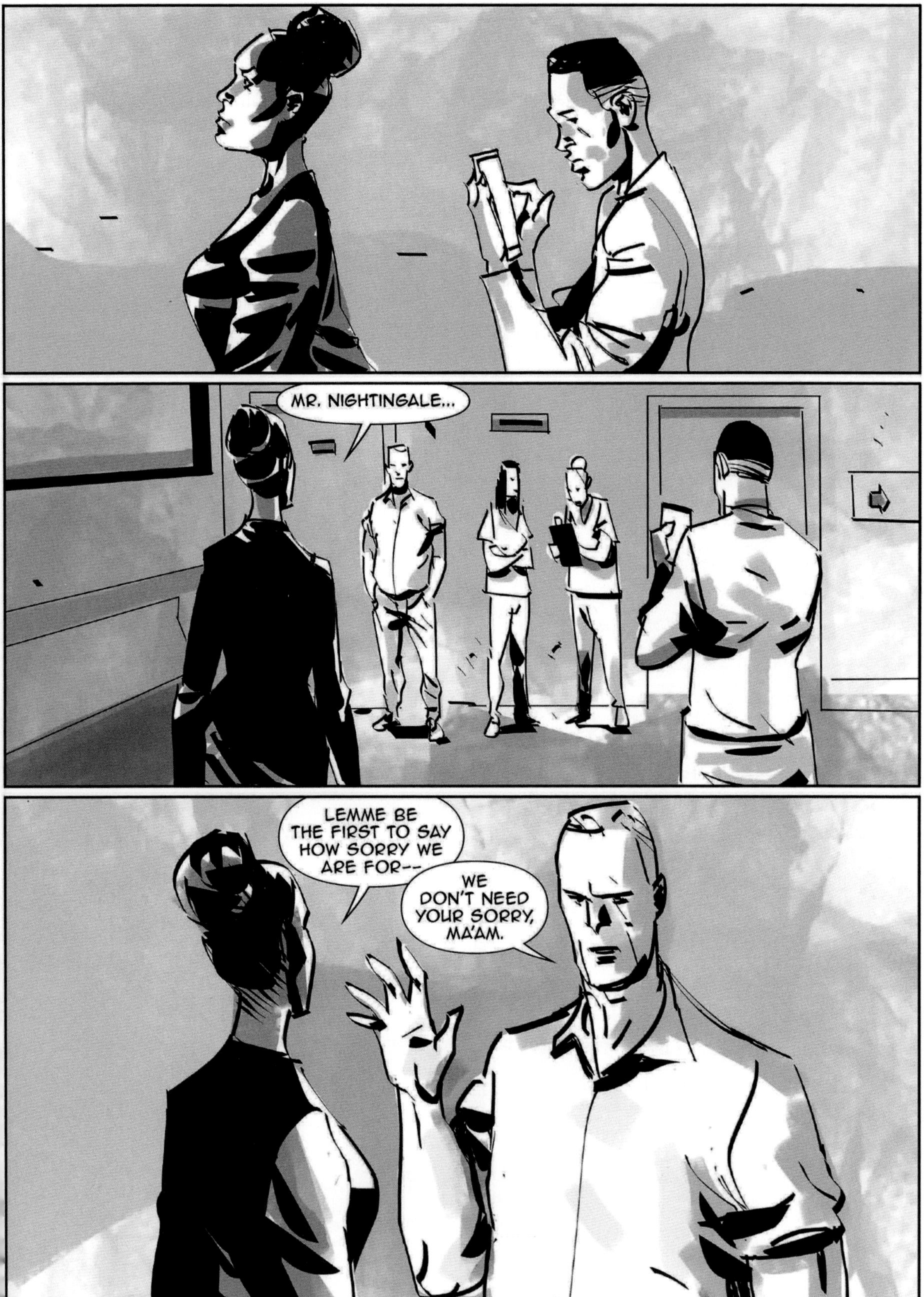
MR. NIGHTINGALE...
LEMME BE THE FIRST TO SAY HOW SORRY WE ARE FOR--
WE DON'T NEED YOUR SORRY, MA'AM.

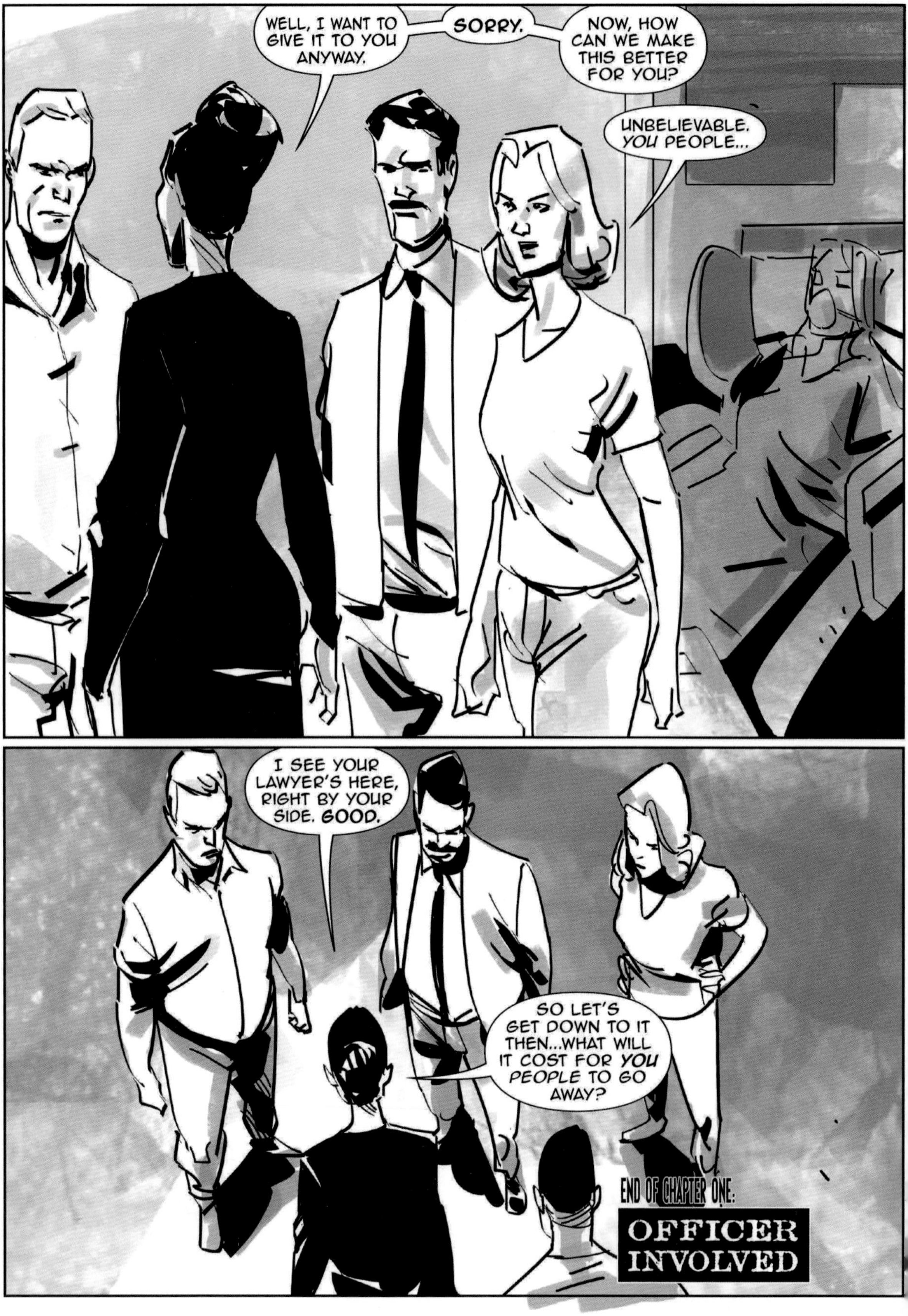
WELL, I WANT TO GIVE IT TO YOU ANYWAY.
SORRY.
NOW, HOW CAN WE MAKE THIS BETTER FOR YOU?
UNBELIEVABLE. YOU PEOPLE...
I SEE YOUR LAWYER'S HERE, RIGHT BY YOUR SIDE. GOOD.
SO LET'S GET DOWN TO IT THEN...WHAT WILL IT COST FOR YOU PEOPLE TO GO AWAY?
END OF CHAPTER ONE:
OFFICER INVOLVED

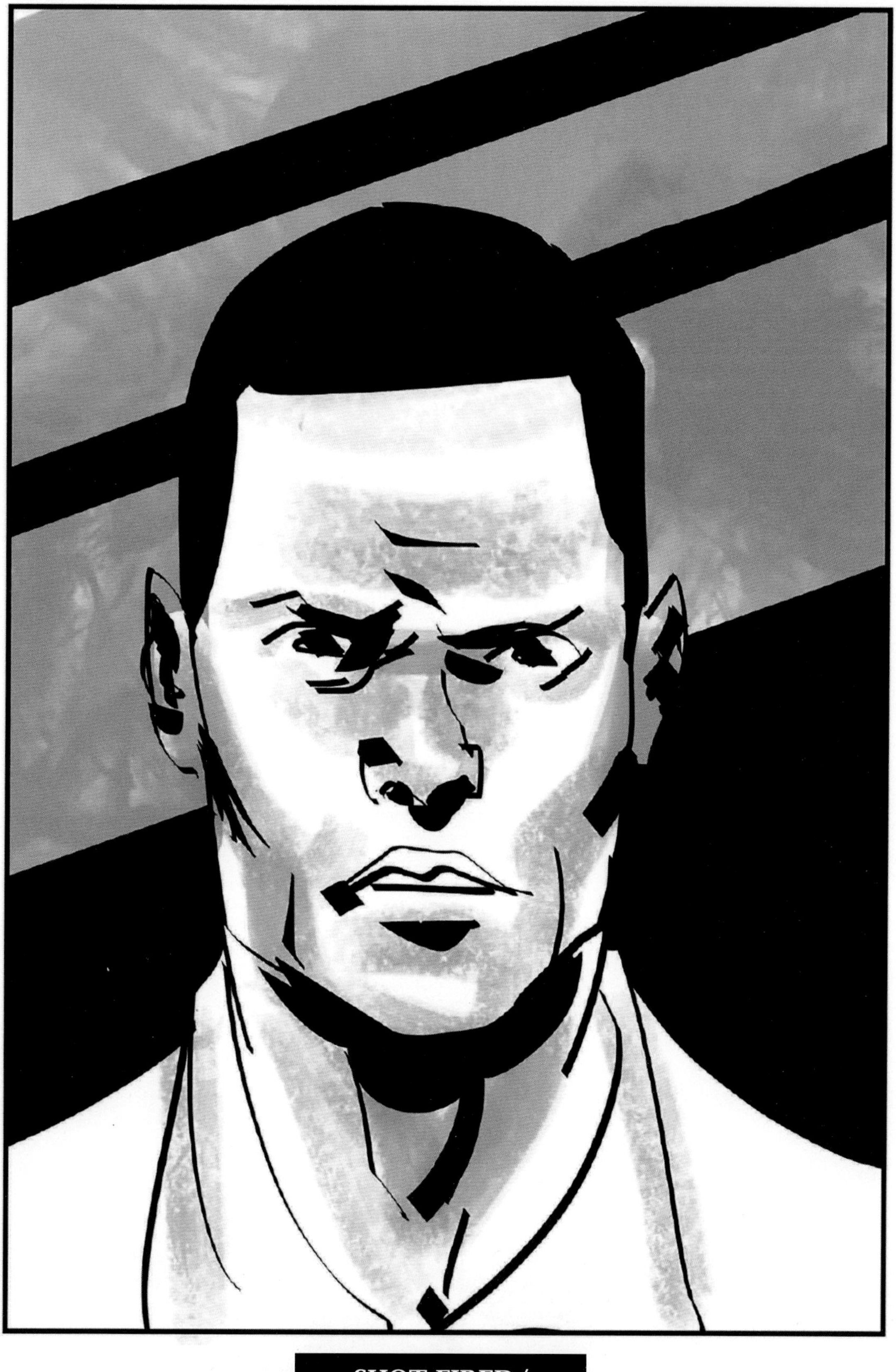

SHOT FIRED/
OFFICER INVOLVED

CHAPTER
2

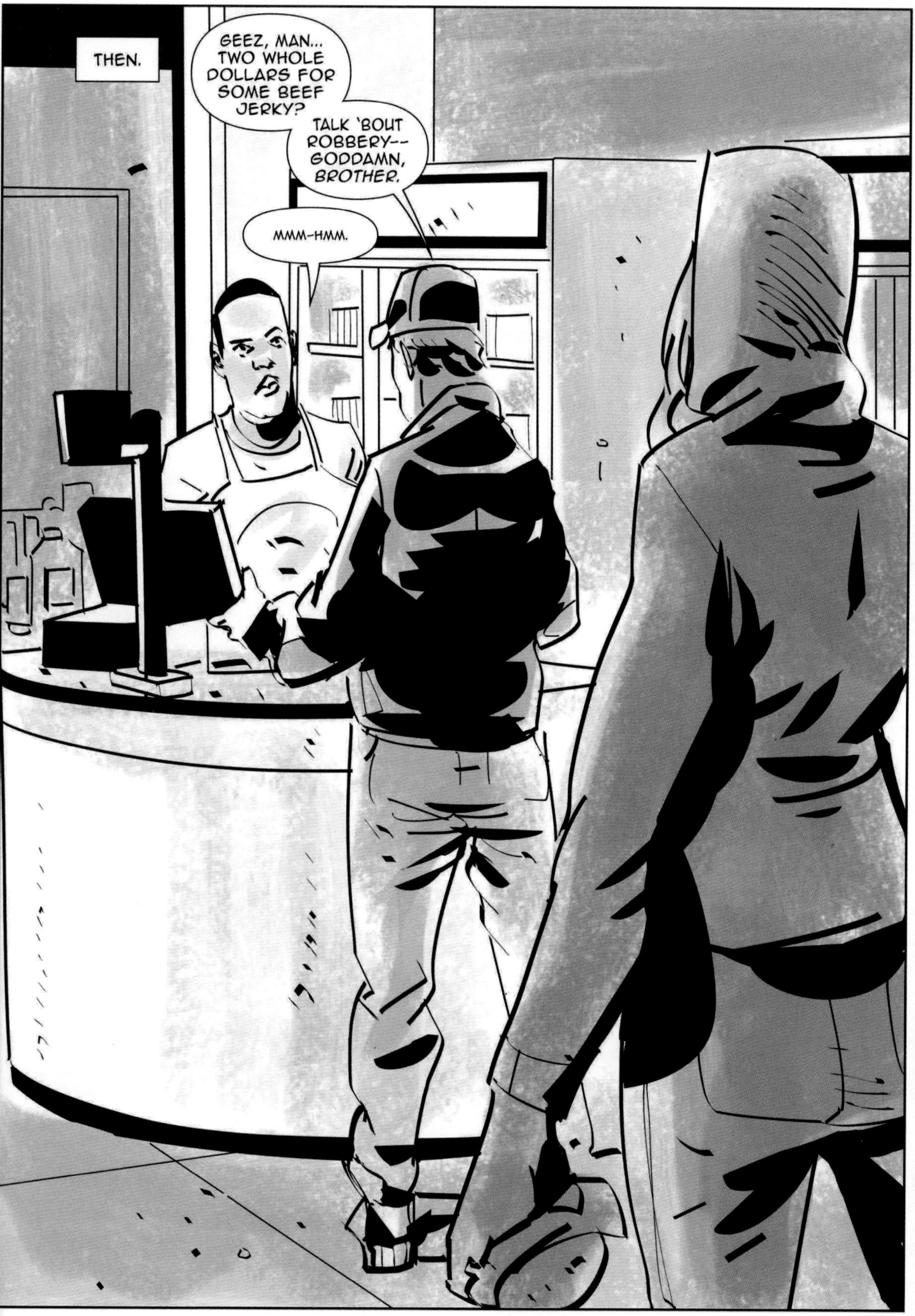
THEN.
GEEZ, MAN... TWO WHOLE DOLLARS FOR SOME BEEF JERKY?
TALK 'BOUT ROBBERY-- GODDAMN, BROTHER.
MMM-HMM.

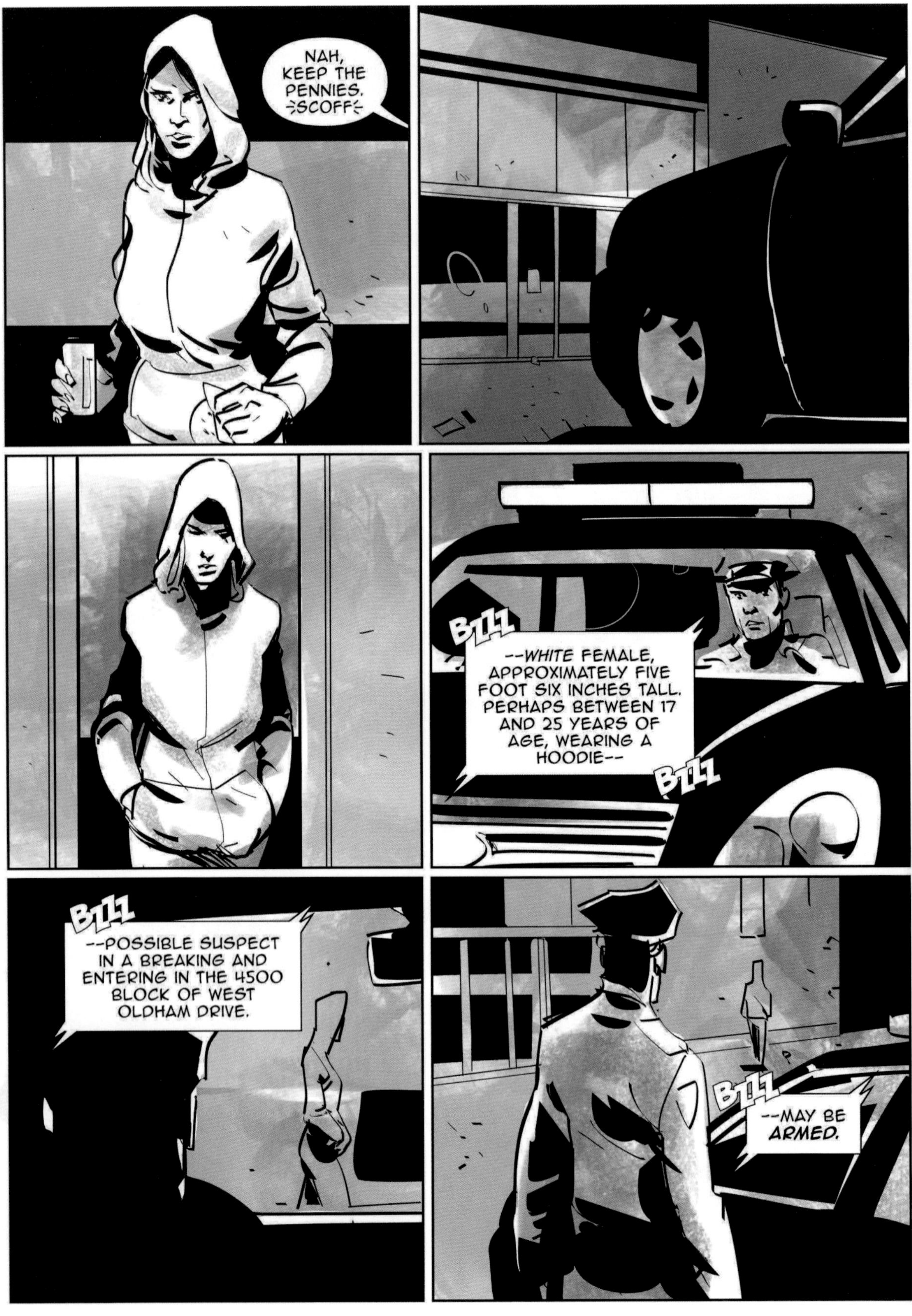
NAH, KEEP THE PENNIES. SCOFF
BZZZ
--WHITE FEMALE, APPROXIMATELY FIVE FOOT SIX INCHES TALL. PERHAPS BETWEEN 17 AND 25 YEARS OF AGE, WEARING A HOODIE--
BZZZ
BZZZ
--POSSIBLE SUSPECT IN A BREAKING AND ENTERING IN THE 4500 BLOCK OF WEST OLDHAM DRIVE.
BZZZ
--MAY BE ARMED.

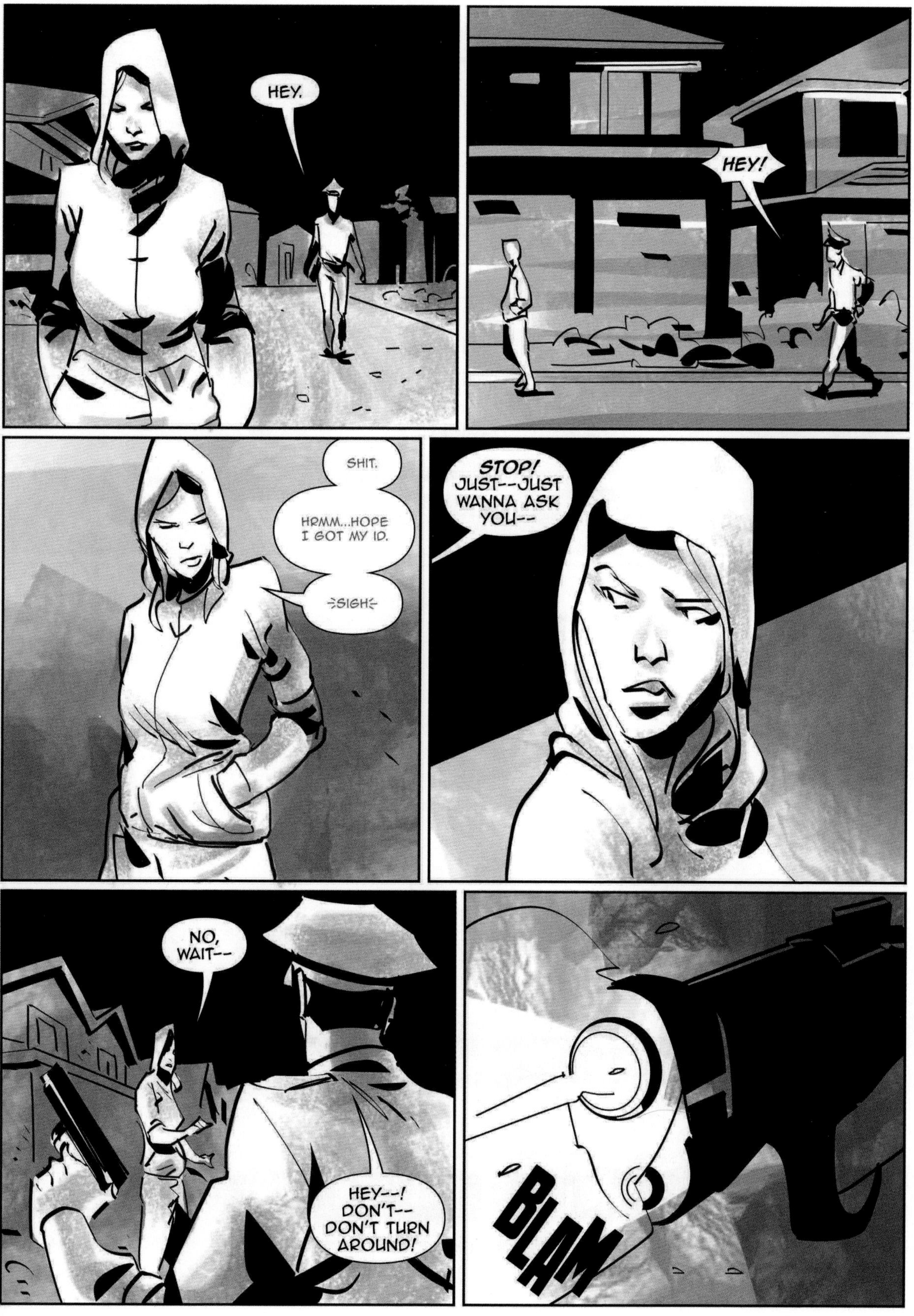
HEY.
HEY!
SHIT.
HRMM...HOPE I GOT MY ID.
~SIGH~
STOP! JUST--JUST WANNA ASK YOU--
NO, WAIT--
HEY--! DON'T-- DON'T TURN AROUND!
BLAM

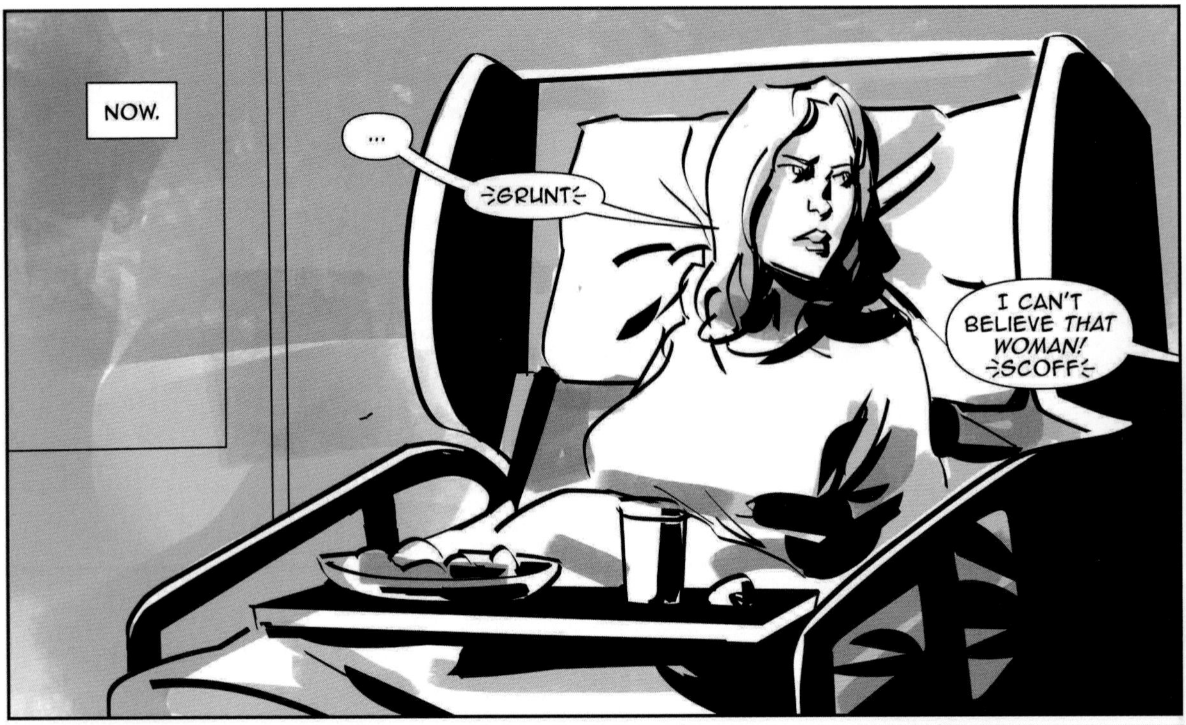
NOW.
...
GRUNT
I CAN'T BELIEVE THAT WOMAN! SCOFF

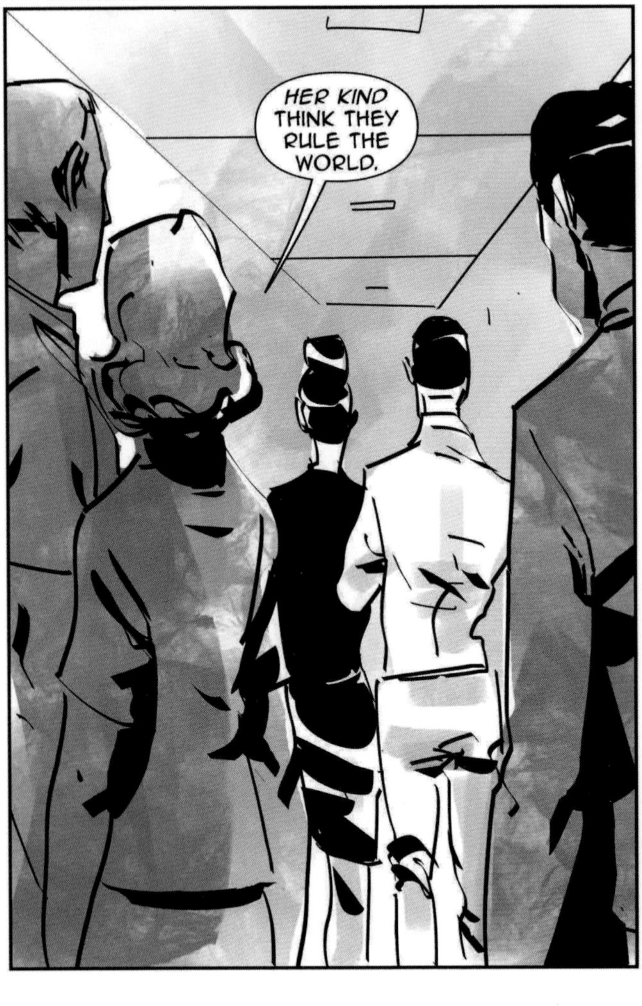
HER KIND THINK THEY RULE THE WORLD.

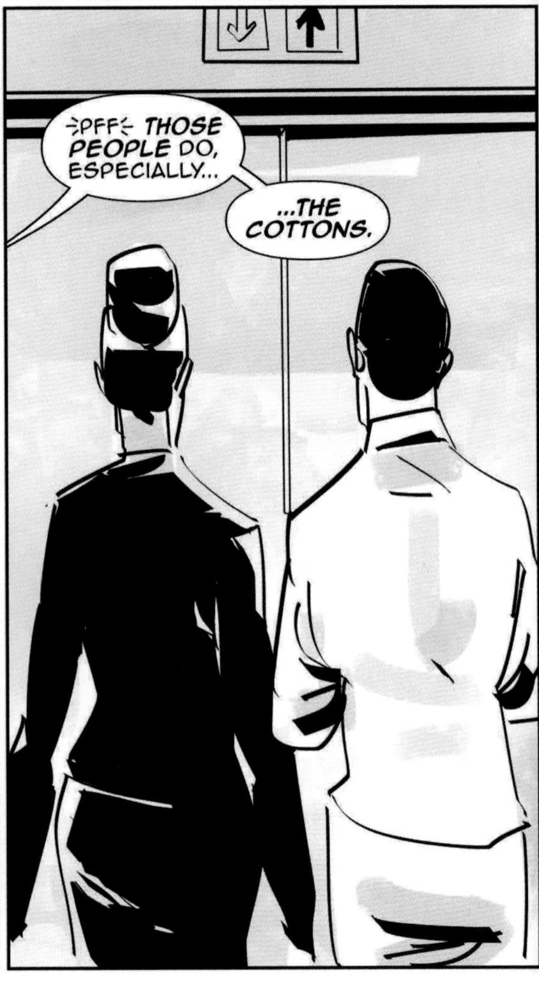
PFF THOSE PEOPLE DO, ESPECIALLY...
...THE COTTONS.

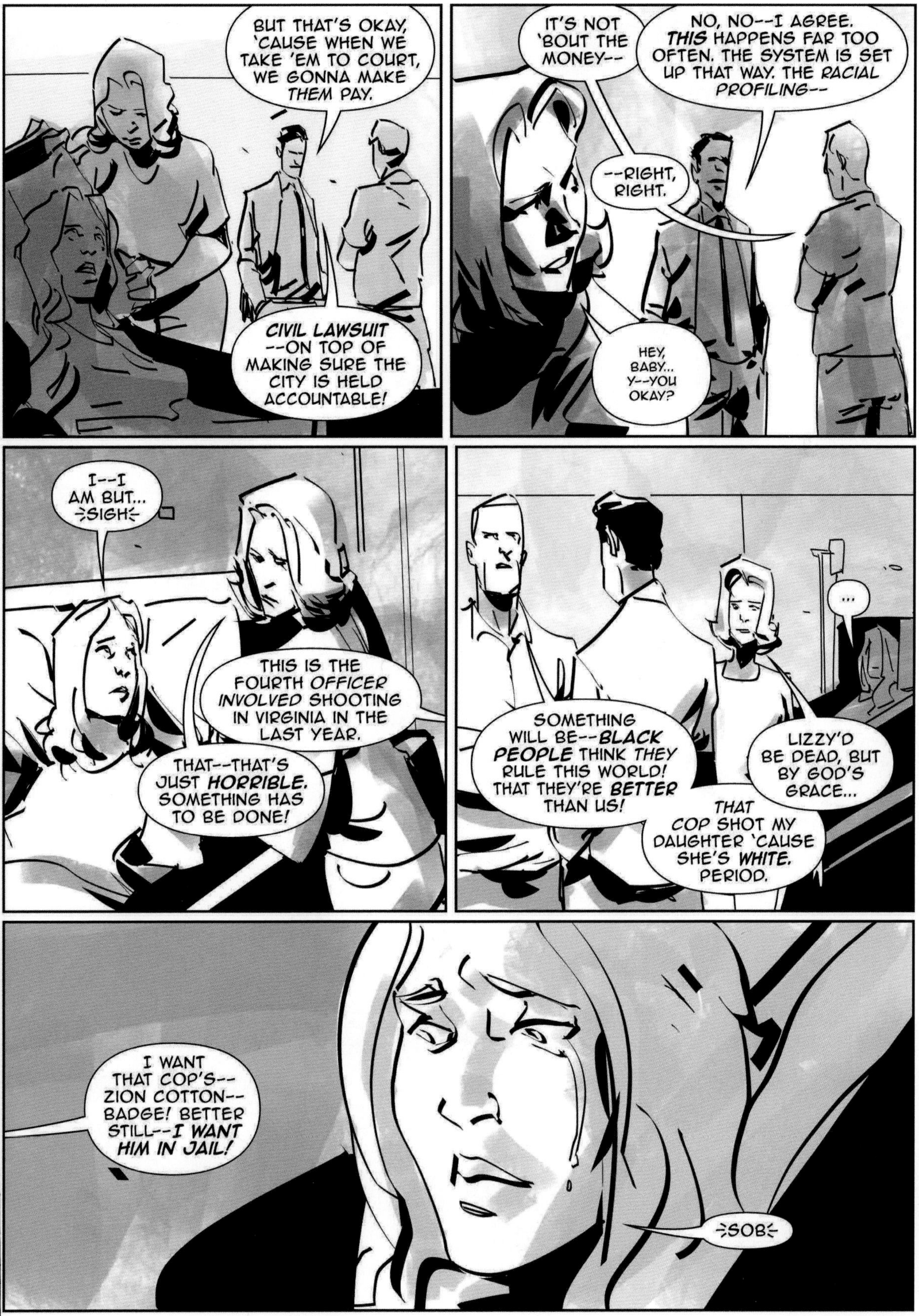
BUT THAT'S OKAY, 'CAUSE WHEN WE TAKE 'EM TO COURT, WE GONNA MAKE THEM PAY.
CIVIL LAWSUIT --ON TOP OF MAKING SURE THE CITY IS HELD ACCOUNTABLE!
IT'S NOT 'BOUT THE MONEY--
NO, NO--I AGREE. THIS HAPPENS FAR TOO OFTEN. THE SYSTEM IS SET UP THAT WAY. THE RACIAL PROFILING--
--RIGHT, RIGHT.
HEY, BABY... Y--YOU OKAY?
I--I AM BUT... SIGH
THIS IS THE FOURTH OFFICER INVOLVED SHOOTING IN VIRGINIA IN THE LAST YEAR.
THAT--THAT'S JUST HORRIBLE. SOMETHING HAS TO BE DONE!
...
LIZZY'D BE DEAD, BUT BY GOD'S GRACE...
SOMETHING WILL BE--BLACK PEOPLE THINK THEY RULE THIS WORLD! THAT THEY'RE BETTER THAN US!
THAT COP SHOT MY DAUGHTER 'CAUSE SHE'S WHITE. PERIOD.
I WANT THAT COP'S-- ZION COTTON-- BADGE! BETTER STILL--I WANT HIM IN JAIL!
SOB

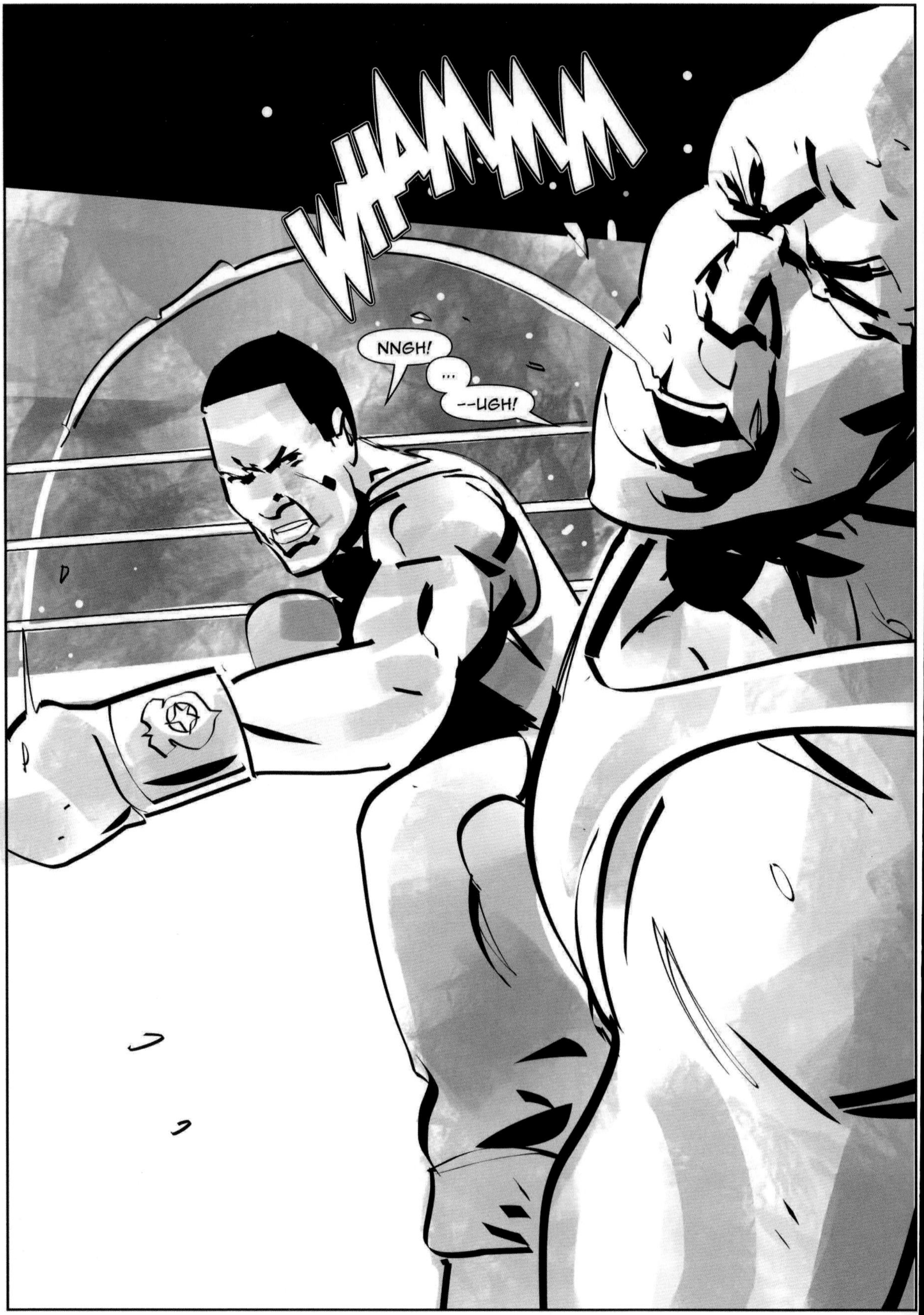
WHAMMM
NNGH!
...
--UGH!

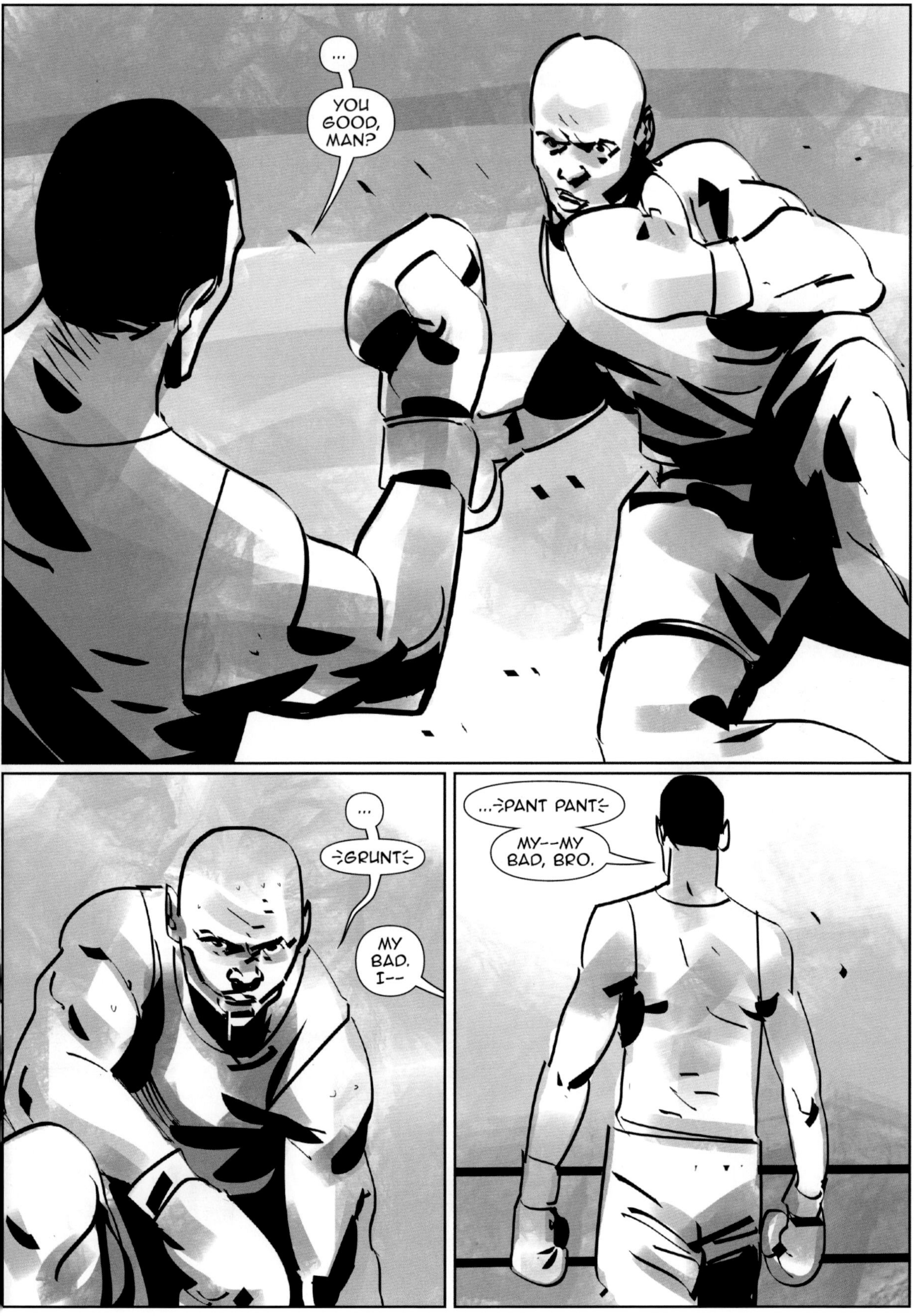
...
YOU GOOD, MAN?
...
=GRUNT=
MY BAD. I--
...=PANT PANT=
MY--MY BAD, BRO.

NAH, F*#! THAT...
AAARGH--!
BAMM
NNGH! ADE--
WHOOOSH
...

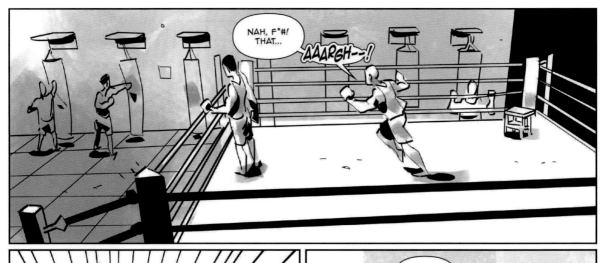

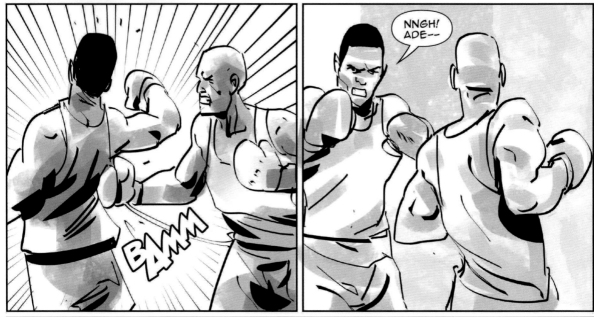

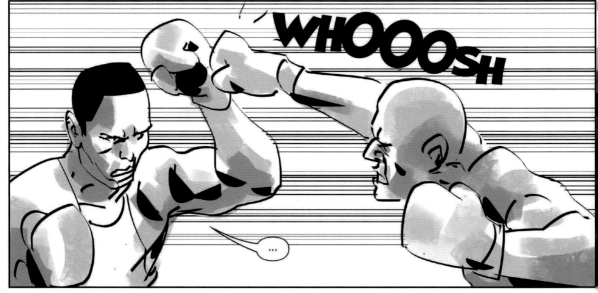

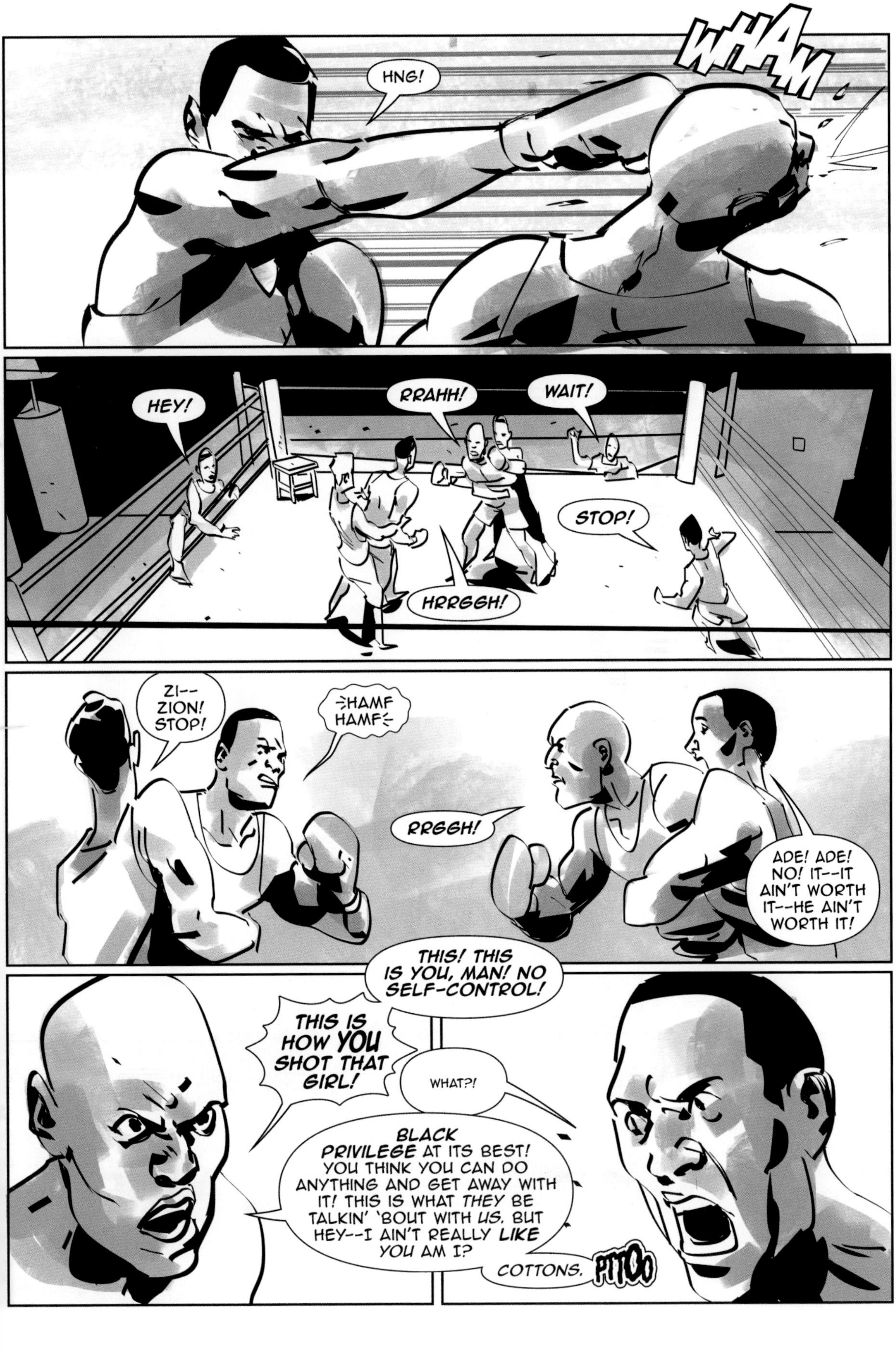
WHAM
HNG!
HEY!
RRAHH!
WAIT!
STOP!
HRRGGH!
ZI-- ZION! STOP!
HAMF HAMF
RRGGH!
ADE! ADE! NO! IT--IT AIN'T WORTH IT--HE AIN'T WORTH IT!
THIS! THIS IS YOU, MAN! NO SELF-CONTROL!
THIS IS HOW YOU SHOT THAT GIRL!
WHAT?!
BLACK PRIVILEGE AT ITS BEST! YOU THINK YOU CAN DO ANYTHING AND GET AWAY WITH IT! THIS IS WHAT THEY BE TALKIN' 'BOUT WITH US. BUT HEY--I AIN'T REALLY LIKE YOU AM I?
COTTONS.
PTTOO

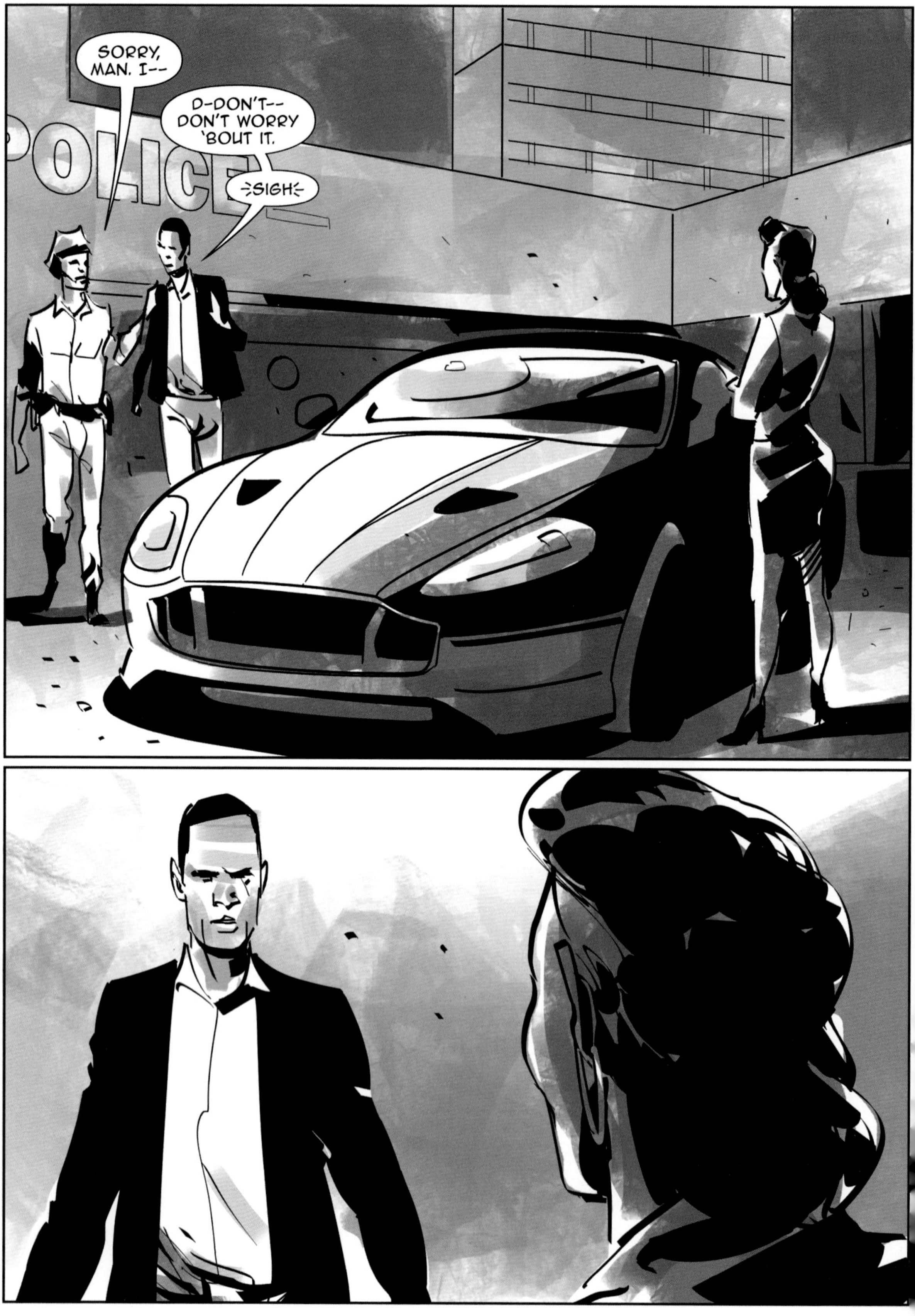
SORRY, MAN. I--
D-DON'T--
DON'T WORRY 'BOUT IT.
-SIGH-
POLICE

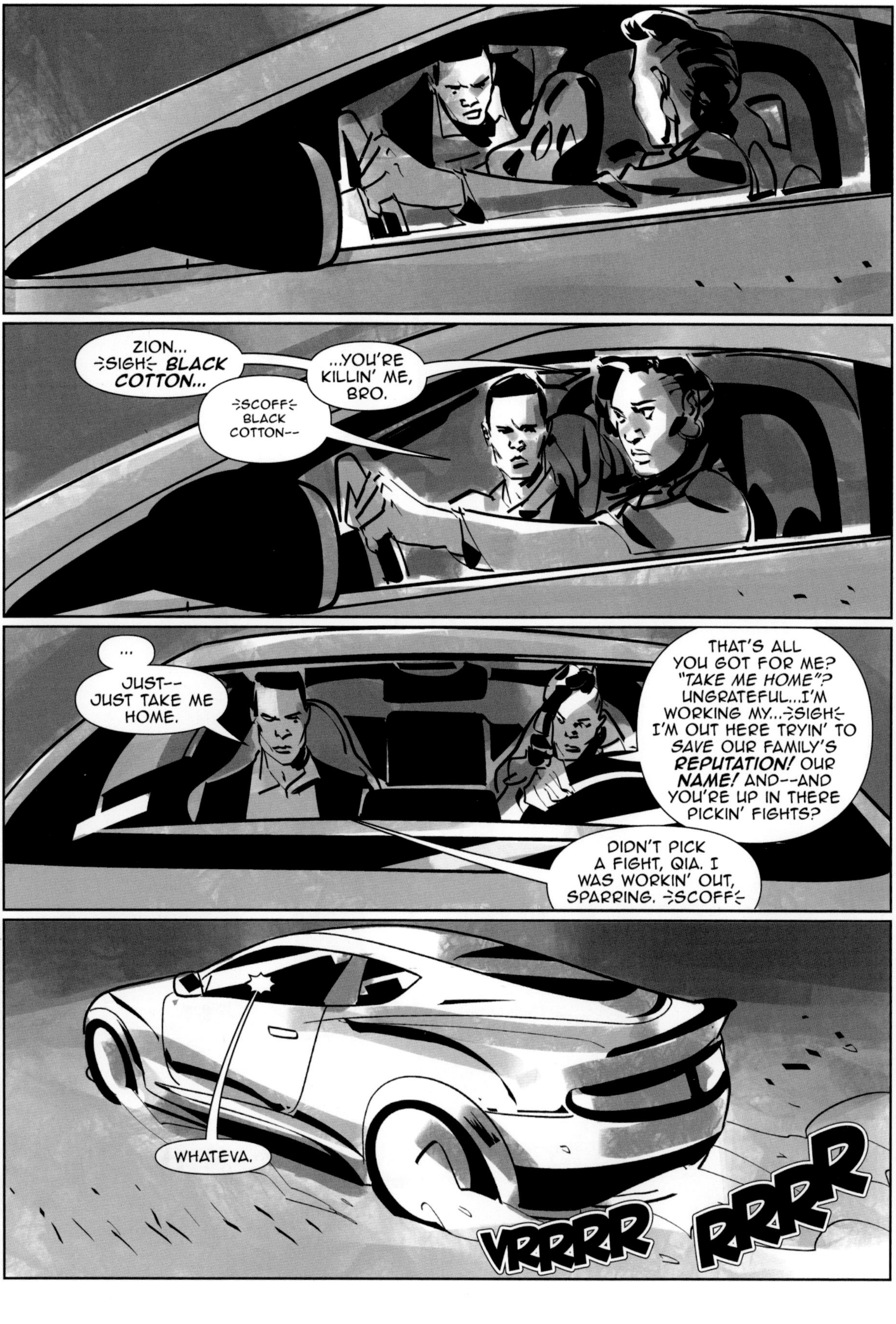
ZION... ⋟SIGH⋞ BLACK COTTON...
⋟SCOFF⋞ BLACK COTTON--
...YOU'RE KILLIN' ME, BRO.
...
JUST-- JUST TAKE ME HOME.
THAT'S ALL YOU GOT FOR ME? "TAKE ME HOME"? UNGRATEFUL...I'M WORKING MY...⋟SIGH⋞ I'M OUT HERE TRYIN' TO SAVE OUR FAMILY'S REPUTATION! OUR NAME! AND--AND YOU'RE UP IN THERE PICKIN' FIGHTS?
DIDN'T PICK A FIGHT, QIA. I WAS WORKIN' OUT, SPARRING. ⋟SCOFF⋞
WHATEVA.
VRRRR RRRR

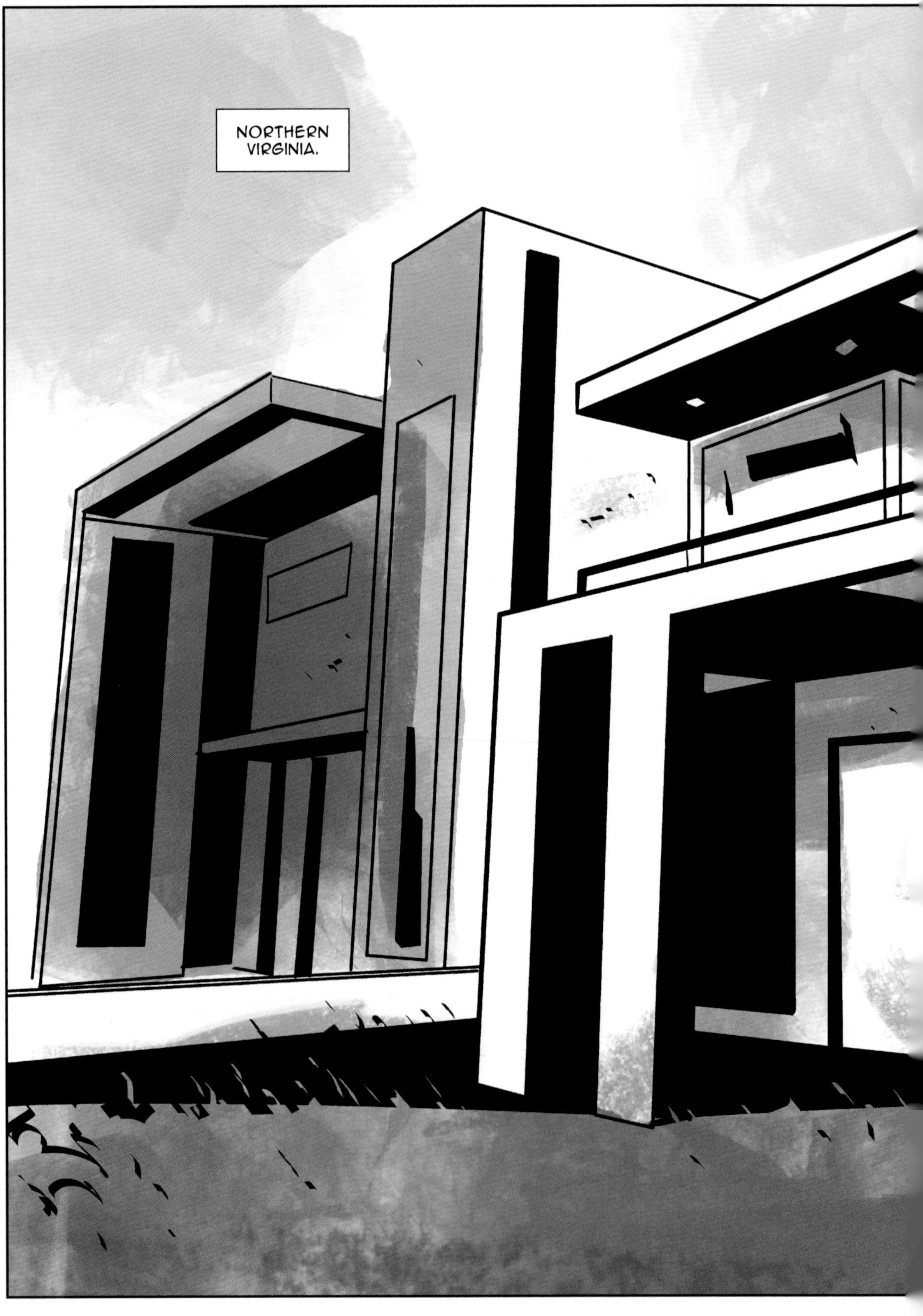
NORTHERN VIRGINIA.

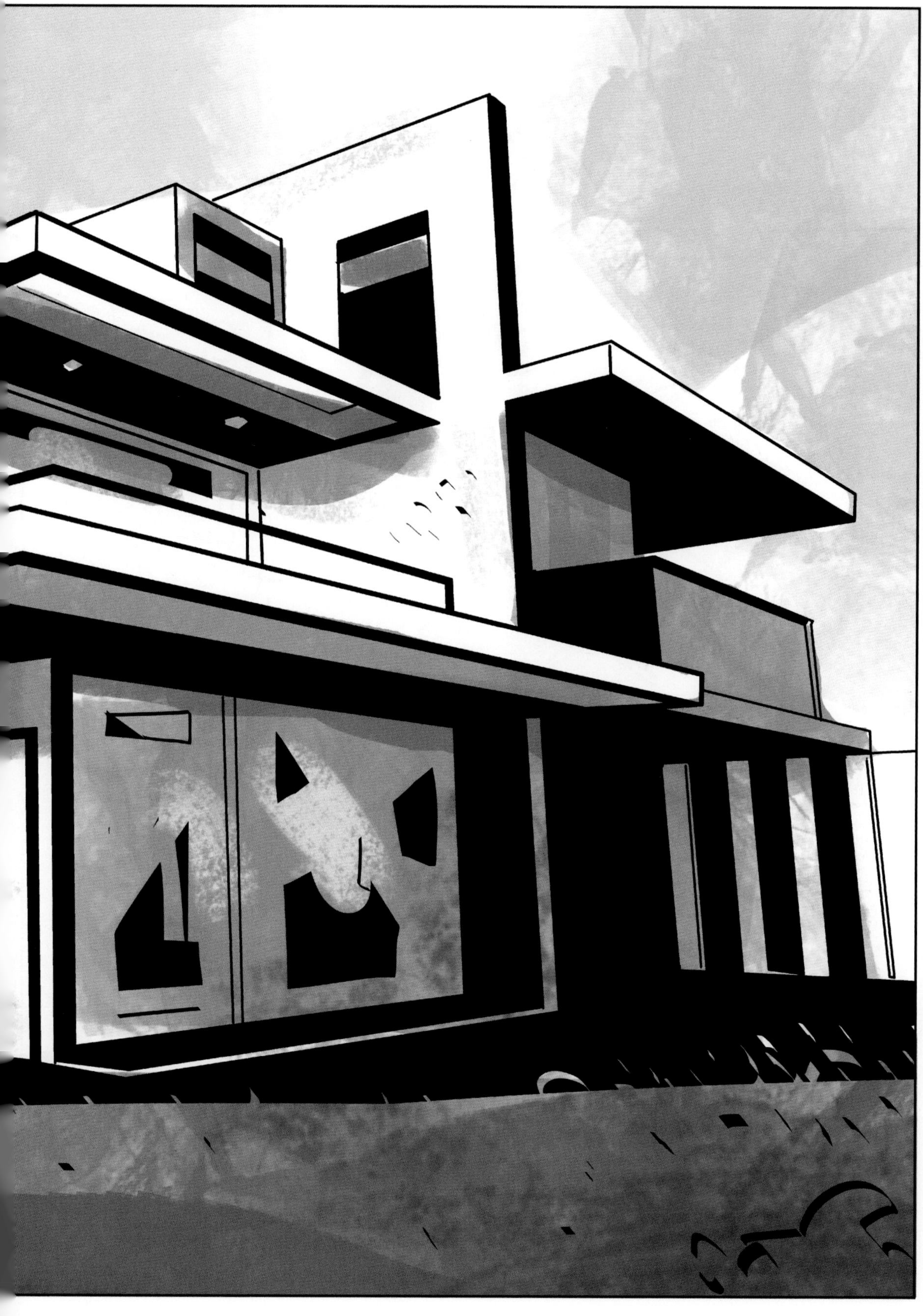

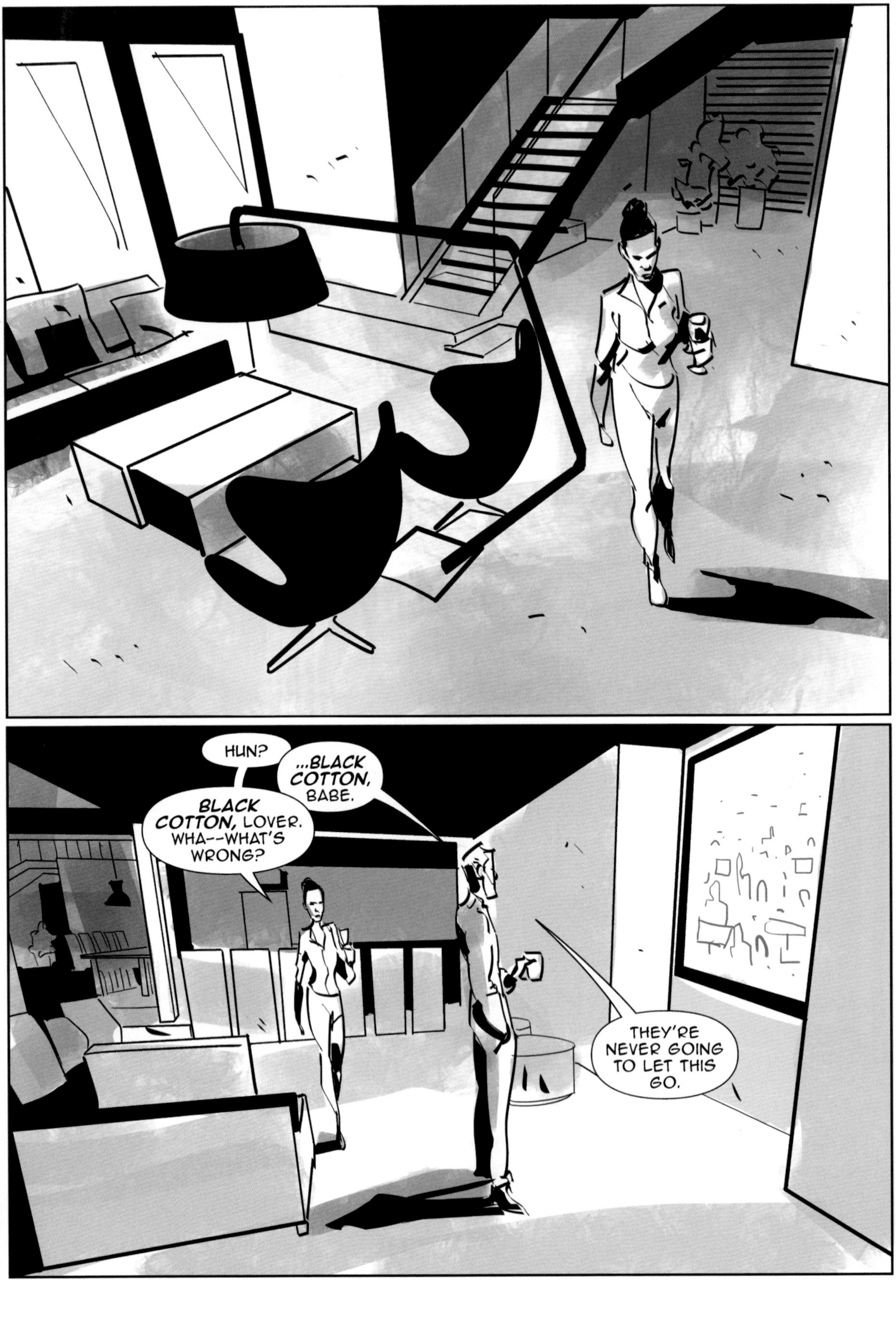
HUN?
...BLACK COTTON, BABE.
BLACK COTTON, LOVER. WHA--WHAT'S WRONG?
THEY'RE NEVER GOING TO LET THIS GO.

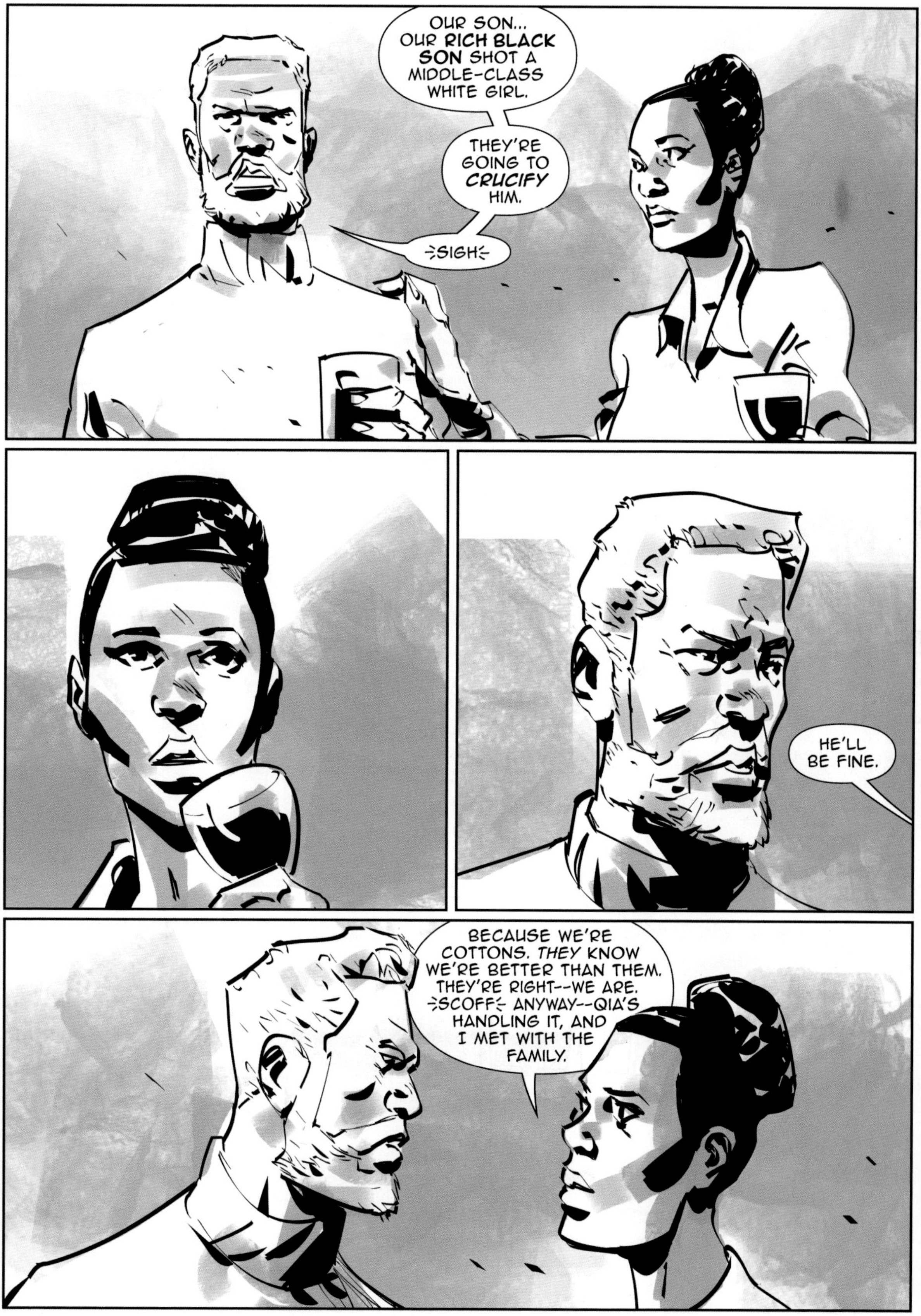
OUR SON... OUR **RICH BLACK SON** SHOT A MIDDLE-CLASS WHITE GIRL.
THEY'RE GOING TO ***CRUCIFY*** HIM.
SIGH
HE'LL BE FINE.
BECAUSE WE'RE COTTONS. *THEY* KNOW WE'RE BETTER THAN THEM. THEY'RE RIGHT--WE ARE. SCOFF ANYWAY--QIA'S HANDLING IT, AND I MET WITH THE FAMILY.

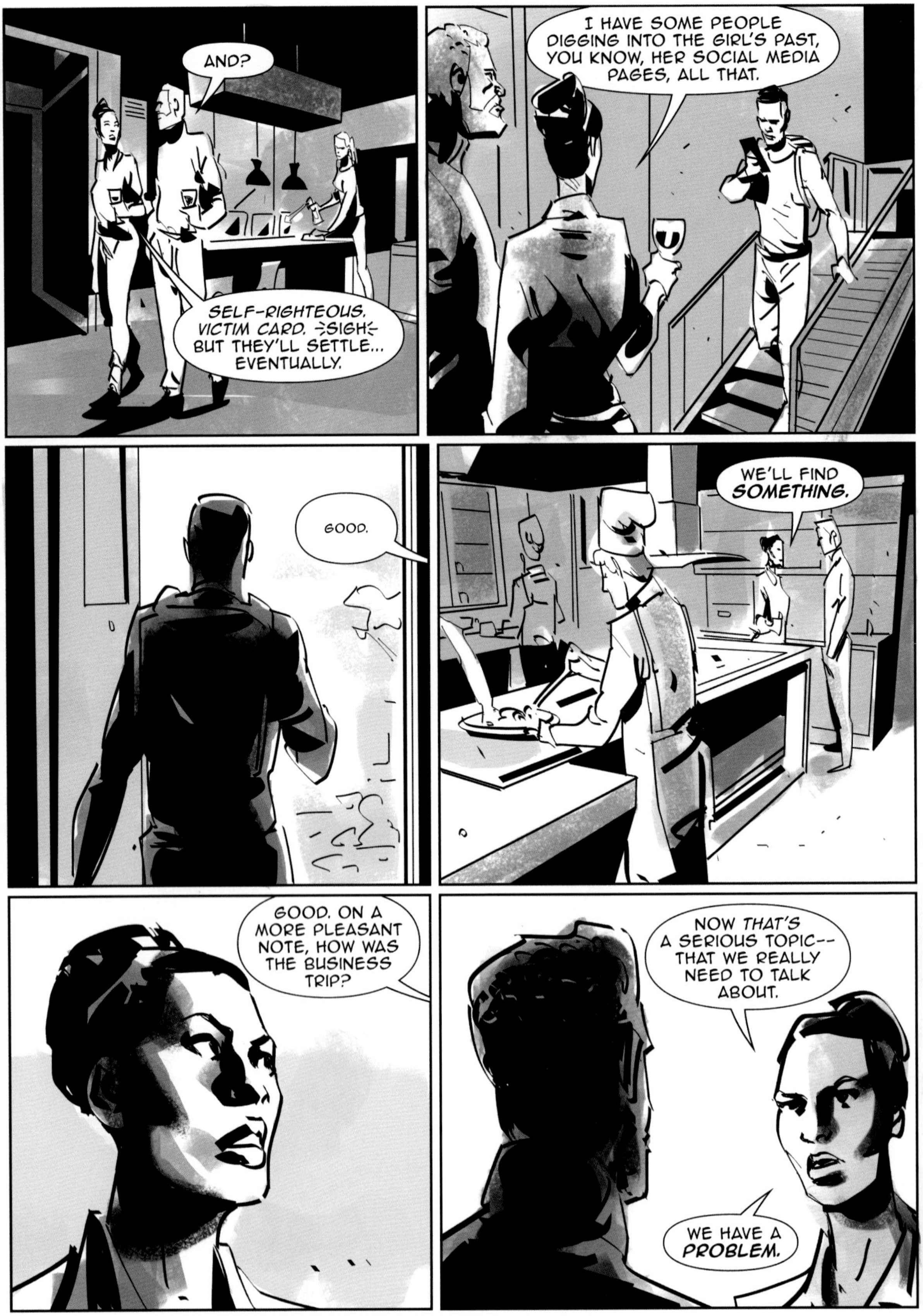
AND?
SELF-RIGHTEOUS. VICTIM CARD. ⇒SIGH⇐ BUT THEY'LL SETTLE... EVENTUALLY.
I HAVE SOME PEOPLE DIGGING INTO THE GIRL'S PAST, YOU KNOW, HER SOCIAL MEDIA PAGES, ALL THAT.
GOOD.
WE'LL FIND *SOMETHING.*
GOOD. ON A MORE PLEASANT NOTE, HOW WAS THE BUSINESS TRIP?
NOW *THAT'S* A SERIOUS TOPIC-- THAT WE REALLY NEED TO TALK ABOUT.
WE HAVE A *PROBLEM.*

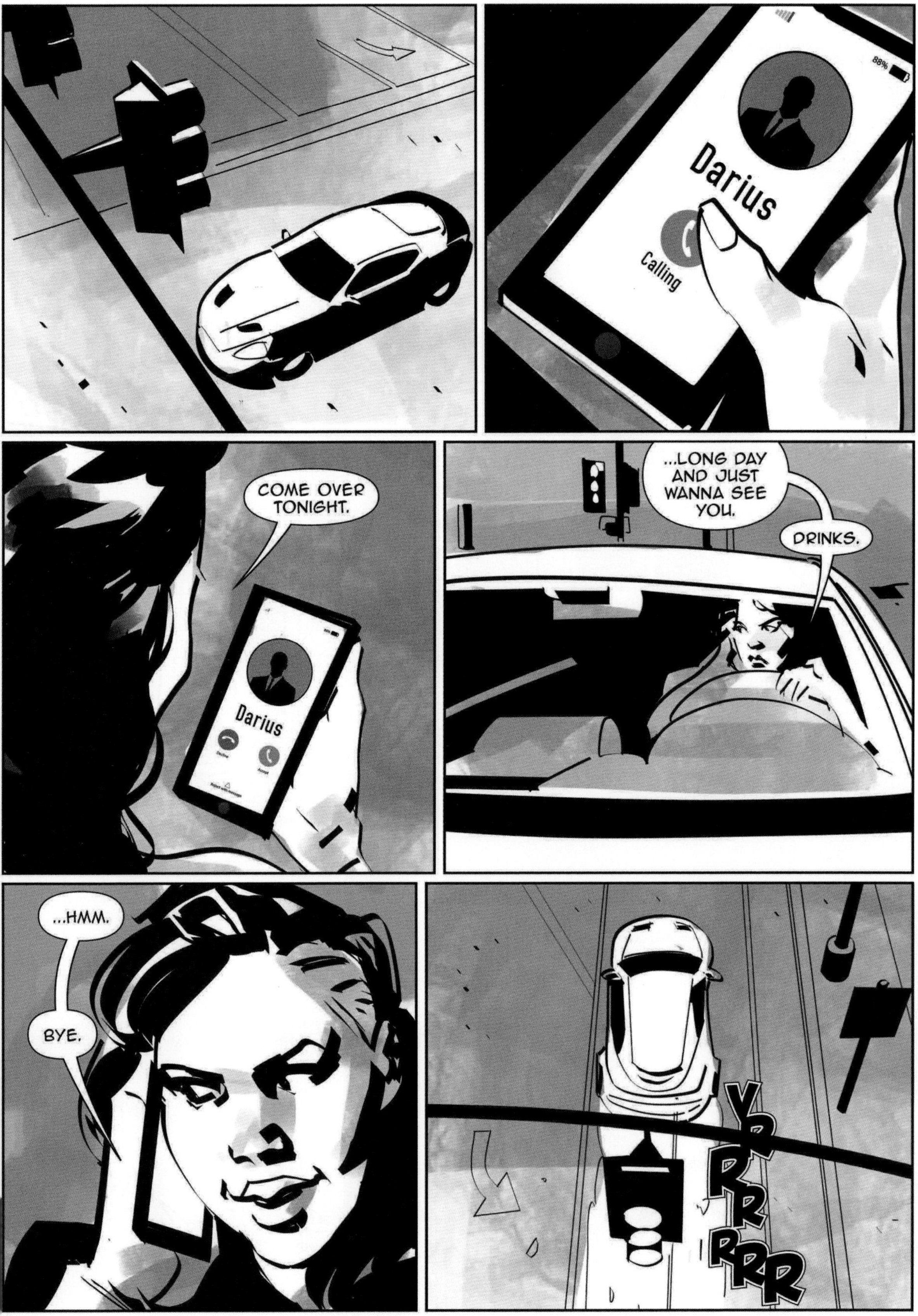
88%
Darius
Calling
COME OVER TONIGHT.
Darius
...LONG DAY AND JUST WANNA SEE YOU.
DRINKS.
...HMM.
BYE.
VRRRRRR

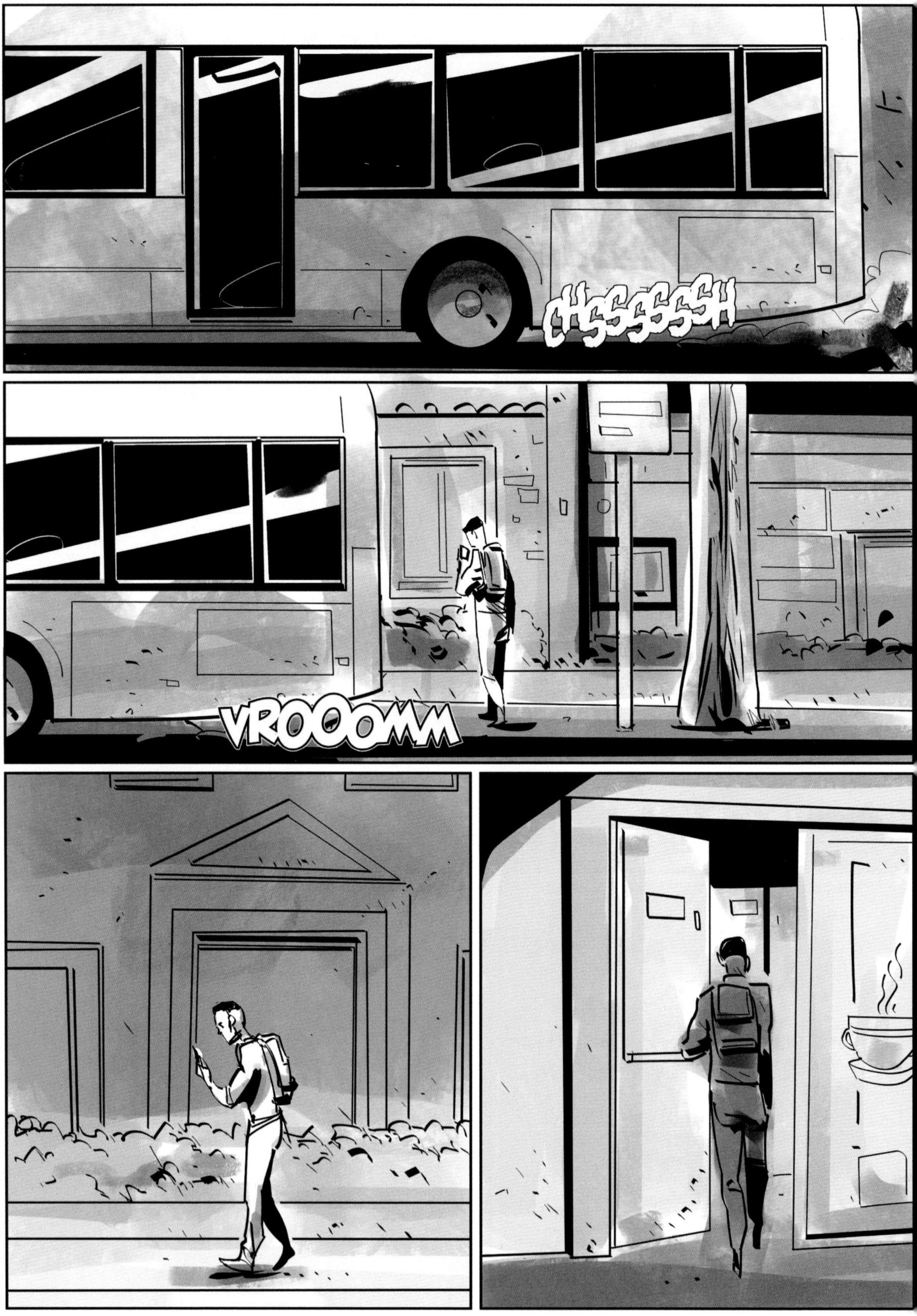
CHSSSSSSH
VROOOMM

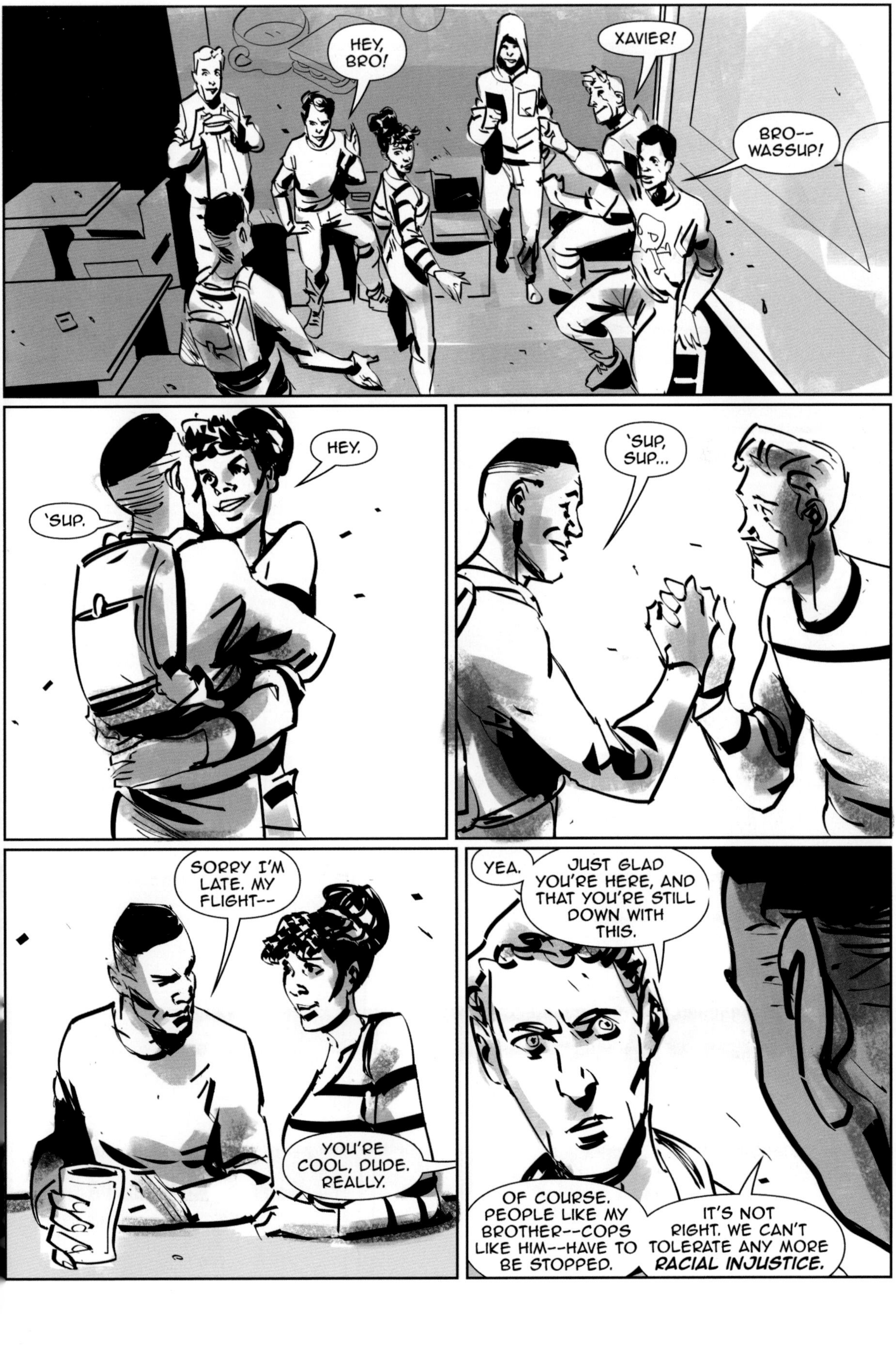
HEY, BRO!
XAVIER!
BRO-- WASSUP!
HEY.
'SUP.
'SUP, SUP...
SORRY I'M LATE. MY FLIGHT--
YOU'RE COOL, DUDE. REALLY.
YEA.
JUST GLAD YOU'RE HERE, AND THAT YOU'RE STILL DOWN WITH THIS.
OF COURSE. PEOPLE LIKE MY BROTHER--COPS LIKE HIM--HAVE TO BE STOPPED.
IT'S NOT RIGHT. WE CAN'T TOLERATE ANY MORE RACIAL INJUSTICE.

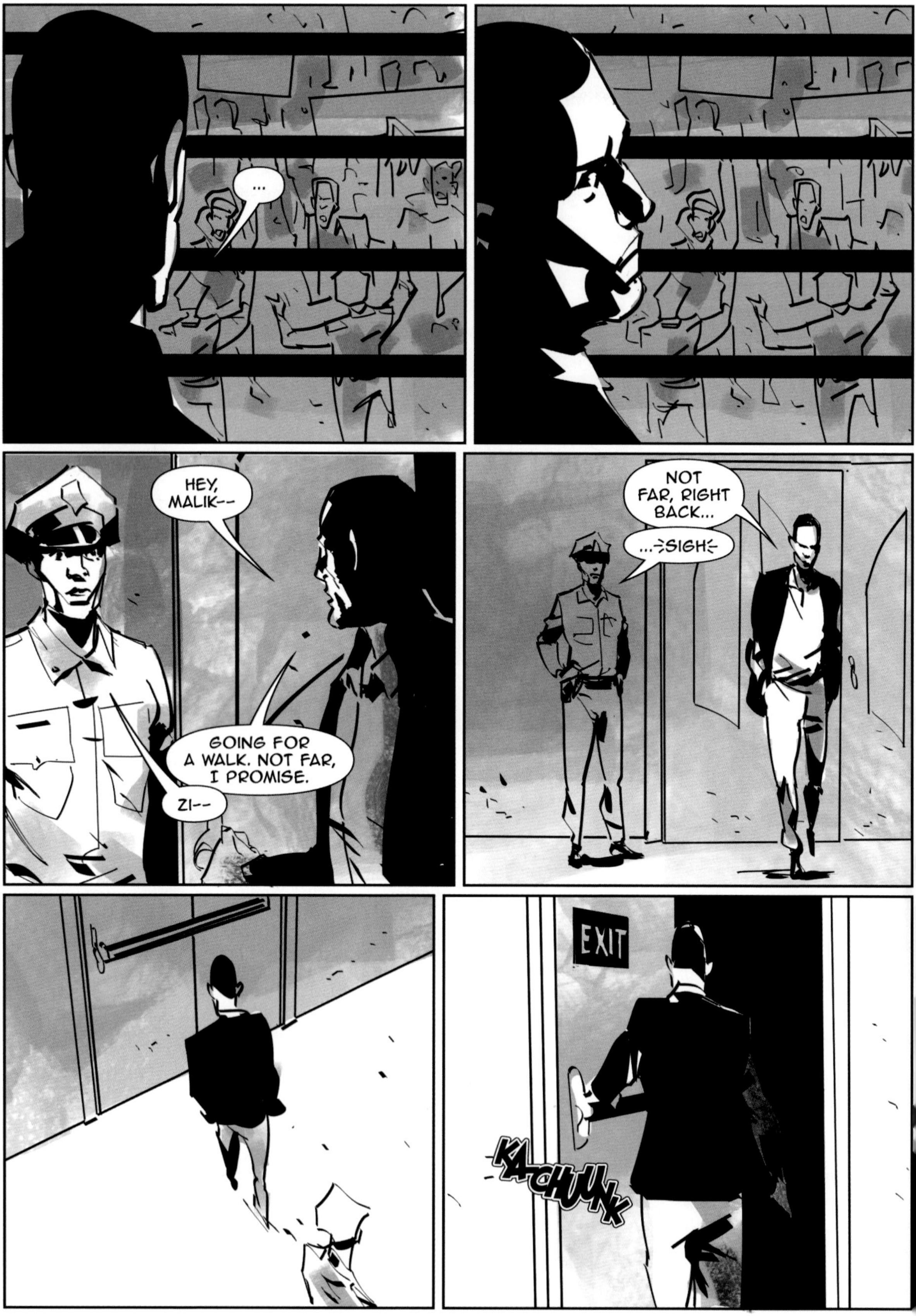
...
HEY, MALIK--
GOING FOR A WALK. NOT FAR, I PROMISE.
ZI--
NOT FAR, RIGHT BACK...
...SIGH
EXIT
KA-CHUNK

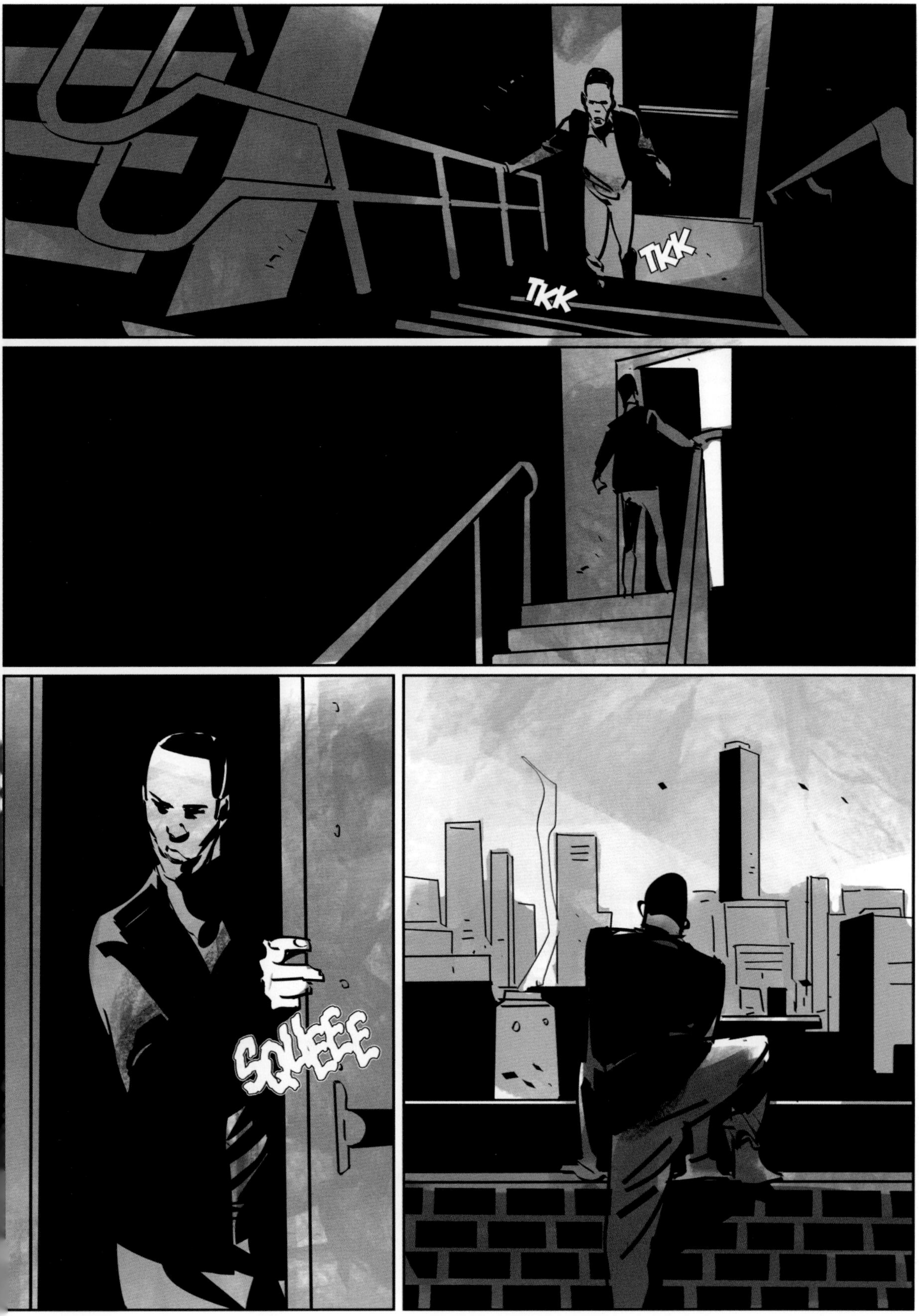
TKK
TKK
SQUEEE

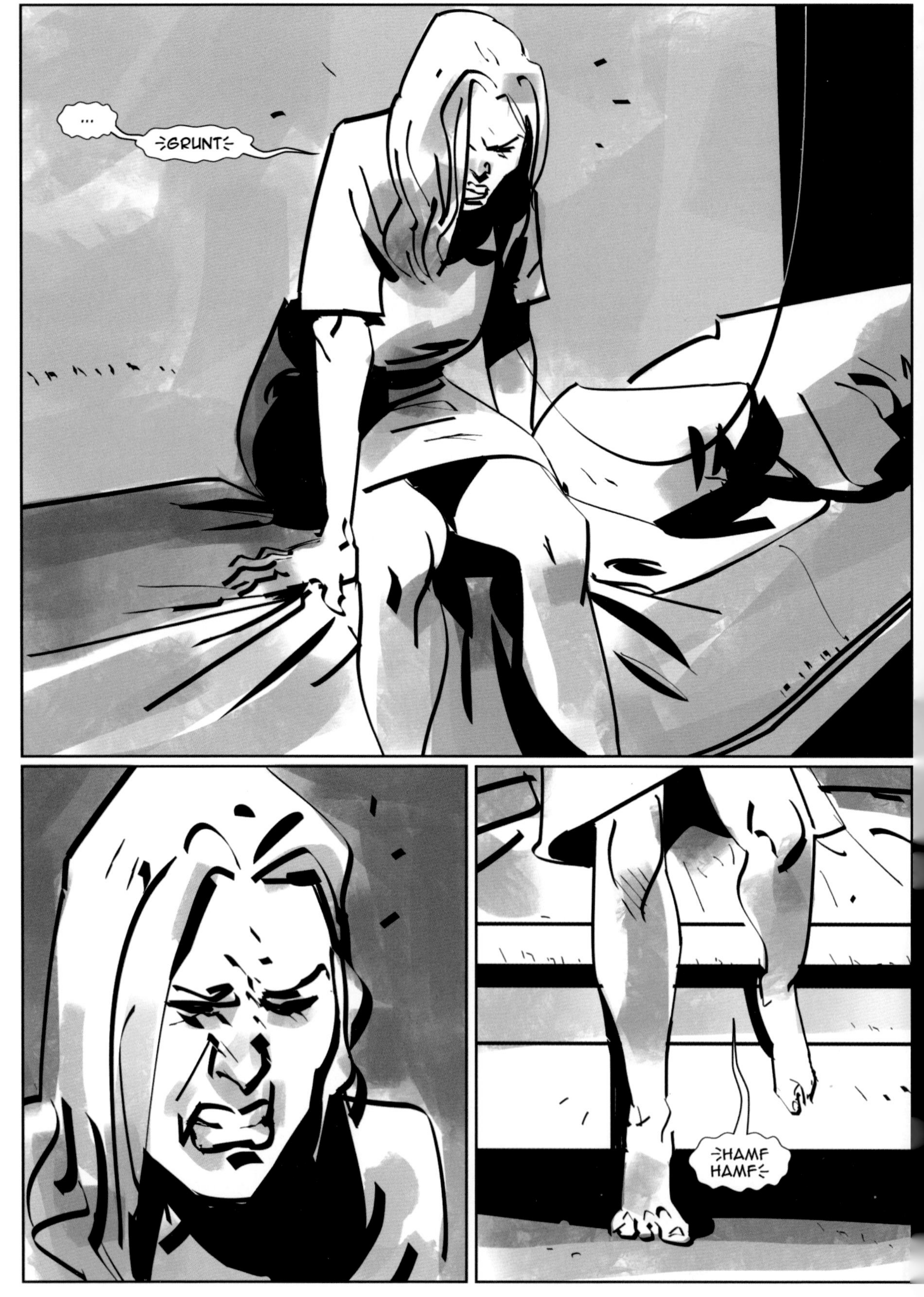
...
GRUNT
HAMF HAMF

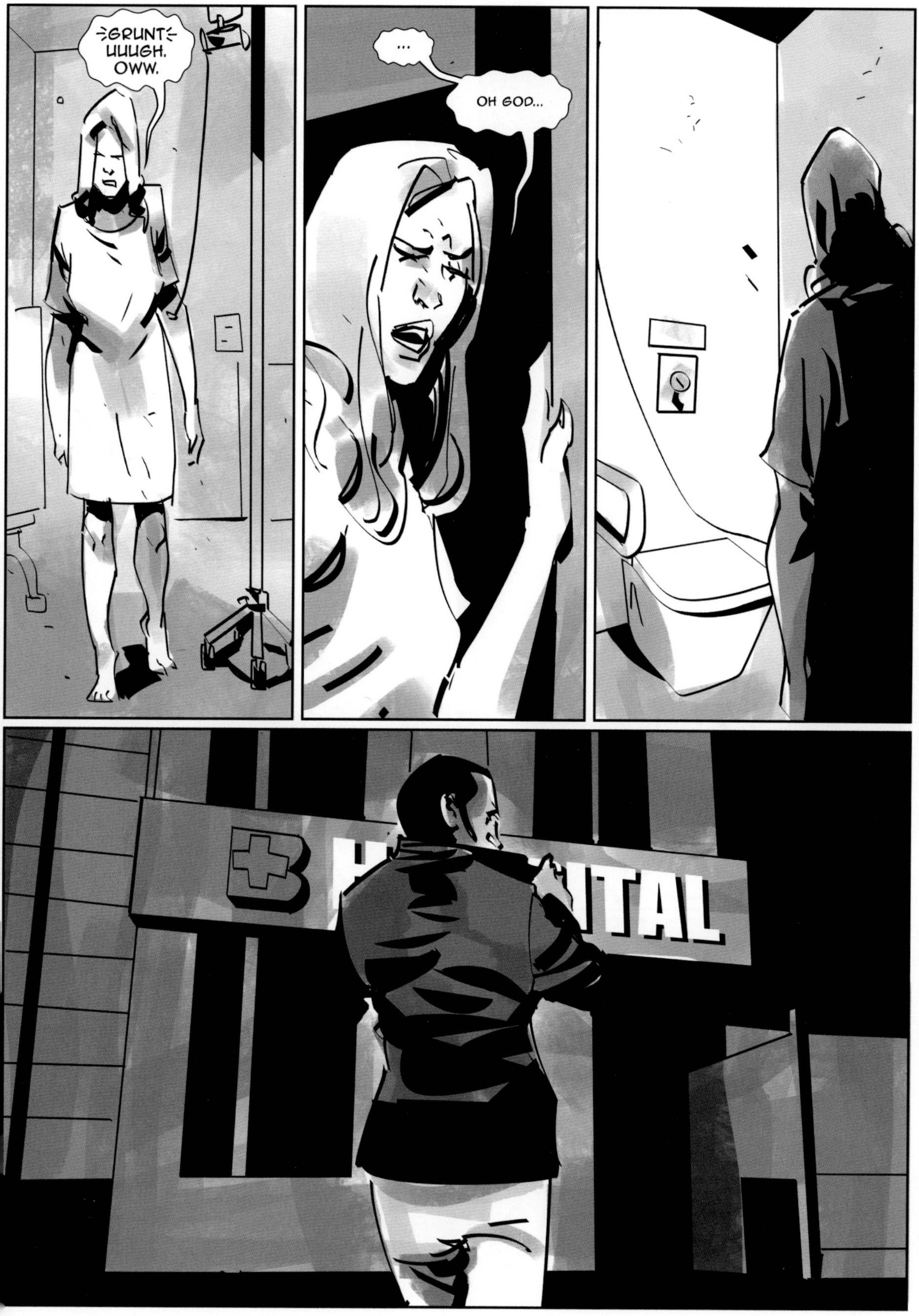

GRUNT
UUUGH. OWW.
...
OH GOD...
TAL

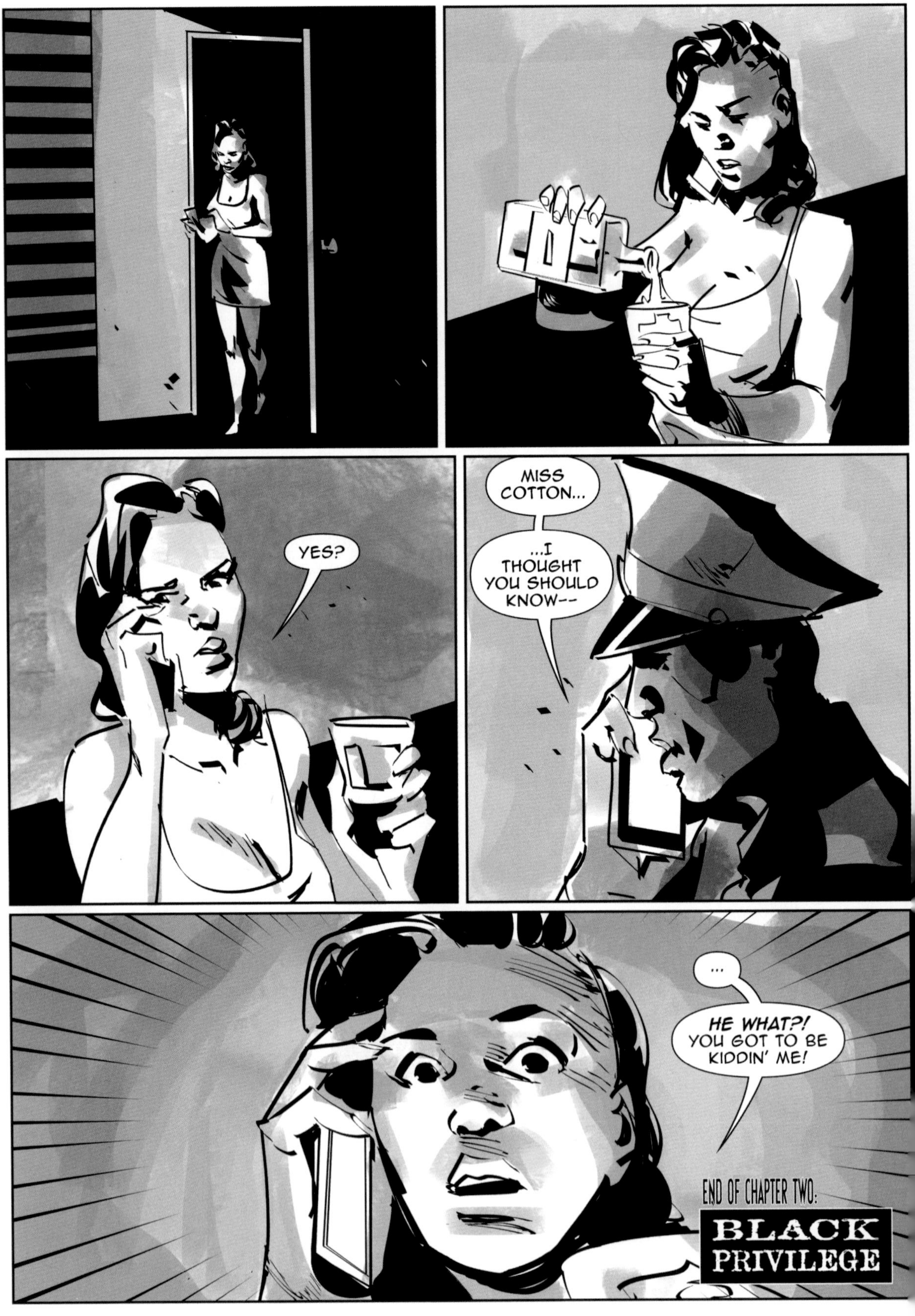

YES?
MISS COTTON...
...I THOUGHT YOU SHOULD KNOW--
...
HE WHAT?! YOU GOT TO BE KIDDIN' ME!
END OF CHAPTER TWO:
BLACK PRIVILEGE

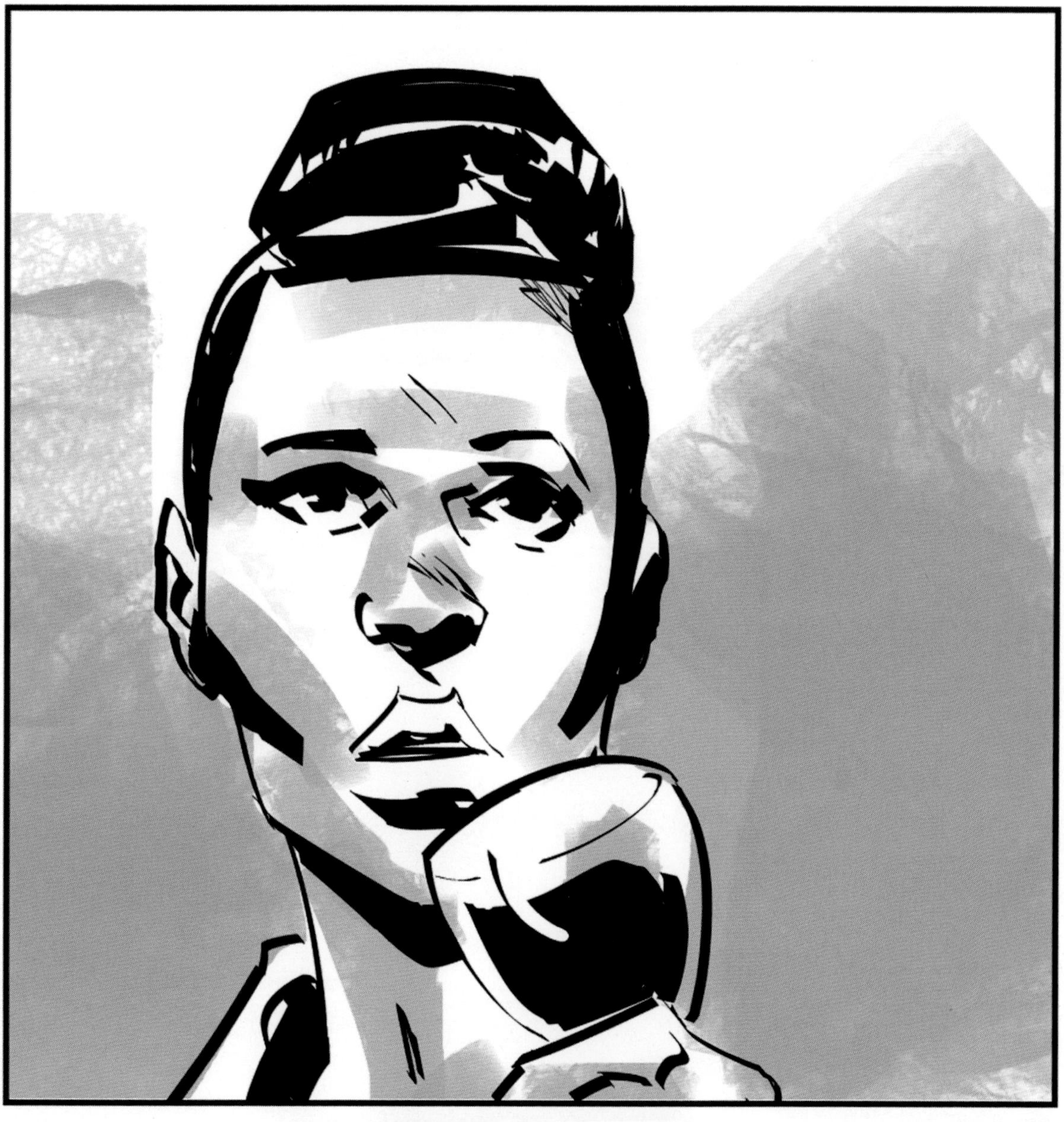

AFTER SHOT/
BLACK PRIVILEGE

CHAPTER
3

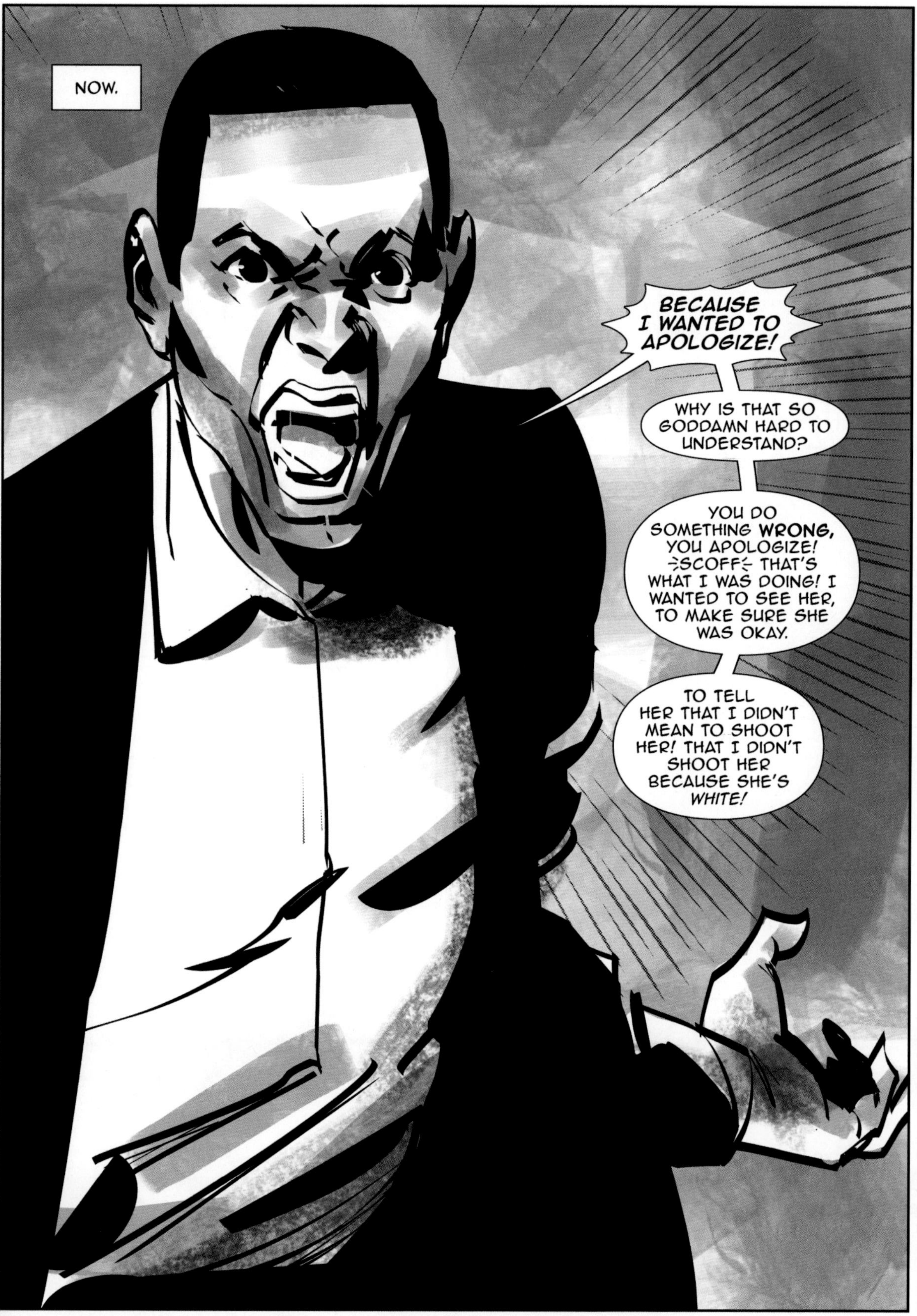
NOW.
BECAUSE I WANTED TO APOLOGIZE!
WHY IS THAT SO GODDAMN HARD TO UNDERSTAND?
YOU DO SOMETHING **WRONG,** YOU APOLOGIZE! ~SCOFF~ THAT'S WHAT I WAS DOING! I WANTED TO SEE HER, TO MAKE SURE SHE WAS OKAY.
TO TELL HER THAT I DIDN'T MEAN TO SHOOT HER! THAT I DIDN'T SHOOT HER BECAUSE SHE'S *WHITE!*

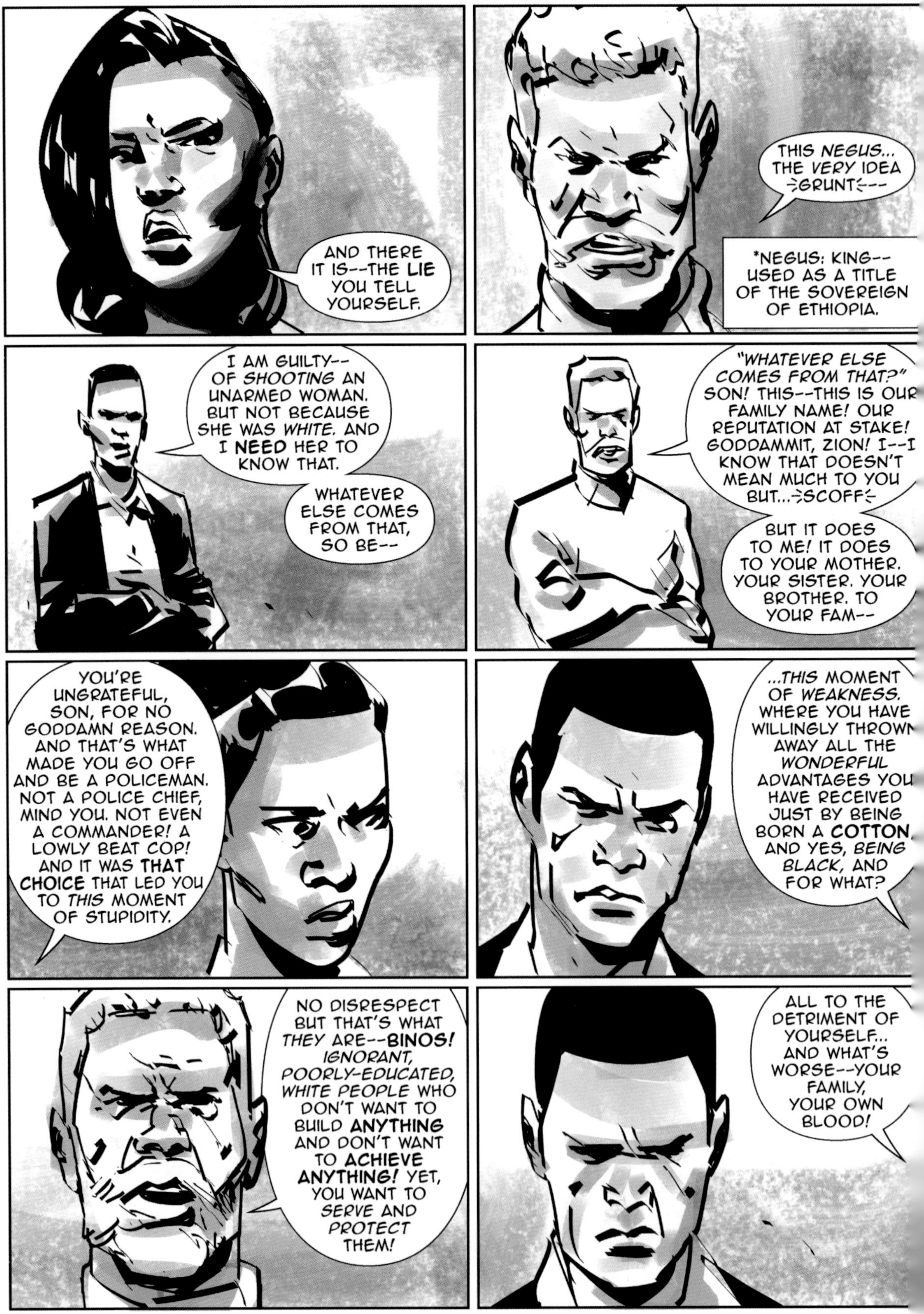
AND THERE IT IS--THE LIE YOU TELL YOURSELF.
THIS NEGUS... THE VERY IDEA ⋟GRUNT⋞--
*NEGUS: KING-- USED AS A TITLE OF THE SOVEREIGN OF ETHIOPIA.
I AM GUILTY-- OF SHOOTING AN UNARMED WOMAN. BUT NOT BECAUSE SHE WAS WHITE. AND I NEED HER TO KNOW THAT.
WHATEVER ELSE COMES FROM THAT, SO BE--
"WHATEVER ELSE COMES FROM THAT?" SON! THIS--THIS IS OUR FAMILY NAME! OUR REPUTATION AT STAKE! GODDAMMIT, ZION! I--I KNOW THAT DOESN'T MEAN MUCH TO YOU BUT...⋟SCOFF⋞
BUT IT DOES TO ME! IT DOES TO YOUR MOTHER. YOUR SISTER. YOUR BROTHER. TO YOUR FAM--
YOU'RE UNGRATEFUL, SON, FOR NO GODDAMN REASON. AND THAT'S WHAT MADE YOU GO OFF AND BE A POLICEMAN. NOT A POLICE CHIEF, MIND YOU. NOT EVEN A COMMANDER! A LOWLY BEAT COP! AND IT WAS THAT CHOICE THAT LED YOU TO THIS MOMENT OF STUPIDITY.
...THIS MOMENT OF WEAKNESS. WHERE YOU HAVE WILLINGLY THROWN AWAY ALL THE WONDERFUL ADVANTAGES YOU HAVE RECEIVED JUST BY BEING BORN A COTTON, AND YES, BEING BLACK, AND FOR WHAT?
NO DISRESPECT BUT THAT'S WHAT THEY ARE--BINOS! IGNORANT, POORLY-EDUCATED, WHITE PEOPLE WHO DON'T WANT TO BUILD ANYTHING AND DON'T WANT TO ACHIEVE ANYTHING! YET, YOU WANT TO SERVE AND PROTECT THEM!
ALL TO THE DETRIMENT OF YOURSELF... AND WHAT'S WORSE--YOUR FAMILY, YOUR OWN BLOOD!

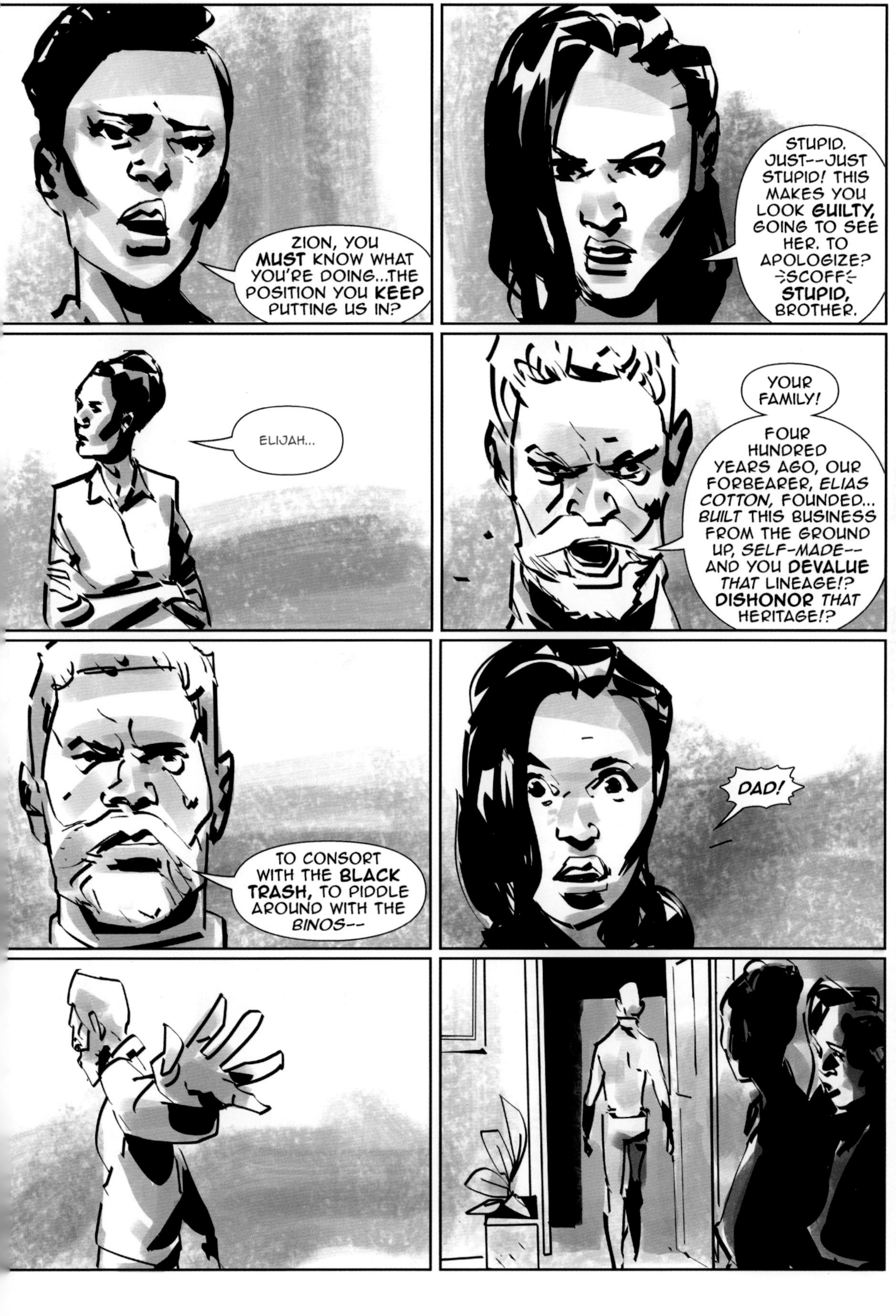
ZION, YOU **MUST** KNOW WHAT YOU'RE DOING...THE POSITION YOU **KEEP** PUTTING US IN?
STUPID. JUST--JUST STUPID! THIS MAKES YOU LOOK **GUILTY,** GOING TO SEE HER. TO APOLOGIZE? *SCOFF* **STUPID,** BROTHER.
ELIJAH...
YOUR FAMILY!
FOUR HUNDRED YEARS AGO, OUR FORBEARER, *ELIAS COTTON,* FOUNDED... *BUILT* THIS BUSINESS FROM THE GROUND UP, *SELF-MADE--* AND YOU **DEVALUE** *THAT* LINEAGE!? **DISHONOR** *THAT* HERITAGE!?
TO CONSORT WITH THE **BLACK TRASH,** TO PIDDLE AROUND WITH THE *BINOS--*
DAD!

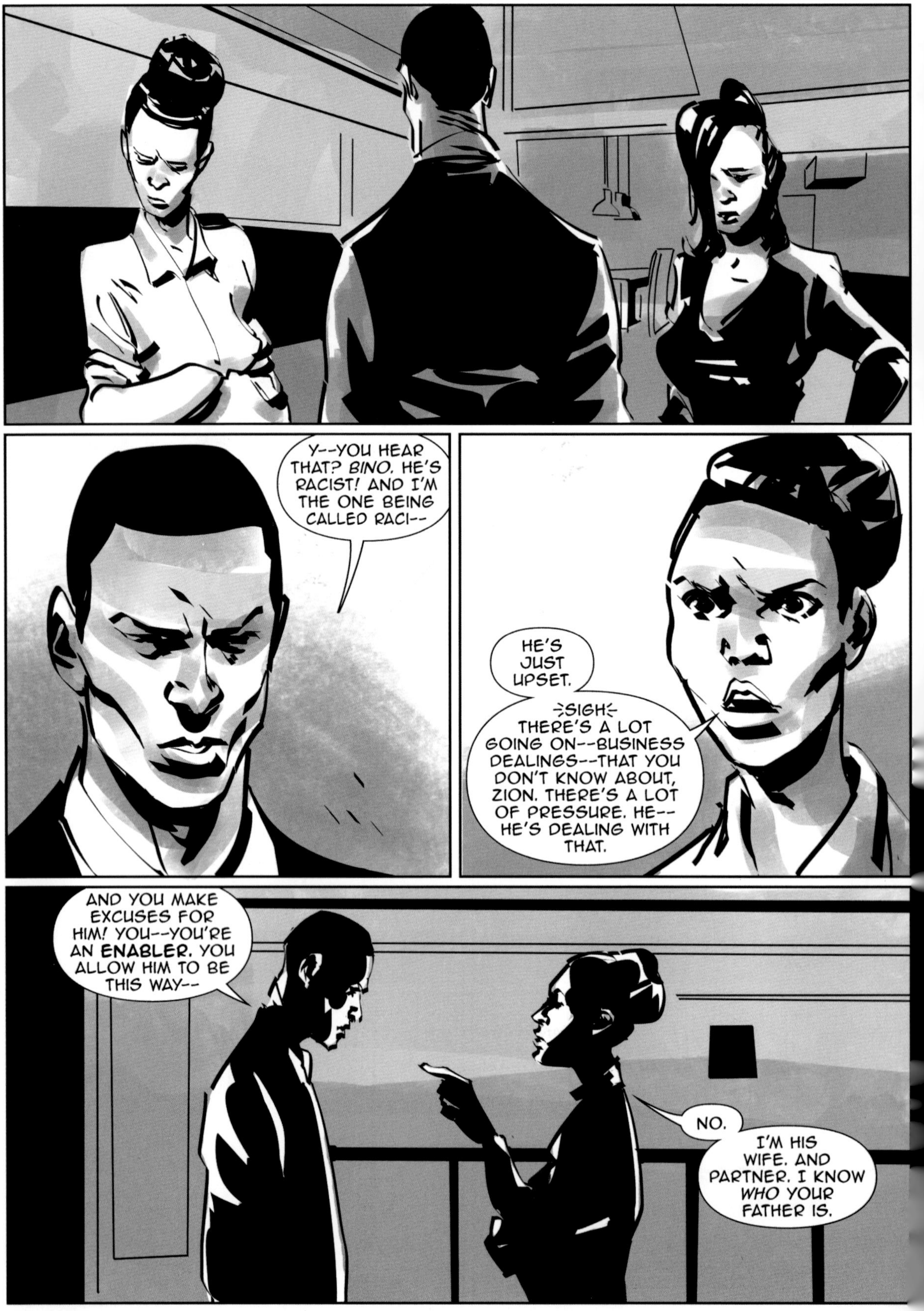

Y--YOU HEAR THAT? *BINO.* HE'S RACIST! AND I'M THE ONE BEING CALLED RACI--
HE'S JUST UPSET.
-SIGH- THERE'S A LOT GOING ON--BUSINESS DEALINGS--THAT YOU DON'T KNOW ABOUT, ZION. THERE'S A LOT OF PRESSURE. HE--HE'S DEALING WITH THAT.
AND YOU MAKE EXCUSES FOR HIM! YOU--YOU'RE AN **ENABLER.** YOU ALLOW HIM TO BE THIS WAY--
NO.
I'M HIS WIFE. AND PARTNER. I KNOW *WHO* YOUR FATHER IS.

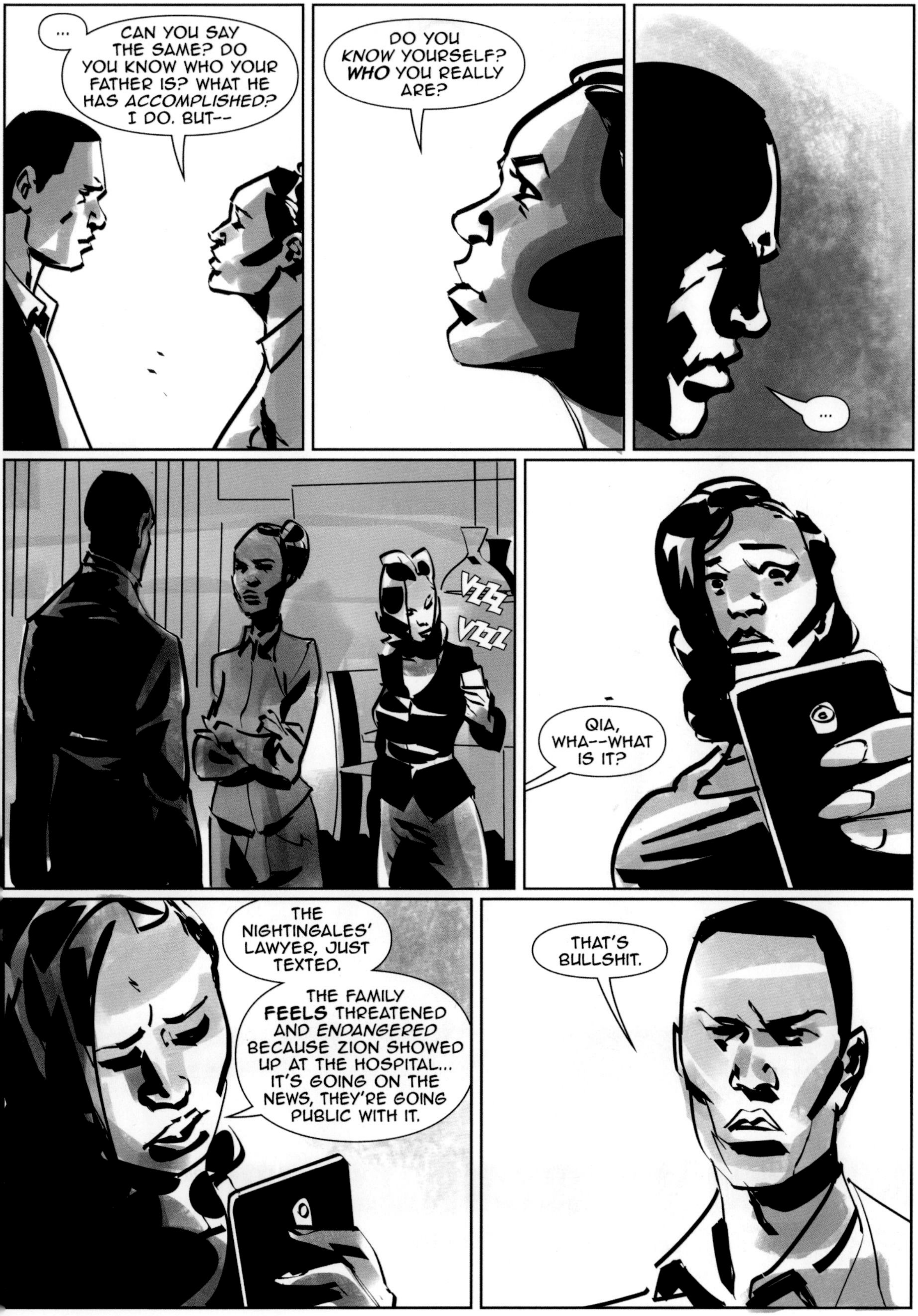
...
CAN YOU SAY THE SAME? DO YOU KNOW WHO YOUR FATHER IS? WHAT HE HAS ACCOMPLISHED? I DO. BUT--
DO YOU KNOW YOURSELF? WHO YOU REALLY ARE?
...
VZZZ
VZZZ
QIA, WHA--WHAT IS IT?
THE NIGHTINGALES' LAWYER, JUST TEXTED.
THE FAMILY FEELS THREATENED AND ENDANGERED BECAUSE ZION SHOWED UP AT THE HOSPITAL... IT'S GOING ON THE NEWS, THEY'RE GOING PUBLIC WITH IT.
THAT'S BULLSHIT.

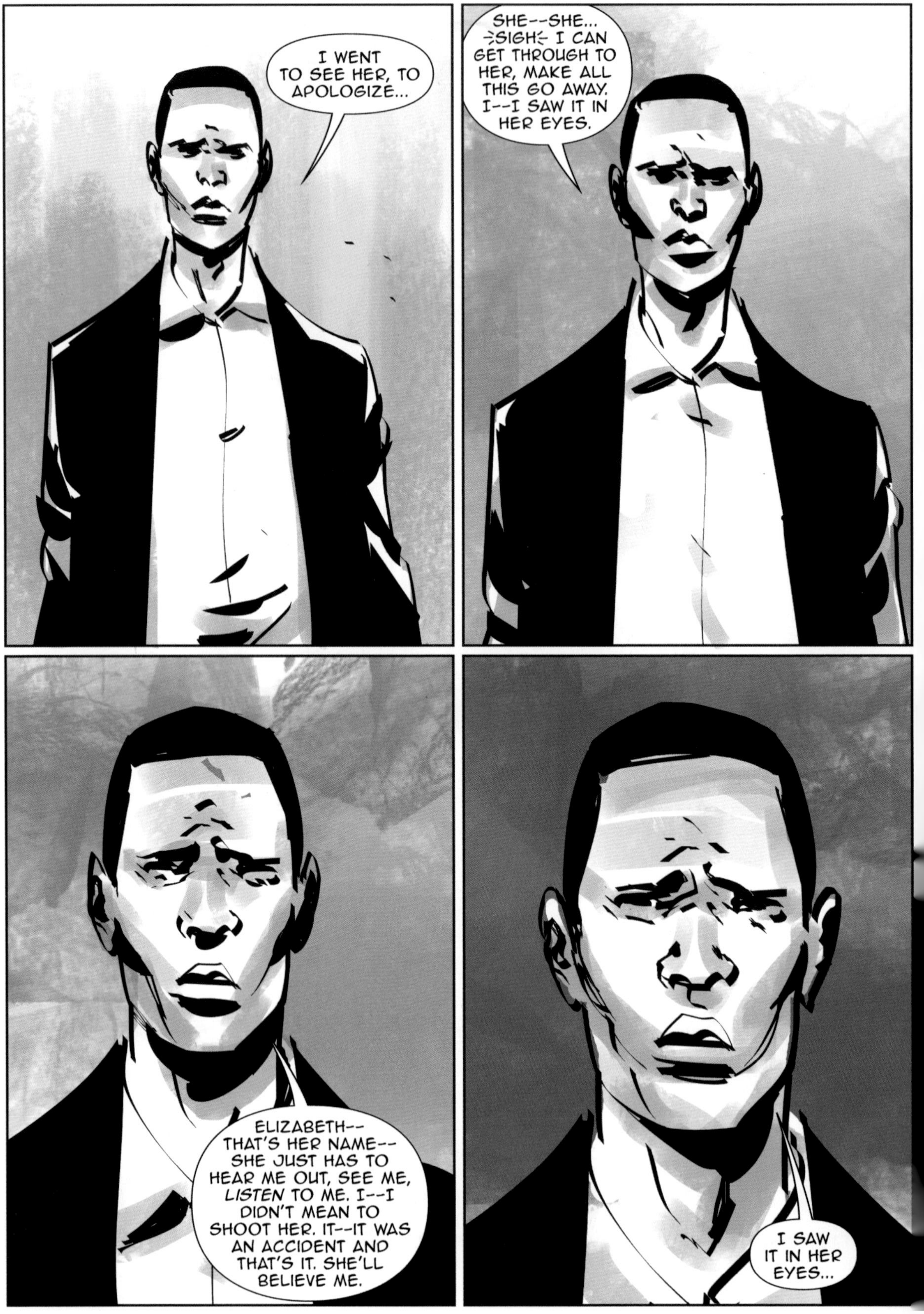
I WENT TO SEE HER, TO APOLOGIZE...
SHE--SHE... -SIGH- I CAN GET THROUGH TO HER, MAKE ALL THIS GO AWAY. I--I SAW IT IN HER EYES.
ELIZABETH-- THAT'S HER NAME-- SHE JUST HAS TO HEAR ME OUT, SEE ME, *LISTEN* TO ME. I--I DIDN'T MEAN TO SHOOT HER. IT--IT WAS AN ACCIDENT AND THAT'S IT. SHE'LL BELIEVE ME.
I SAW IT IN HER EYES...

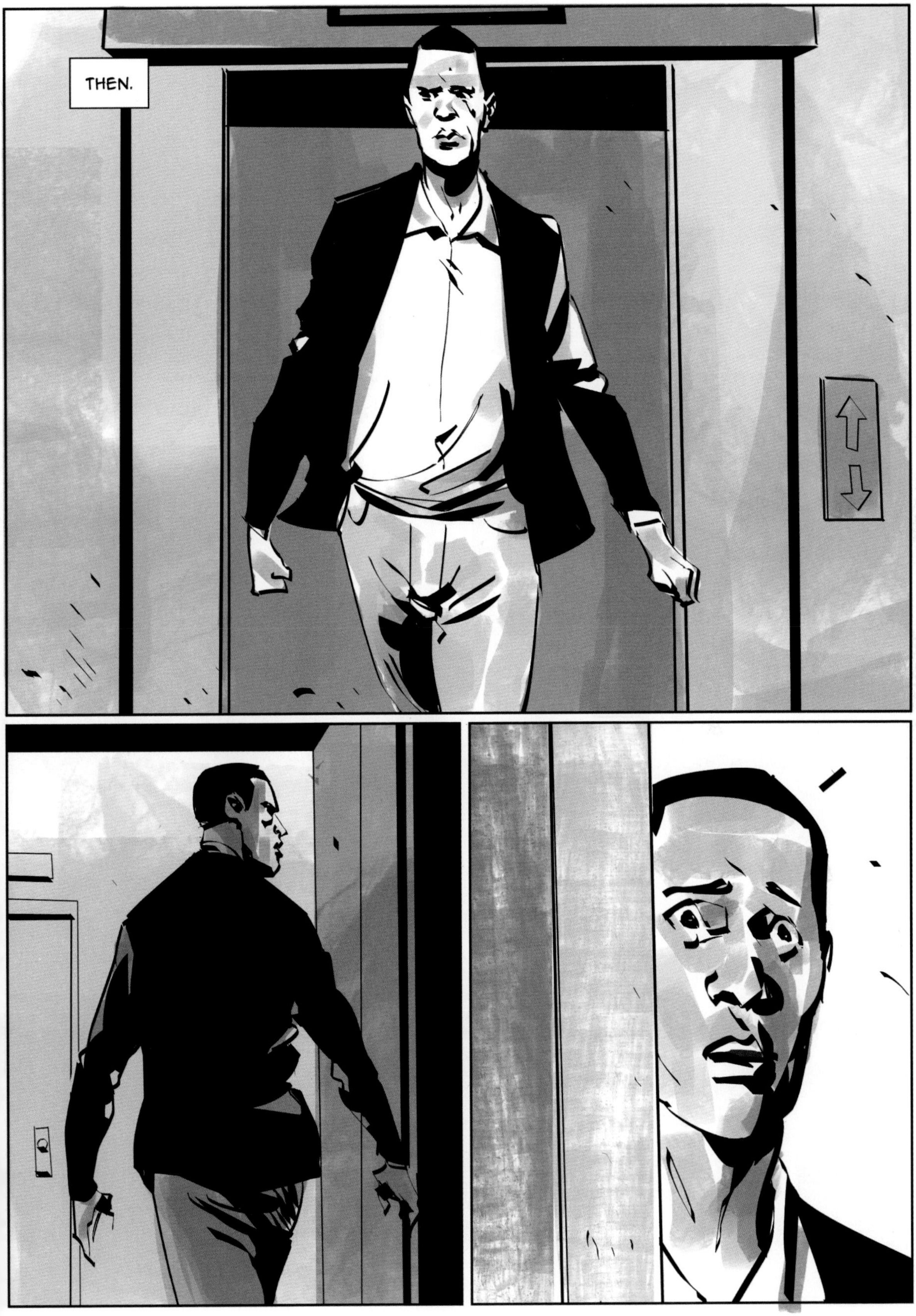
THEN.

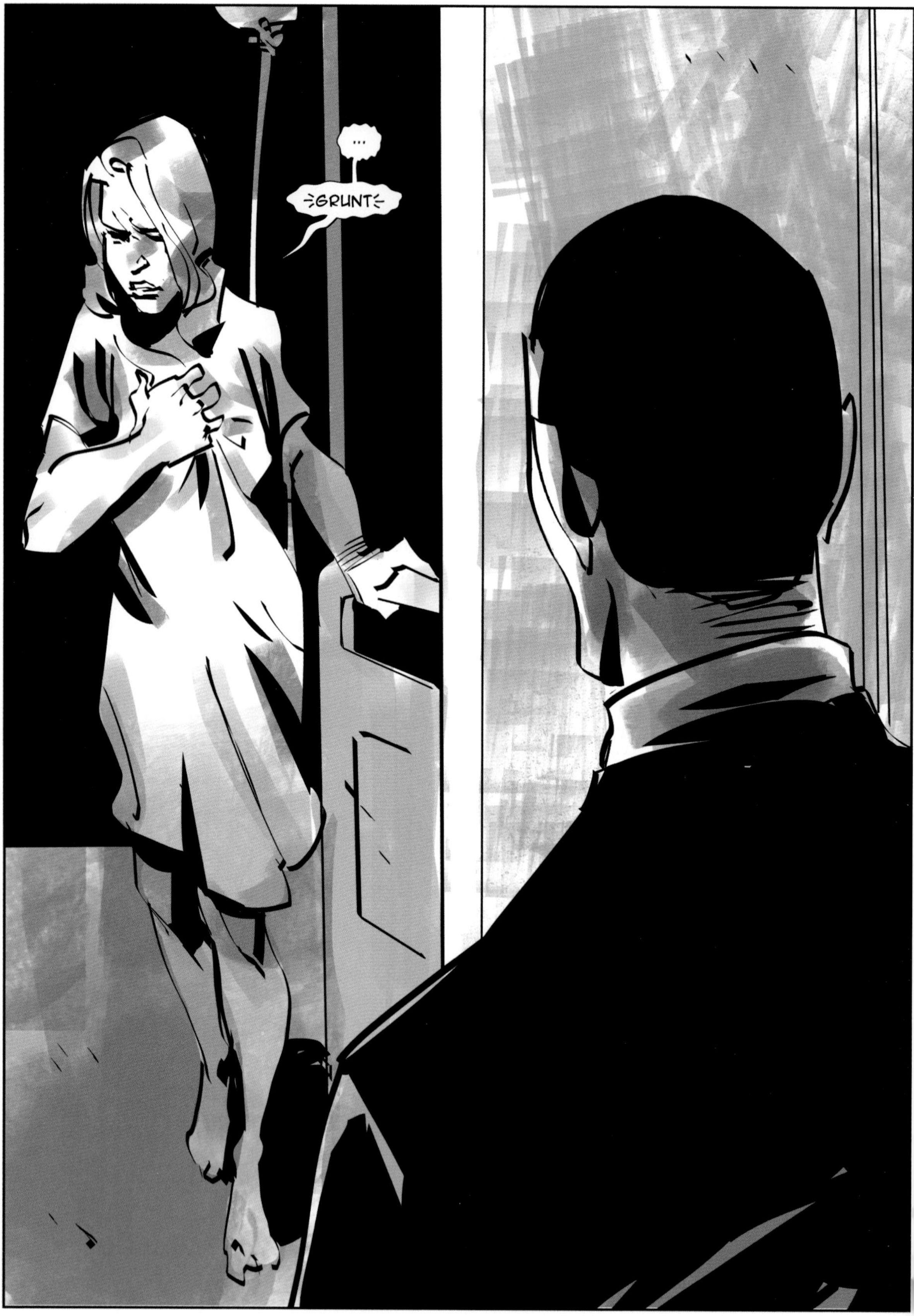
...
GRUNT

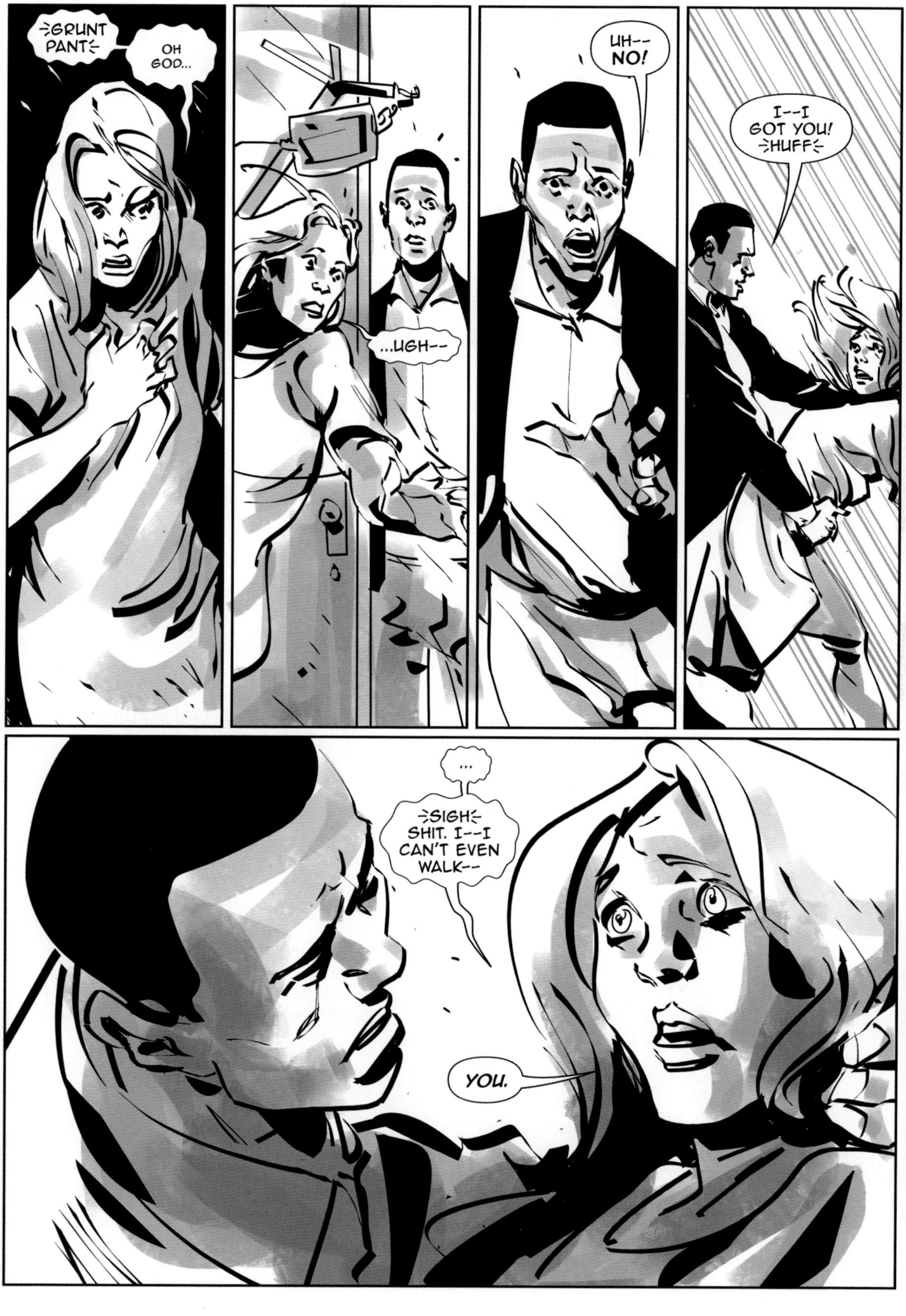

GRUNT PANT
OH GOD...
...UGH--
UH-- NO!
I--I GOT YOU! HUFF
...
SIGH SHIT. I--I CAN'T EVEN WALK--
YOU.

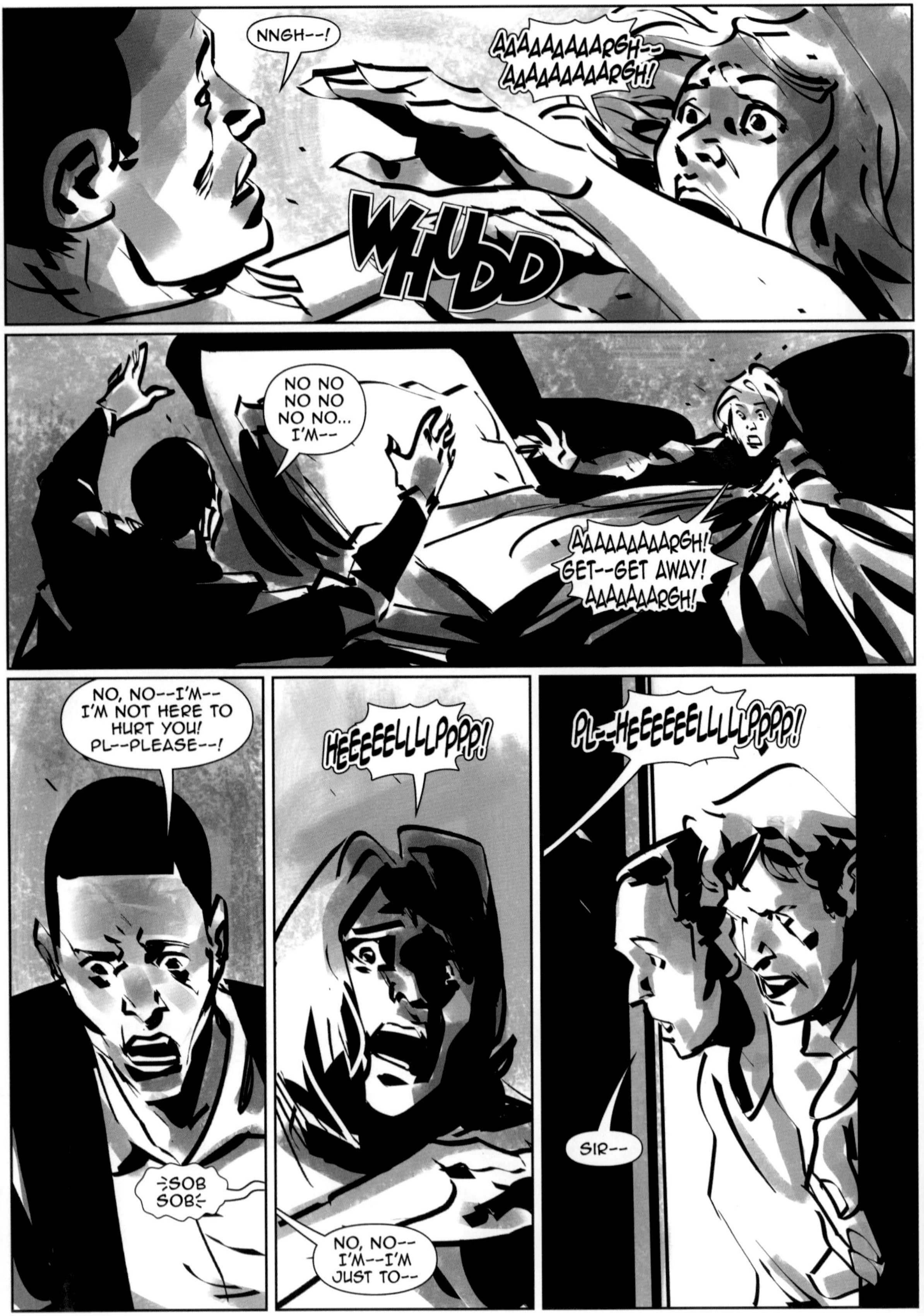
NNGH--!
AAAAAAAAARGH--
AAAAAAAAARGH!
WHUDD
NO NO NO NO NO NO... I'M--
AAAAAAAAARGH! GET--GET AWAY! AAAAAAARGH!
NO, NO--I'M-- I'M NOT HERE TO HURT YOU! PL--PLEASE--!
SOB SOB
HEEEEELLLLPPPP!
NO, NO-- I'M--I'M JUST TO--
PL--HEEEEEELLLLLPPPP!
SIR--

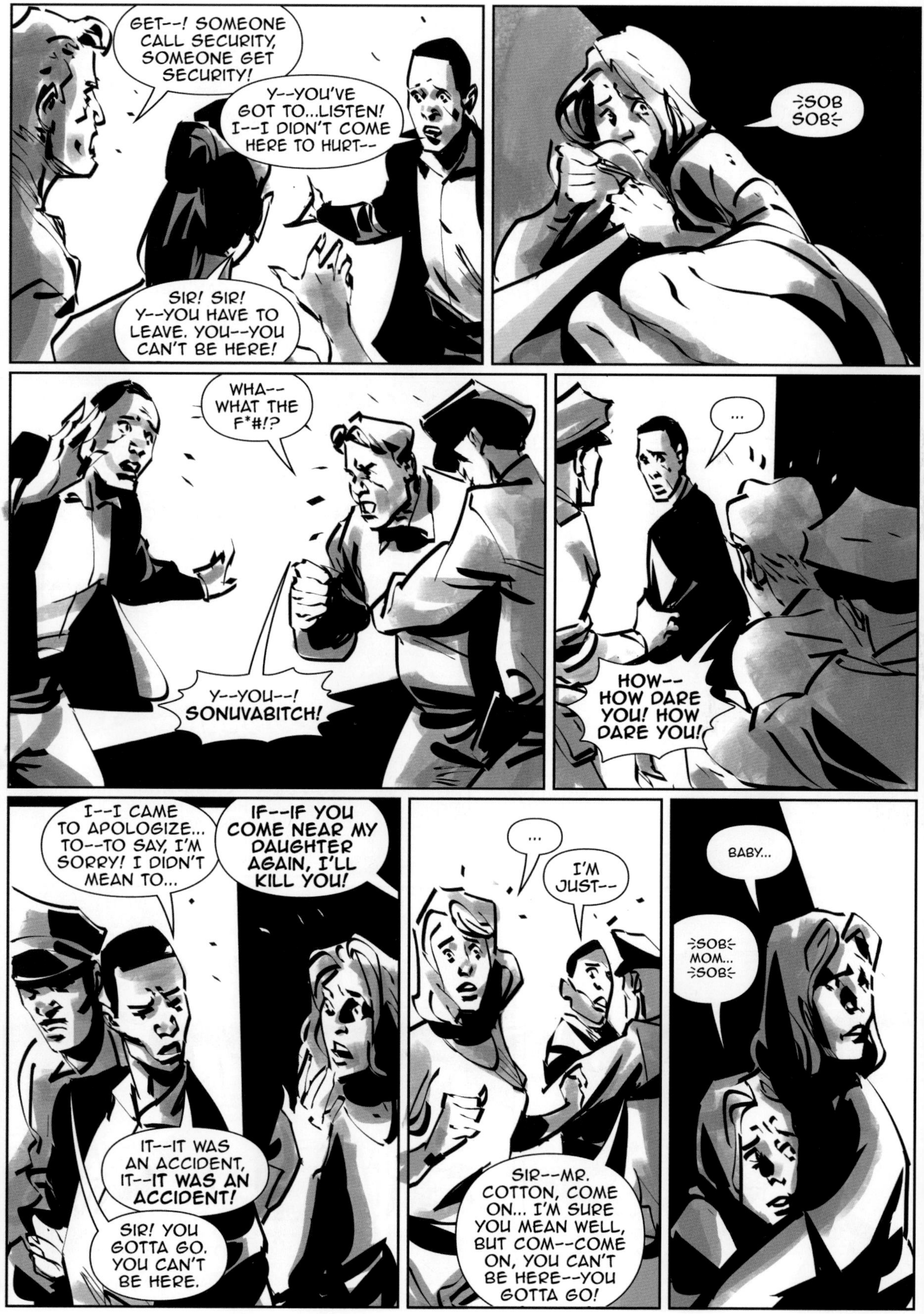
GET--! SOMEONE CALL SECURITY, SOMEONE GET SECURITY!
Y--YOU'VE GOT TO...LISTEN! I--I DIDN'T COME HERE TO HURT--
SIR! SIR! Y--YOU HAVE TO LEAVE. YOU--YOU CAN'T BE HERE!
SOB SOB
WHA-- WHAT THE F*#!?
Y--YOU--! SONUVABITCH!
...
HOW-- HOW DARE YOU! HOW DARE YOU!
I--I CAME TO APOLOGIZE... TO--TO SAY, I'M SORRY! I DIDN'T MEAN TO...
IF--IF YOU COME NEAR MY DAUGHTER AGAIN, I'LL KILL YOU!
IT--IT WAS AN ACCIDENT, IT--IT WAS AN ACCIDENT!
SIR! YOU GOTTA GO. YOU CAN'T BE HERE.
...
I'M JUST--
SIR--MR. COTTON, COME ON... I'M SURE YOU MEAN WELL, BUT COM--COME ON, YOU CAN'T BE HERE--YOU GOTTA GO!
BABY...
SOB MOM... SOB

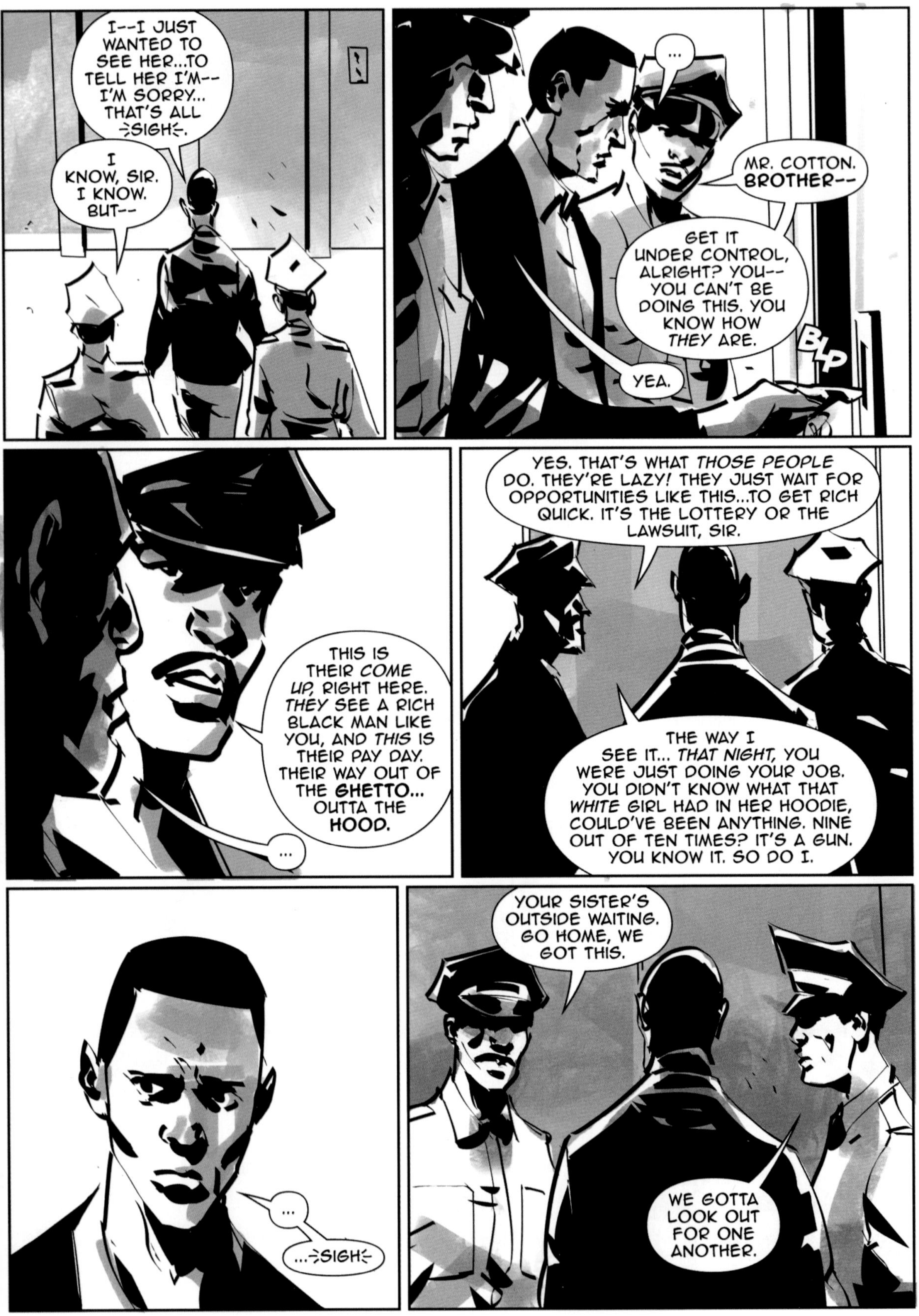
I--I JUST WANTED TO SEE HER...TO TELL HER I'M--I'M SORRY... THAT'S ALL ⇝SIGH⇜.
I KNOW, SIR. I KNOW. BUT--
...
MR. COTTON. BROTHER--
GET IT UNDER CONTROL, ALRIGHT? YOU--YOU CAN'T BE DOING THIS. YOU KNOW HOW THEY ARE.
BLIP
YEA.
THIS IS THEIR COME UP, RIGHT HERE. THEY SEE A RICH BLACK MAN LIKE YOU, AND THIS IS THEIR PAY DAY. THEIR WAY OUT OF THE GHETTO... OUTTA THE HOOD.
...
YES. THAT'S WHAT THOSE PEOPLE DO. THEY'RE LAZY! THEY JUST WAIT FOR OPPORTUNITIES LIKE THIS...TO GET RICH QUICK. IT'S THE LOTTERY OR THE LAWSUIT, SIR.
THE WAY I SEE IT... THAT NIGHT, YOU WERE JUST DOING YOUR JOB. YOU DIDN'T KNOW WHAT THAT WHITE GIRL HAD IN HER HOODIE, COULD'VE BEEN ANYTHING. NINE OUT OF TEN TIMES? IT'S A GUN. YOU KNOW IT. SO DO I.
...
...⇝SIGH⇜
YOUR SISTER'S OUTSIDE WAITING. GO HOME, WE GOT THIS.
WE GOTTA LOOK OUT FOR ONE ANOTHER.

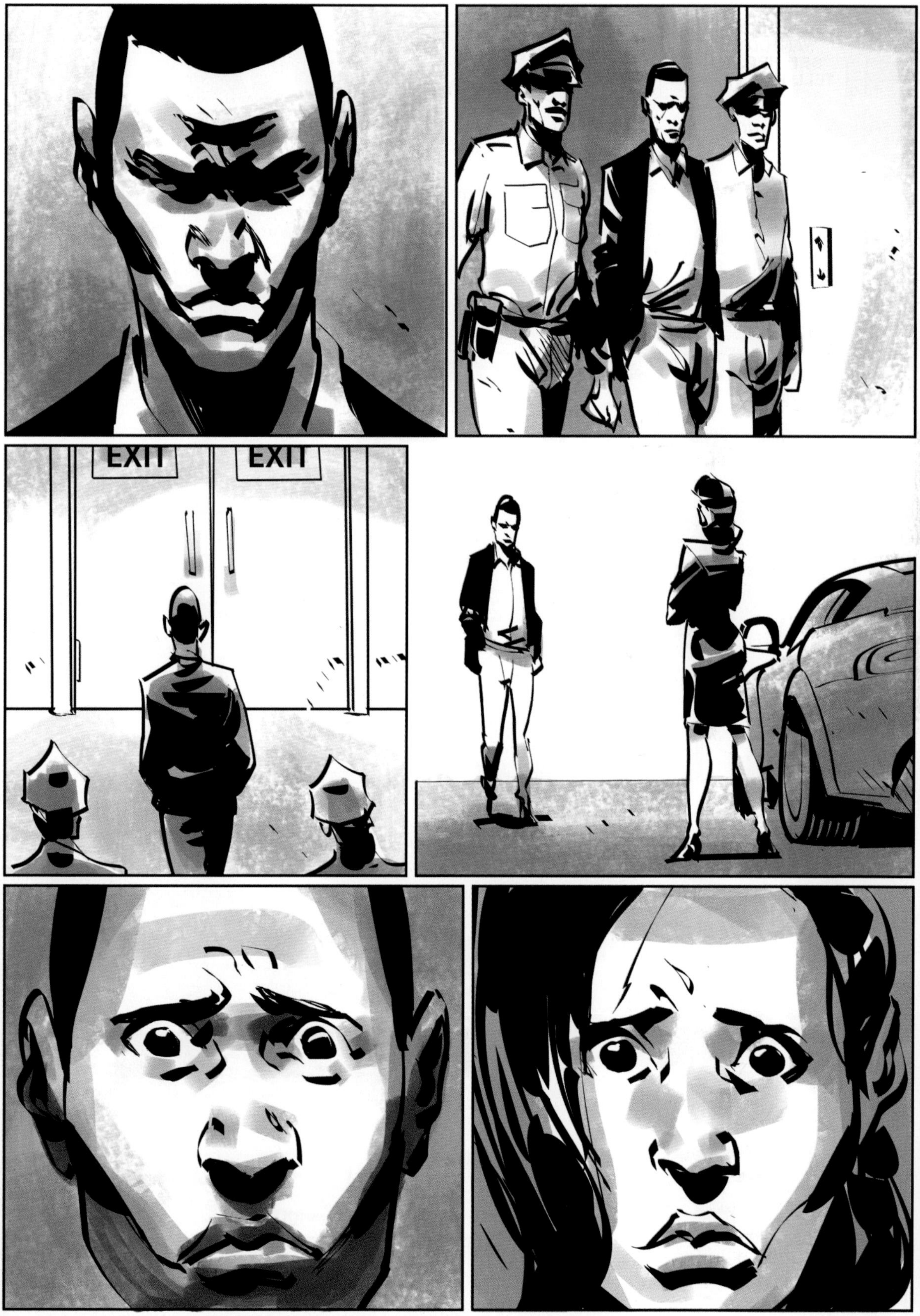
EXIT
EXIT

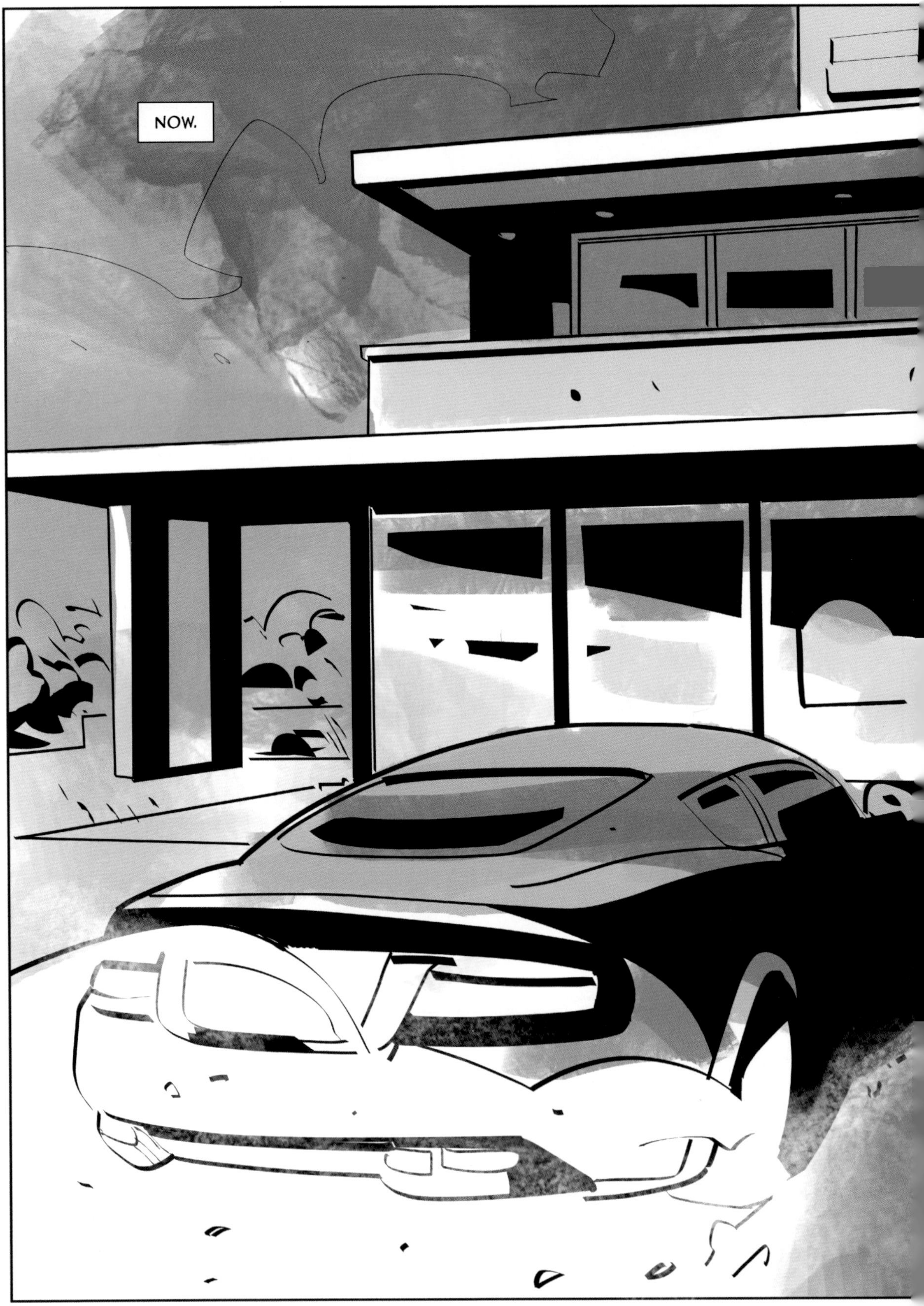
NOW.

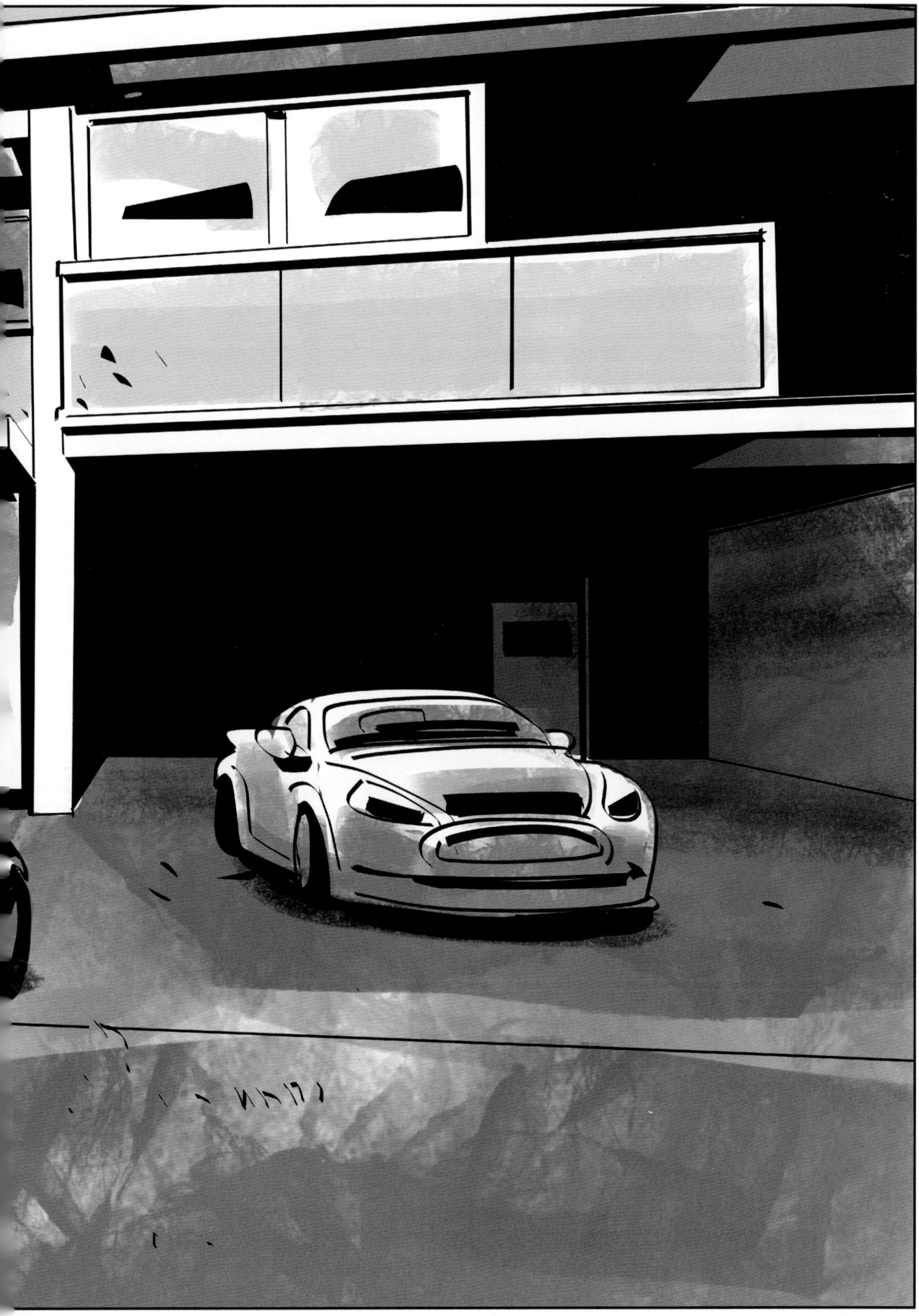

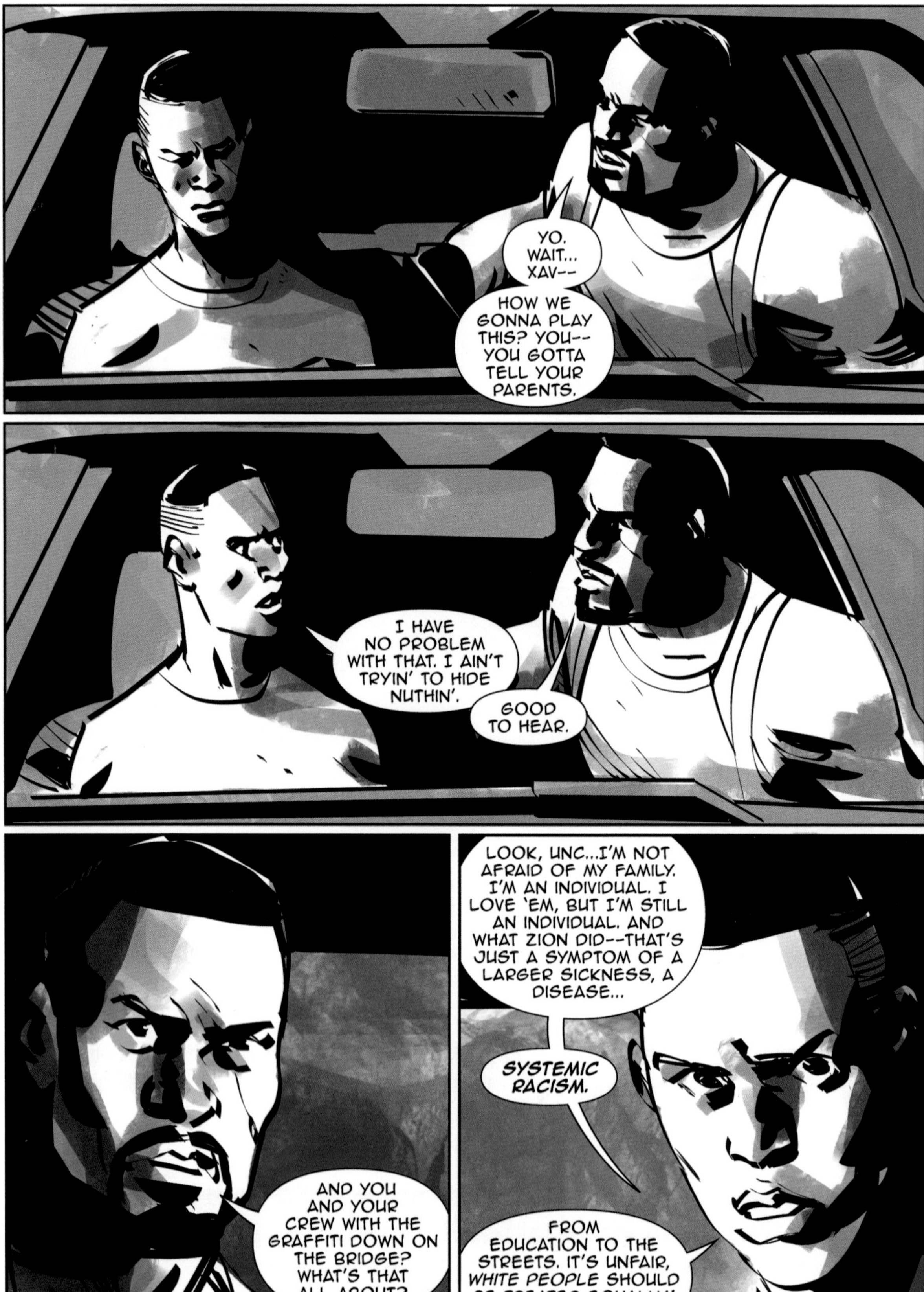
YO. WAIT... XAV--
HOW WE GONNA PLAY THIS? YOU-- YOU GOTTA TELL YOUR PARENTS.
I HAVE NO PROBLEM WITH THAT. I AIN'T TRYIN' TO HIDE NUTHIN'.
GOOD TO HEAR.
AND YOU AND YOUR CREW WITH THE GRAFFITI DOWN ON THE BRIDGE? WHAT'S THAT ALL ABOUT?
LOOK, UNC...I'M NOT AFRAID OF MY FAMILY. I'M AN INDIVIDUAL. I LOVE 'EM, BUT I'M STILL AN INDIVIDUAL. AND WHAT ZION DID--THAT'S JUST A SYMPTOM OF A LARGER SICKNESS, A DISEASE...
SYSTEMIC RACISM.
FROM EDUCATION TO THE STREETS. IT'S UNFAIR, *WHITE PEOPLE* SHOULD BE TREATED EQUALLY! WE'RE ALL EQUAL.

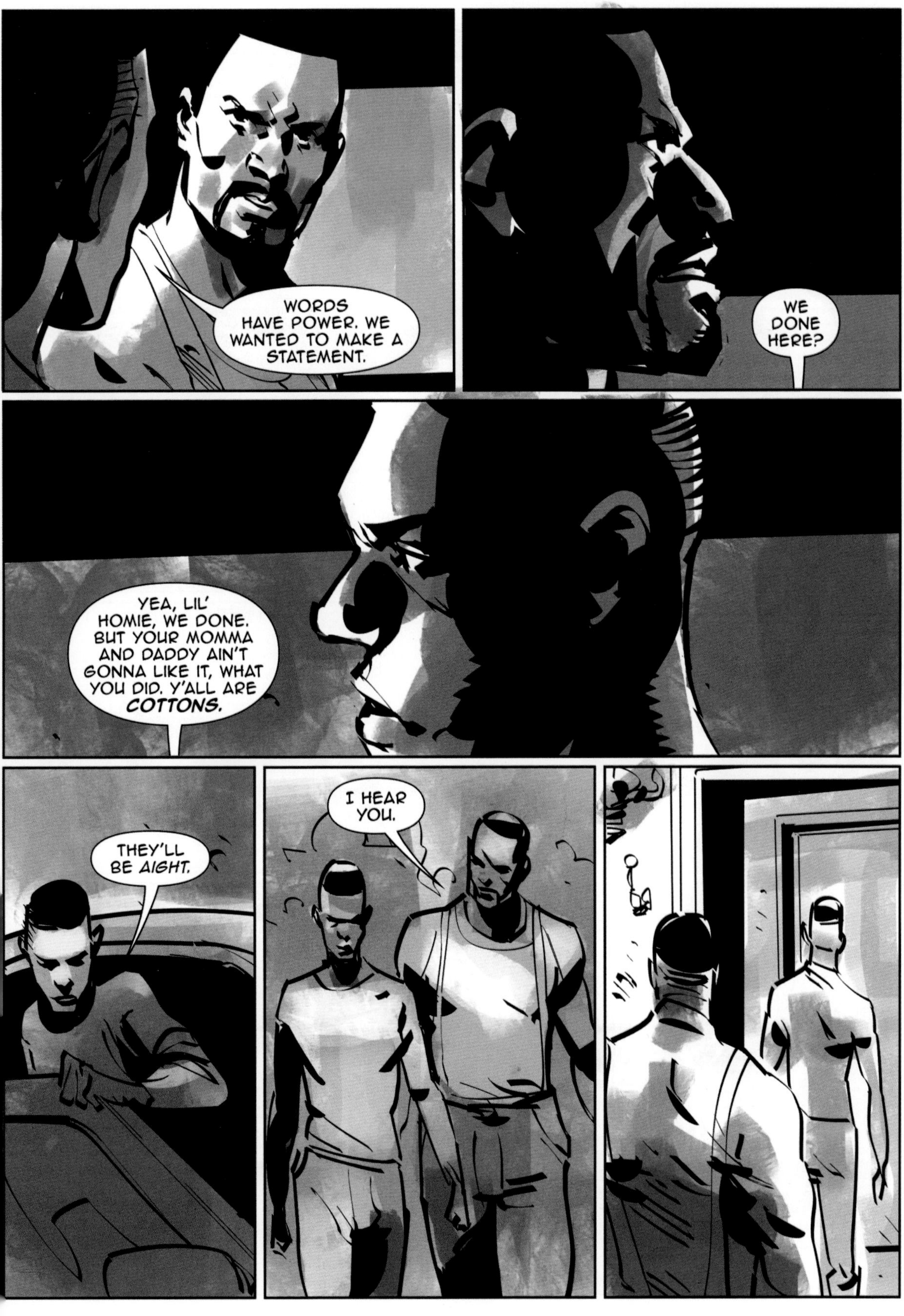
WORDS HAVE POWER. WE WANTED TO MAKE A STATEMENT.
WE DONE HERE?
YEA, LIL' HOMIE, WE DONE. BUT YOUR MOMMA AND DADDY AIN'T GONNA LIKE IT, WHAT YOU DID. Y'ALL ARE *COTTONS.*
THEY'LL BE AIGHT.
I HEAR YOU.

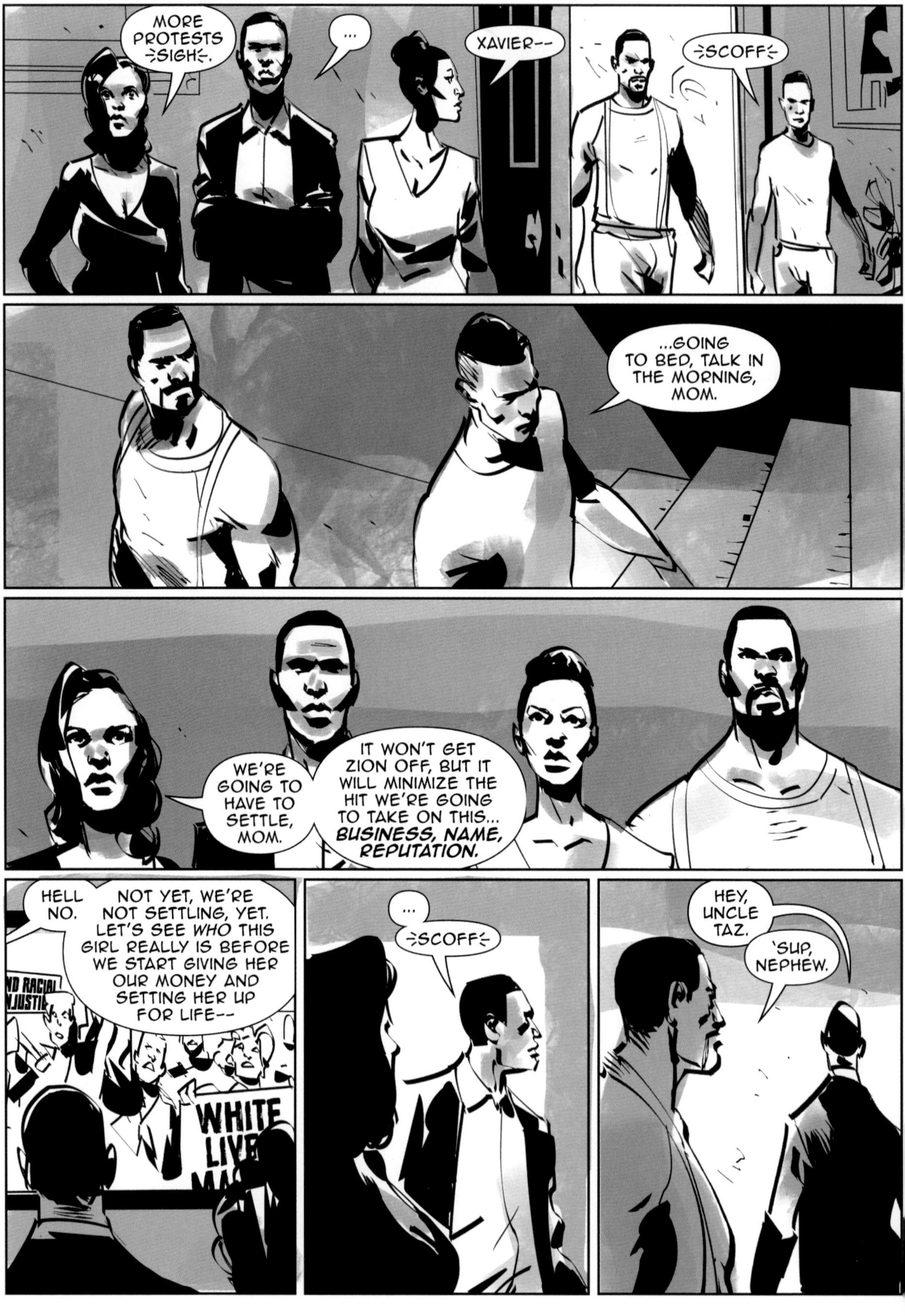
MORE PROTESTS ~SIGH~.
...
XAVIER--
~SCOFF~
...GOING TO BED, TALK IN THE MORNING, MOM.
WE'RE GOING TO HAVE TO SETTLE, MOM.
IT WON'T GET ZION OFF, BUT IT WILL MINIMIZE THE HIT WE'RE GOING TO TAKE ON THIS... BUSINESS, NAME, REPUTATION.
HELL NO.
NOT YET, WE'RE NOT SETTLING, YET. LET'S SEE WHO THIS GIRL REALLY IS BEFORE WE START GIVING HER OUR MONEY AND SETTING HER UP FOR LIFE--
ND RACIAL NJUSTI
WHITE LIVE MA
...
~SCOFF~
HEY, UNCLE TAZ.
'SUP, NEPHEW.

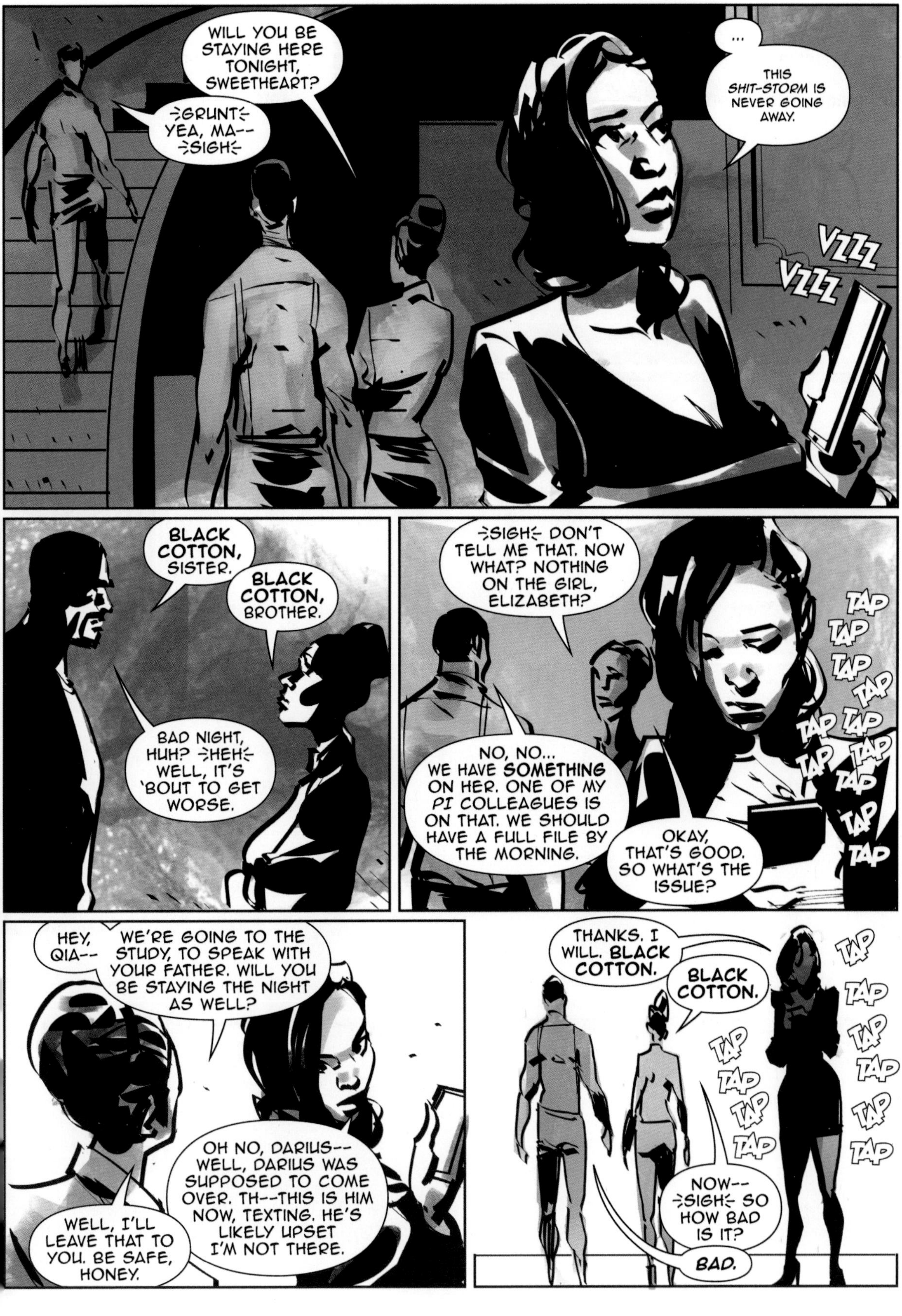
WILL YOU BE STAYING HERE TONIGHT, SWEETHEART?
⁓GRUNT⁓ YEA, MA-- ⁓SIGH⁓
...
THIS SHIT-STORM IS NEVER GOING AWAY.
VZZZ
VZZZ
BLACK COTTON, SISTER.
BLACK COTTON, BROTHER.
BAD NIGHT, HUH? ⁓HEH⁓ WELL, IT'S 'BOUT TO GET WORSE.
⁓SIGH⁓ DON'T TELL ME THAT. NOW WHAT? NOTHING ON THE GIRL, ELIZABETH?
NO, NO... WE HAVE SOMETHING ON HER. ONE OF MY PI COLLEAGUES IS ON THAT. WE SHOULD HAVE A FULL FILE BY THE MORNING.
OKAY, THAT'S GOOD. SO WHAT'S THE ISSUE?
TAP TAP TAP TAP TAP TAP TAP TAP TAP TAP TAP
HEY, QIA--
WE'RE GOING TO THE STUDY, TO SPEAK WITH YOUR FATHER. WILL YOU BE STAYING THE NIGHT AS WELL?
OH NO, DARIUS-- WELL, DARIUS WAS SUPPOSED TO COME OVER. TH--THIS IS HIM NOW, TEXTING. HE'S LIKELY UPSET I'M NOT THERE.
WELL, I'LL LEAVE THAT TO YOU. BE SAFE, HONEY.
THANKS. I WILL. BLACK COTTON.
BLACK COTTON.
TAP TAP TAP TAP TAP TAP TAP TAP TAP TAP
NOW-- ⁓SIGH⁓ SO HOW BAD IS IT?
BAD.

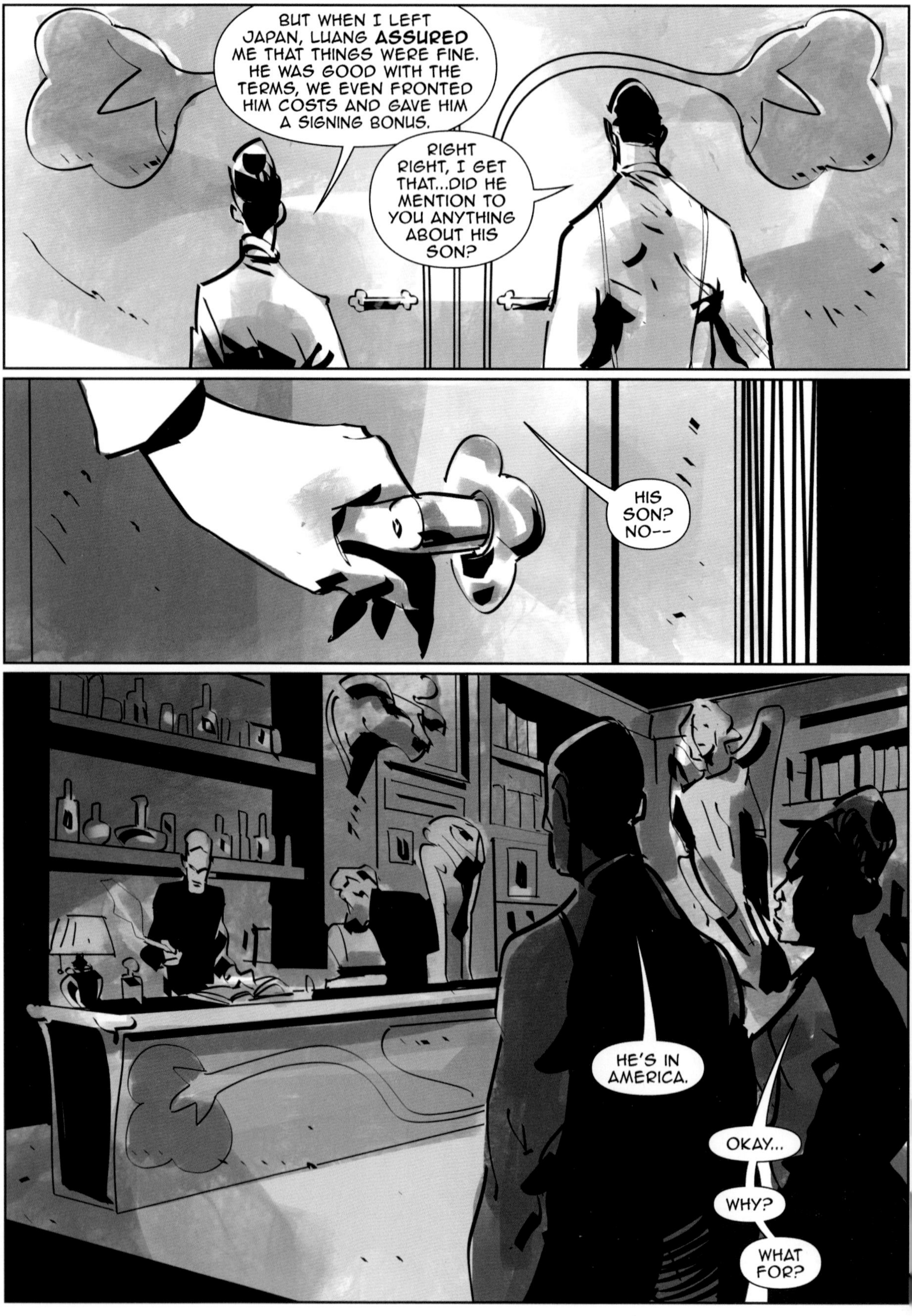
BUT WHEN I LEFT JAPAN, LUANG **ASSURED** ME THAT THINGS WERE FINE. HE WAS GOOD WITH THE TERMS, WE EVEN FRONTED HIM COSTS AND GAVE HIM A SIGNING BONUS.
RIGHT RIGHT, I GET THAT...DID HE MENTION TO YOU ANYTHING ABOUT HIS SON?
HIS SON? NO--
HE'S IN AMERICA.
OKAY...
WHY?
WHAT FOR?

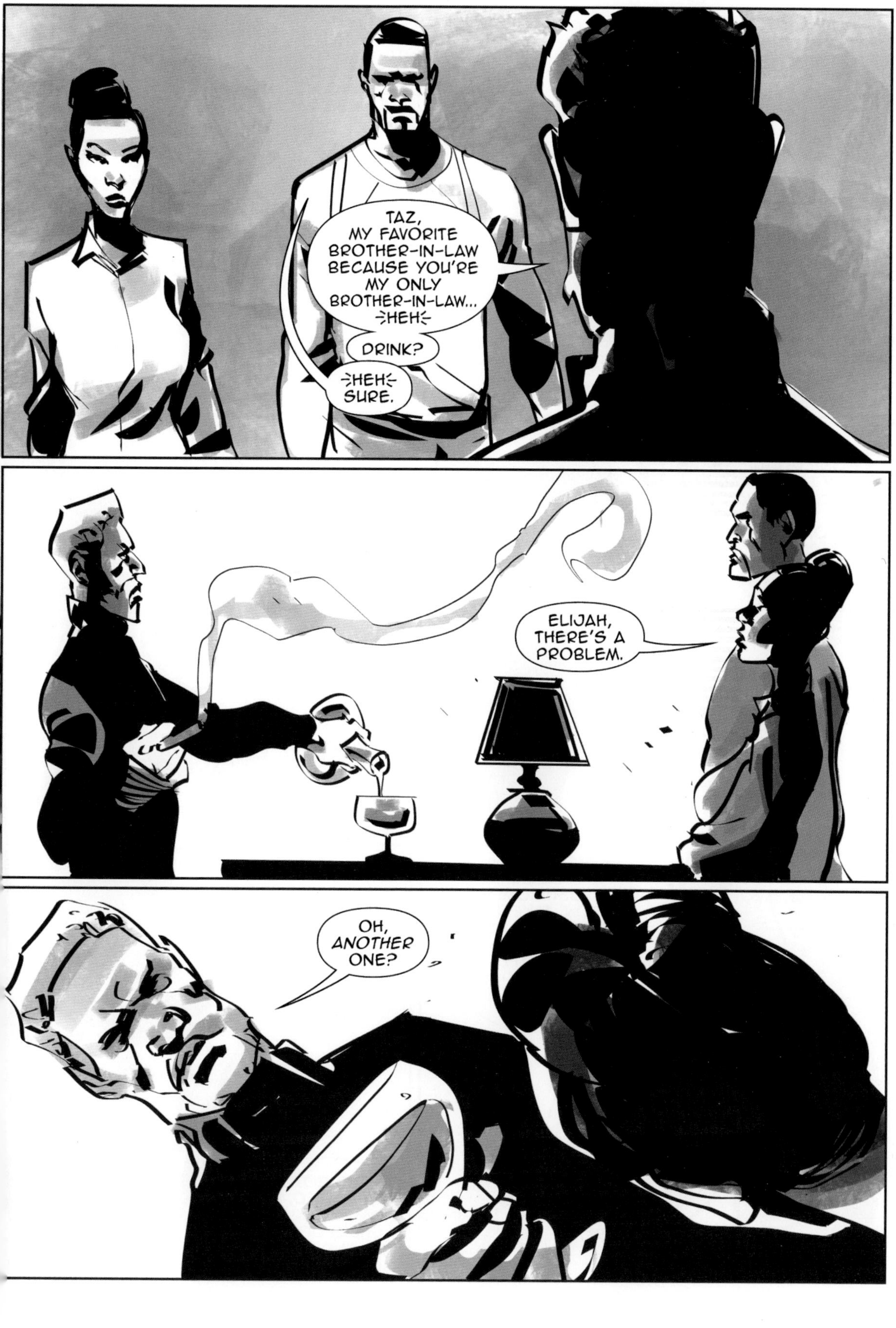
TAZ, MY FAVORITE BROTHER-IN-LAW BECAUSE YOU'RE MY ONLY BROTHER-IN-LAW... HEH
DRINK?
HEH SURE.
ELIJAH, THERE'S A PROBLEM.
OH, ANOTHER ONE?

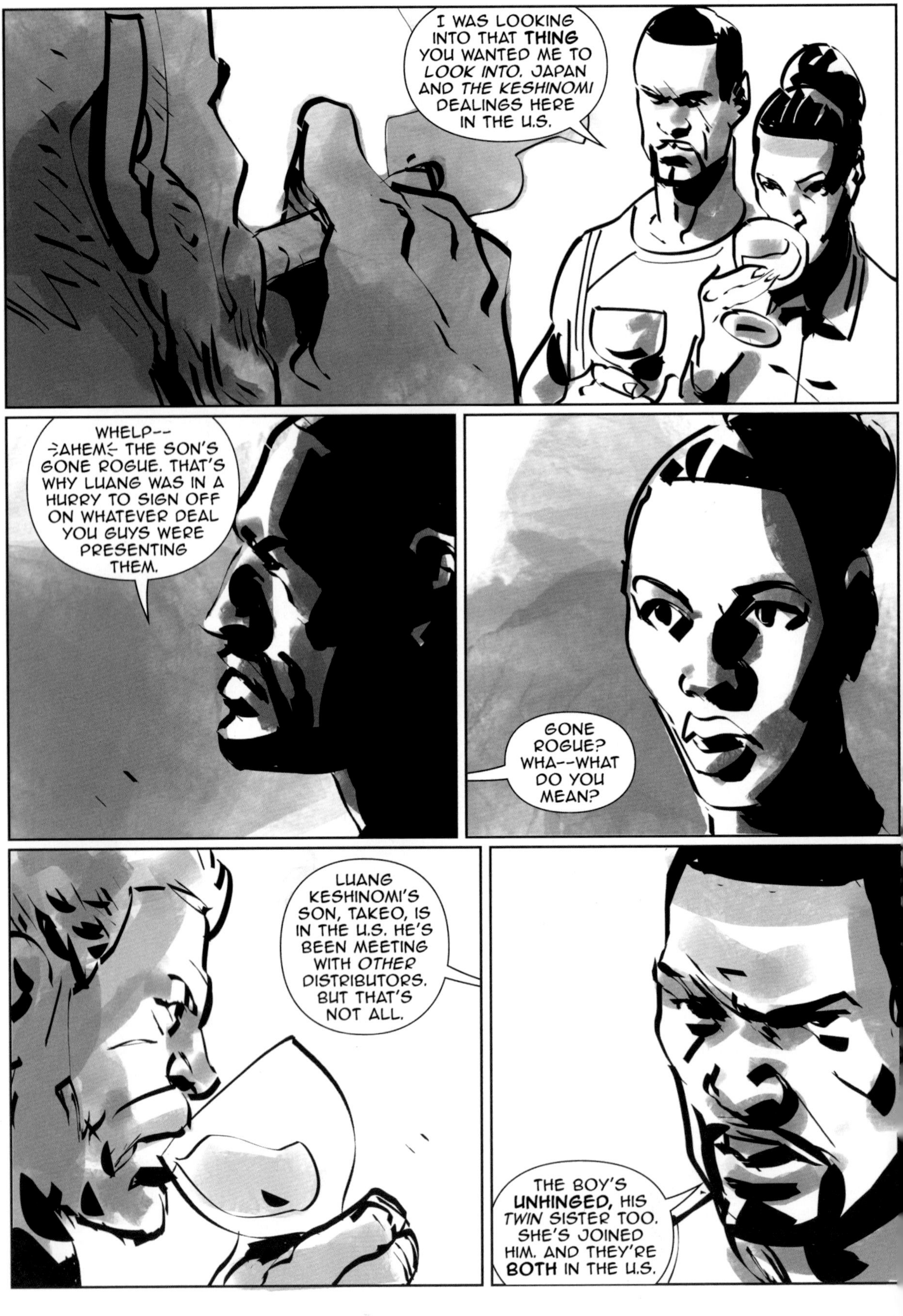

I WAS LOOKING INTO THAT **THING** YOU WANTED ME TO *LOOK INTO.* JAPAN AND *THE KESHINOMI* DEALINGS HERE IN THE U.S.
WHELP-- =AHEM= THE SON'S GONE ROGUE. THAT'S WHY LUANG WAS IN A HURRY TO SIGN OFF ON WHATEVER DEAL YOU GUYS WERE PRESENTING THEM.
GONE ROGUE? WHA--WHAT DO YOU MEAN?
LUANG KESHINOMI'S SON, TAKEO, IS IN THE U.S. HE'S BEEN MEETING WITH *OTHER* DISTRIBUTORS. BUT THAT'S NOT ALL.
THE BOY'S **UNHINGED,** HIS *TWIN* SISTER TOO. SHE'S JOINED HIM. AND THEY'RE **BOTH** IN THE U.S.

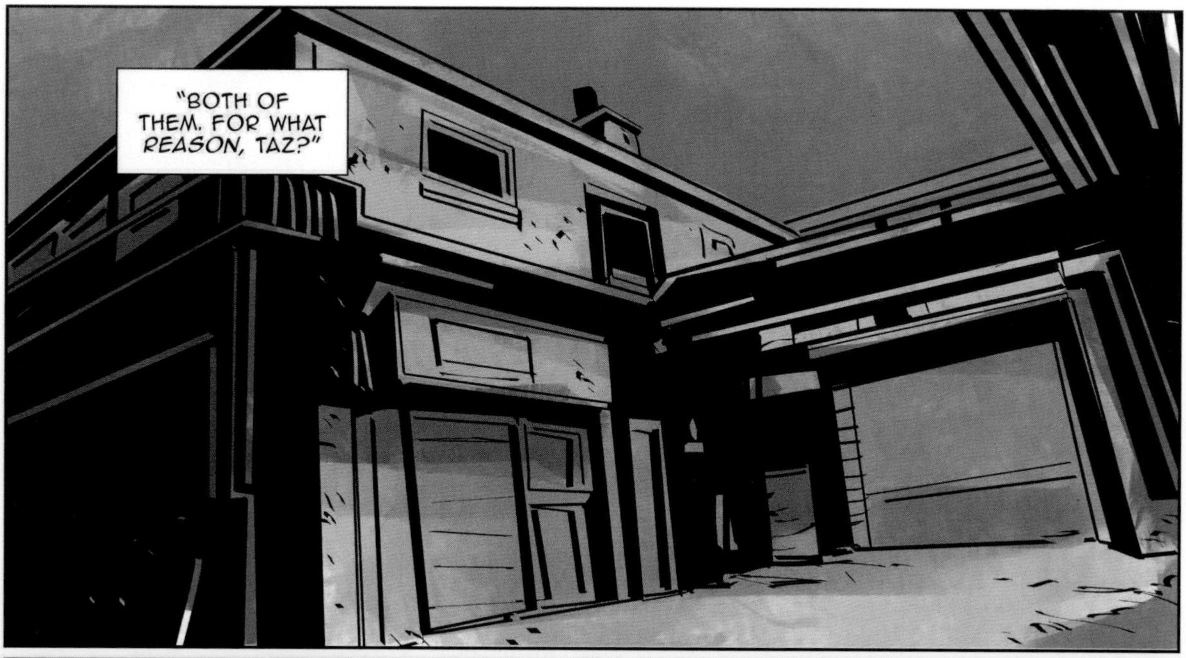
"BOTH OF THEM. FOR WHAT REASON, TAZ?"

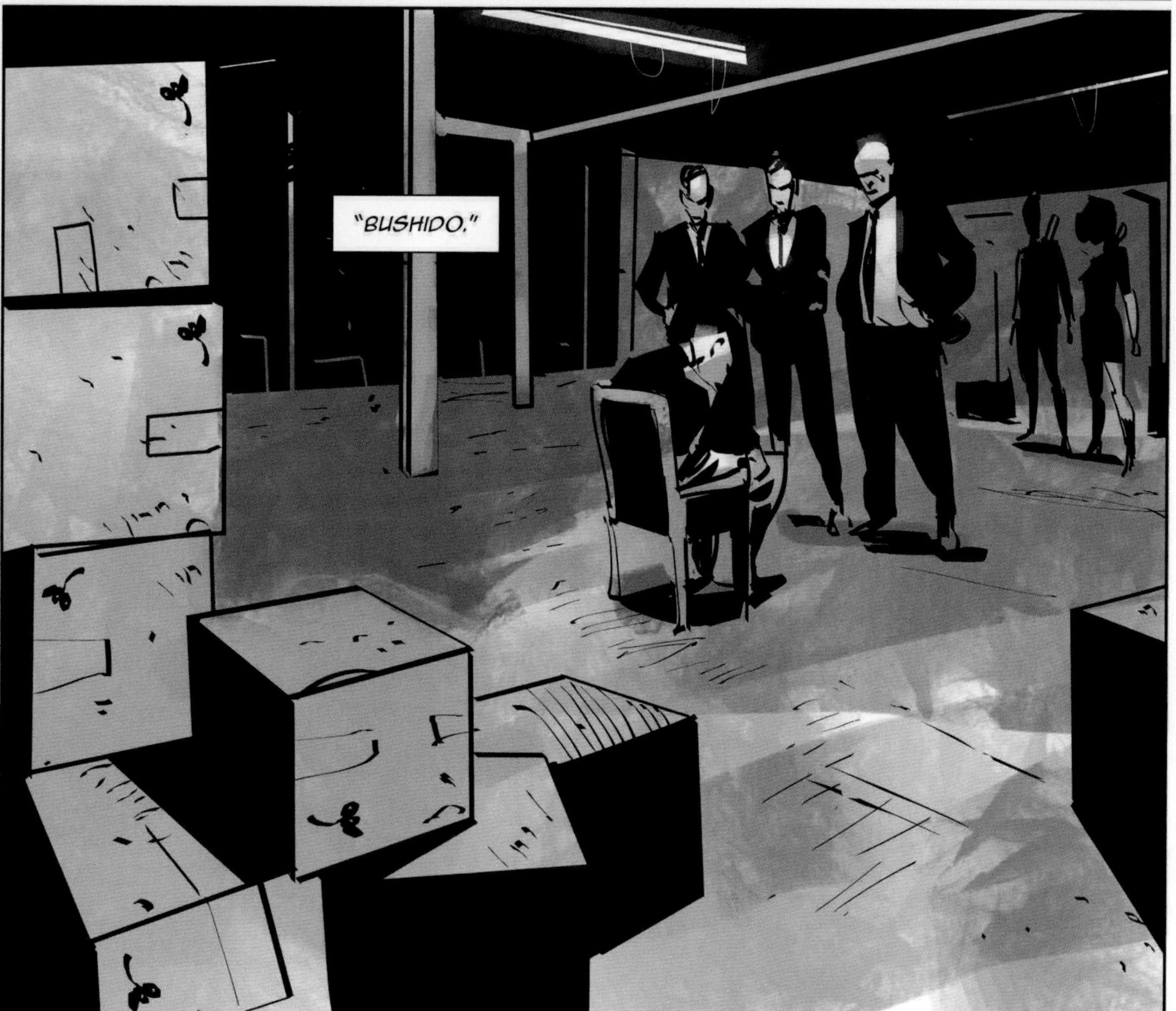
"BUSHIDO."

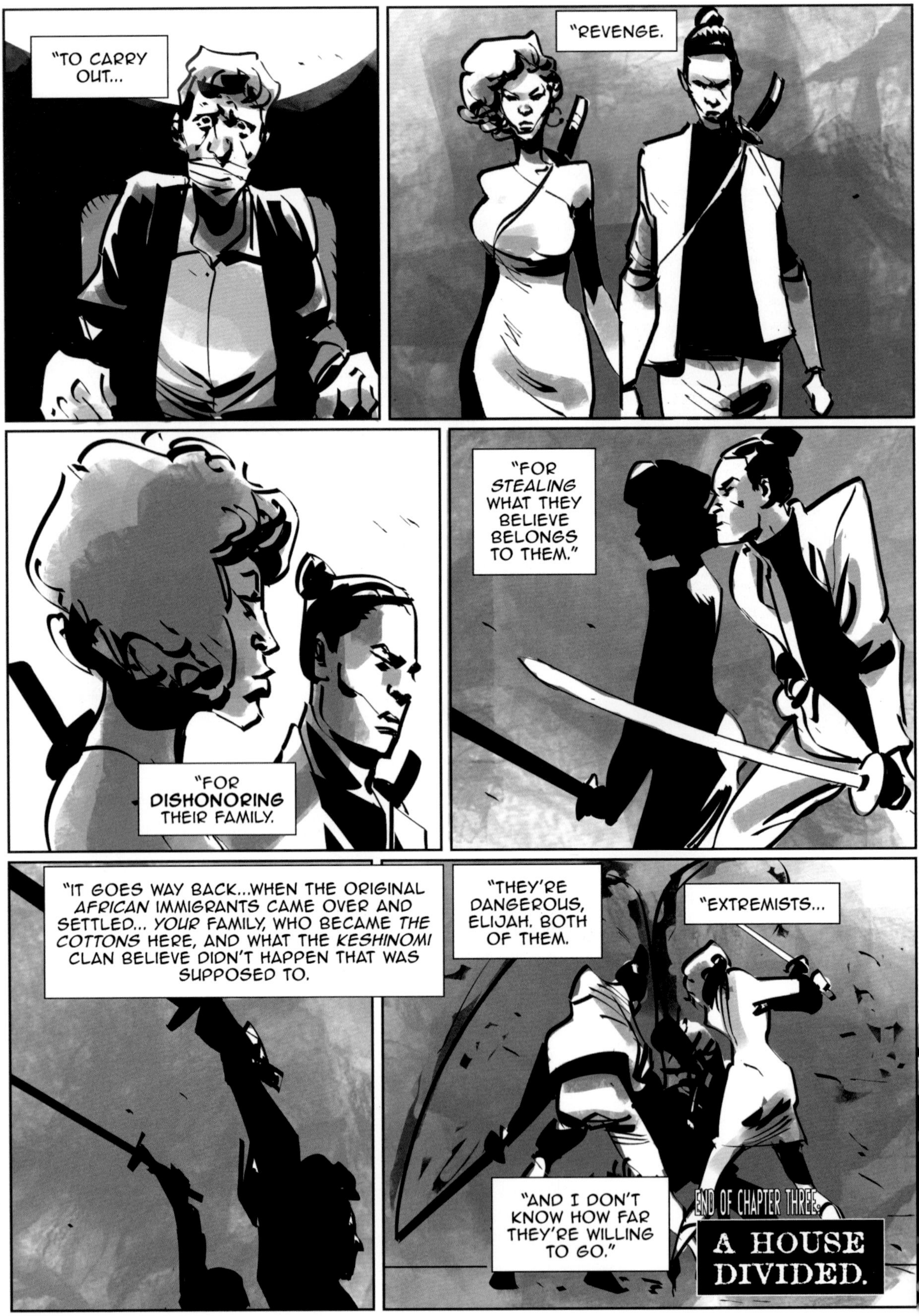
"TO CARRY OUT...
"REVENGE.
"FOR DISHONORING THEIR FAMILY.
"FOR STEALING WHAT THEY BELIEVE BELONGS TO THEM."
"IT GOES WAY BACK...WHEN THE ORIGINAL AFRICAN IMMIGRANTS CAME OVER AND SETTLED... YOUR FAMILY, WHO BECAME THE COTTONS HERE, AND WHAT THE KESHINOMI CLAN BELIEVE DIDN'T HAPPEN THAT WAS SUPPOSED TO.
"THEY'RE DANGEROUS, ELIJAH. BOTH OF THEM.
"EXTREMISTS...
"AND I DON'T KNOW HOW FAR THEY'RE WILLING TO GO."
END OF CHAPTER THREE:
A HOUSE DIVIDED.

LONG SHOT/
A HOUSE DIVIDED

CHAPTER 4

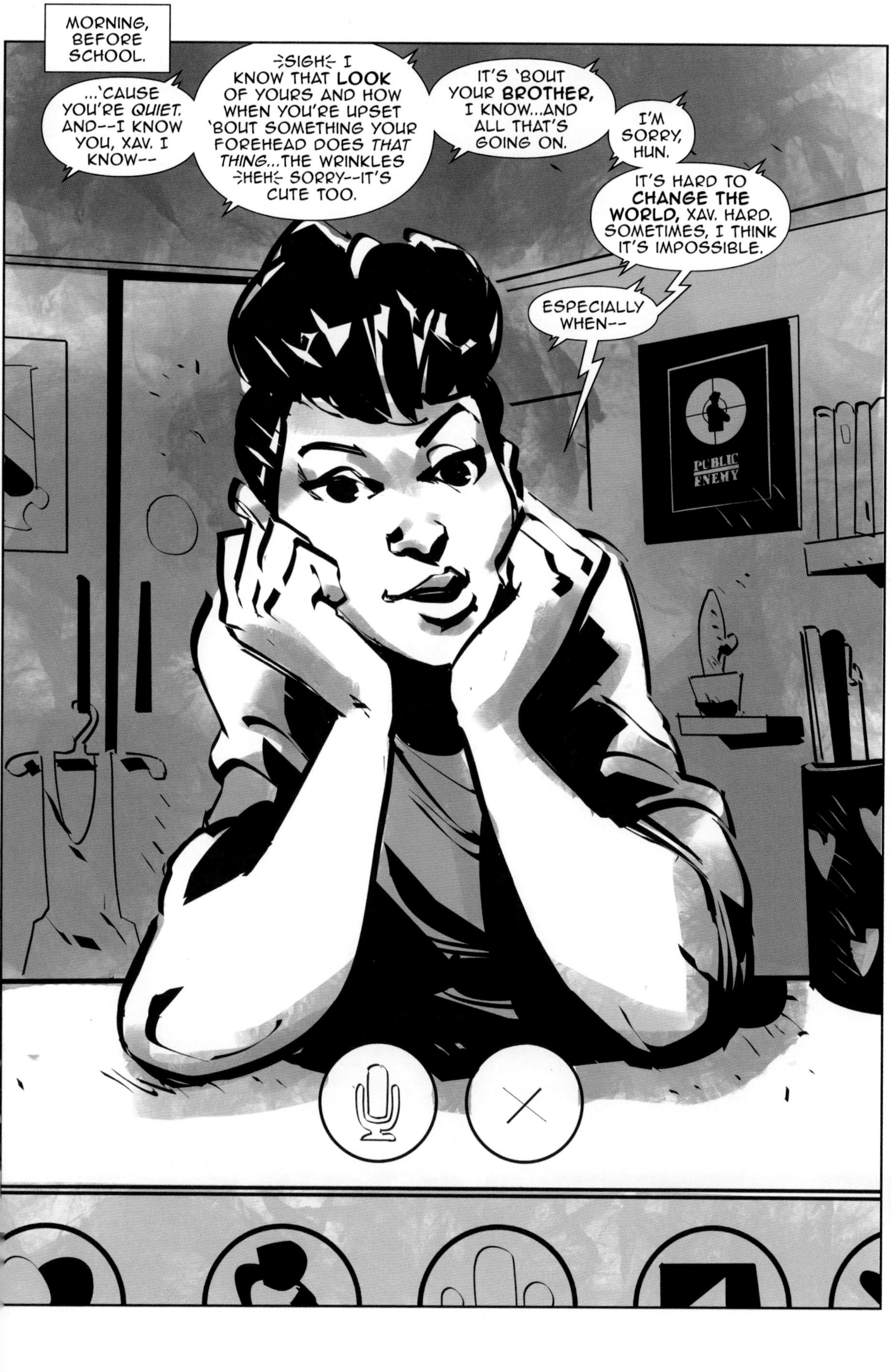
MORNING, BEFORE SCHOOL.
...'CAUSE YOU'RE *QUIET.* AND--I KNOW YOU, XAV. I KNOW--
⸗SIGH⸗ I KNOW THAT **LOOK** OF YOURS AND HOW WHEN YOU'RE UPSET 'BOUT SOMETHING YOUR FOREHEAD DOES *THAT THING*...THE WRINKLES ⸗HEH⸗ SORRY--IT'S CUTE TOO.
IT'S 'BOUT YOUR **BROTHER,** I KNOW...AND ALL THAT'S GOING ON.
I'M SORRY, HUN.
IT'S HARD TO **CHANGE THE WORLD,** XAV. HARD. SOMETIMES, I THINK IT'S IMPOSSIBLE.
ESPECIALLY WHEN--
PUBLIC ENEMY

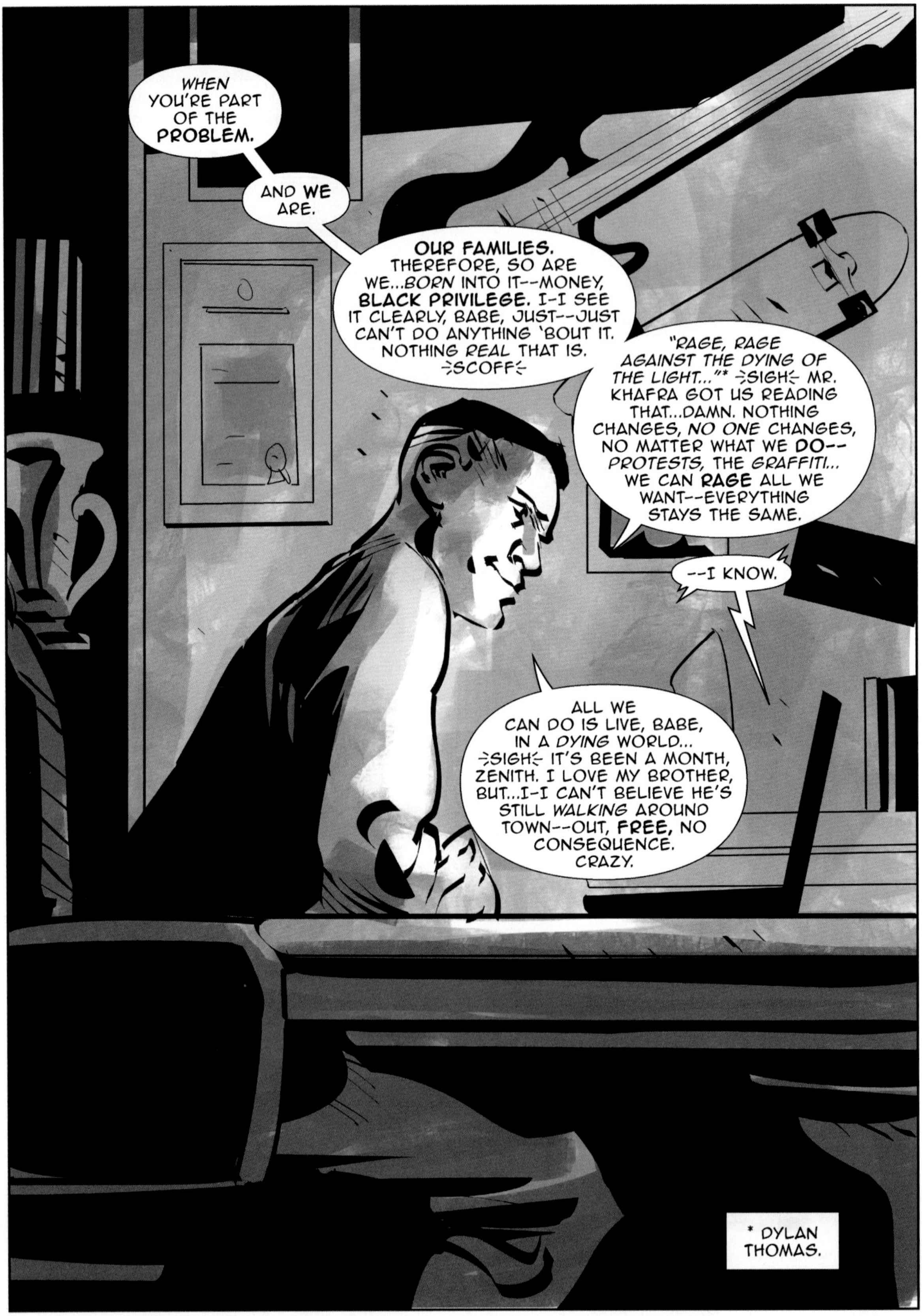
WHEN YOU'RE PART OF THE PROBLEM.
AND WE ARE.
OUR FAMILIES. THEREFORE, SO ARE WE...BORN INTO IT--MONEY, BLACK PRIVILEGE. I-I SEE IT CLEARLY, BABE, JUST--JUST CAN'T DO ANYTHING 'BOUT IT. NOTHING REAL THAT IS. ⋺SCOFF⋲
"RAGE, RAGE AGAINST THE DYING OF THE LIGHT..."* ⋺SIGH⋲ MR. KHAFRA GOT US READING THAT...DAMN. NOTHING CHANGES, NO ONE CHANGES, NO MATTER WHAT WE DO--PROTESTS, THE GRAFFITI... WE CAN RAGE ALL WE WANT--EVERYTHING STAYS THE SAME.
--I KNOW.
ALL WE CAN DO IS LIVE, BABE, IN A DYING WORLD... ⋺SIGH⋲ IT'S BEEN A MONTH, ZENITH. I LOVE MY BROTHER, BUT...I-I CAN'T BELIEVE HE'S STILL WALKING AROUND TOWN--OUT, FREE, NO CONSEQUENCE. CRAZY.
* DYLAN THOMAS.

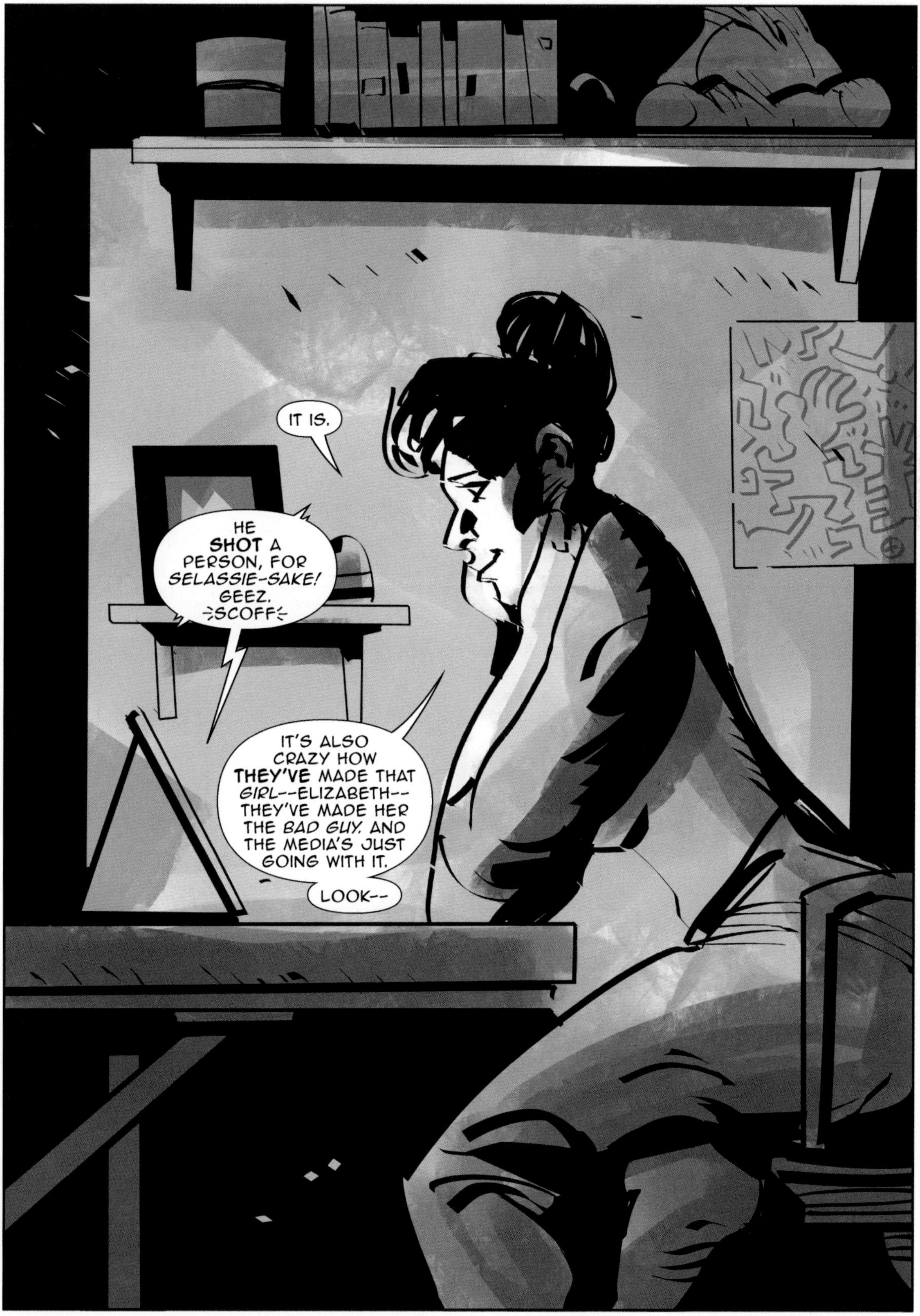
IT IS.
HE SHOT A PERSON, FOR SELASSIE-SAKE! GEEZ. ⁼SCOFF⁼
IT'S ALSO CRAZY HOW THEY'VE MADE THAT GIRL--ELIZABETH--THEY'VE MADE HER THE BAD GUY. AND THE MEDIA'S JUST GOING WITH IT.
LOOK--

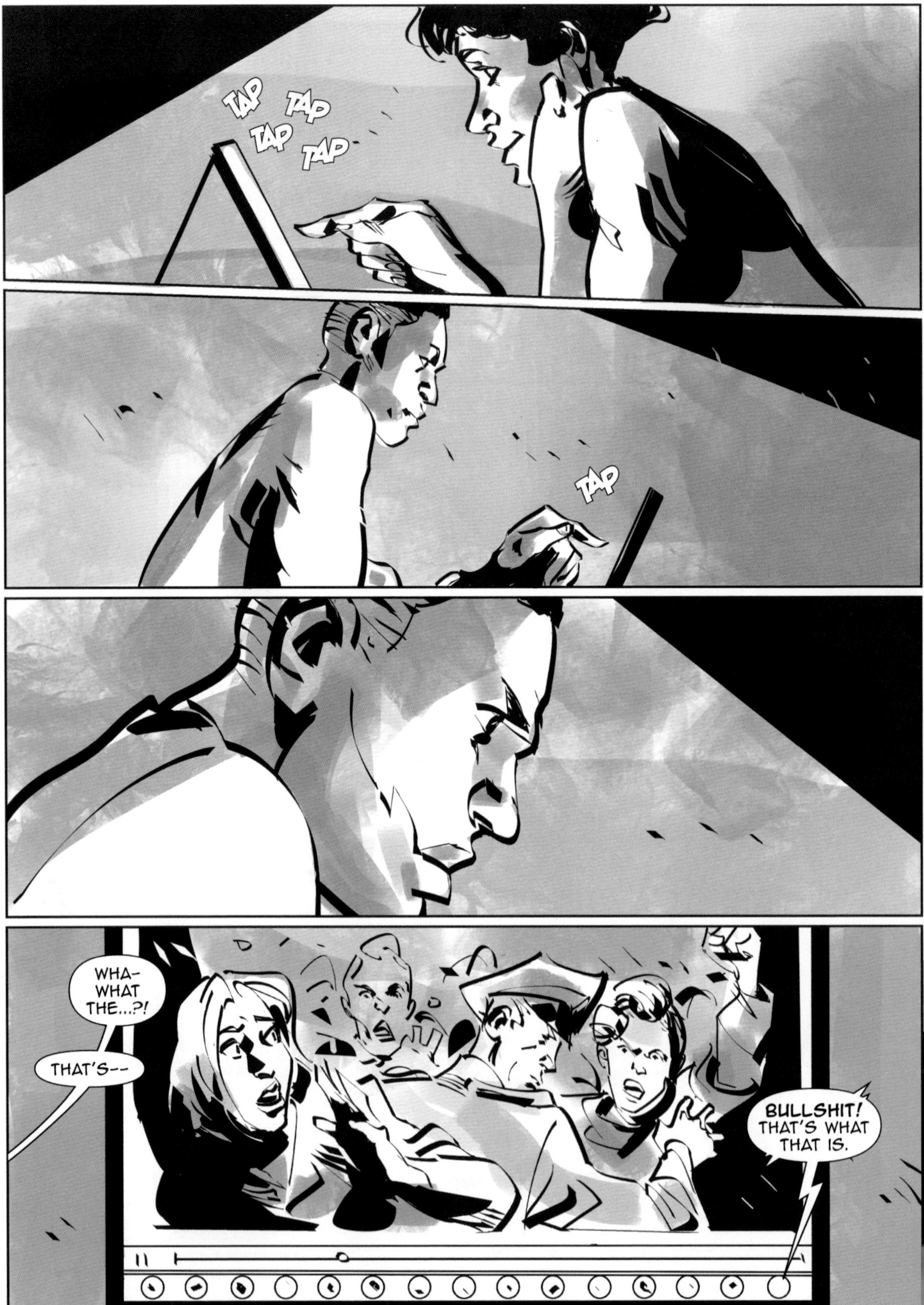
TAP
TAP
TAP
TAP
TAP
WHA-WHAT THE...?!
THAT'S--
BULLSHIT! THAT'S WHAT THAT IS.

THAT WAS LIKE A FEW MONTHS AGO, BEFORE THE SHOOTING. APPARENTLY, *SHE* AND THIS OTHER GIRL GOT INTO IT AT A CLUB--A FIGHT OVER SOME BOY, AT COLLEGE I THINK...

...AND THEN THIS--

...

INFORMATION CONTINUES TO EMERGE, REVEALING SORDID DETAILS REGARDING ELIZABETH NIGHTINGALE'S PAST. MEANWHILE, WE CAN ONLY WAIT TO SEE IF CHARGES WILL BE BROUGHT AGAINST ZION COTTON FOR HIS INVOLVEMENT IN THE SHOOTING.

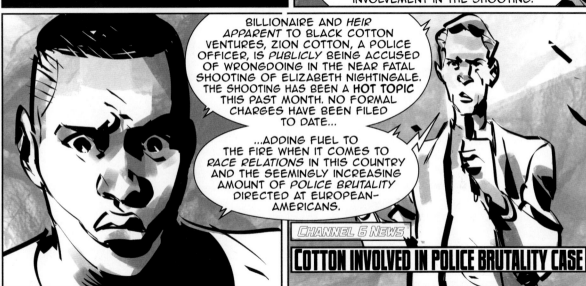

BILLIONAIRE AND *HEIR APPARENT* TO BLACK COTTON VENTURES, ZION COTTON, A POLICE OFFICER, IS *PUBLICLY* BEING ACCUSED OF WRONGDOING IN THE NEAR FATAL SHOOTING OF ELIZABETH NIGHTINGALE. THE SHOOTING HAS BEEN A *HOT TOPIC* THIS PAST MONTH. NO FORMAL CHARGES HAVE BEEN FILED TO DATE...

...ADDING FUEL TO THE FIRE WHEN IT COMES TO *RACE RELATIONS* IN THIS COUNTRY AND THE SEEMINGLY INCREASING AMOUNT OF *POLICE BRUTALITY* DIRECTED AT EUROPEAN-AMERICANS.

CHANNEL 6 NEWS

COTTON INVOLVED IN POLICE BRUTALITY CASE

QUESTIONS ABOUND--DO WE HAVE A *RACE PROBLEM* HERE IN AMERICA?

AND *WHO* IS ELIZABETH NIGHTINGALE?

VIDEOS ARE BEGINNING TO SURFACE THAT PAINT HER IN A LESS THAN *FAVORABLE* LIGHT.

COLLEGE PARTIES, RUMORS OF HOOK-UPS, PROMISCUITY, HER ATHLETIC SCHOLARSHIP ON PROBATION DUE TO LOW GRADES AND POSSIBLE SUBSTANCE ABUSE.

MY GOD... W-WHAT IS MY *FAMILY* DOING TO THIS GIRL?!

...

THEY'RE *DESTROYING* HER LIFE!

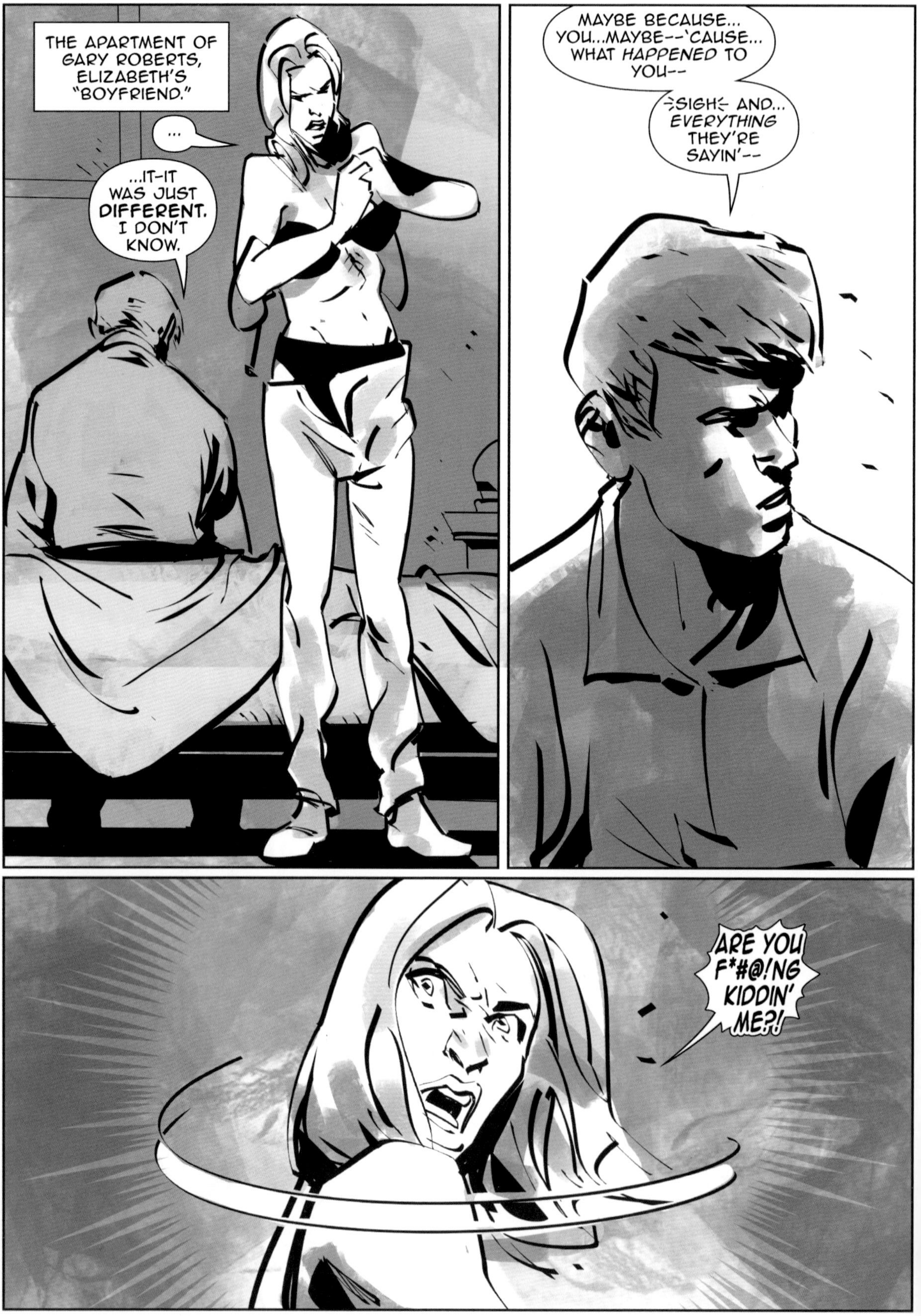
THE APARTMENT OF GARY ROBERTS, ELIZABETH'S "BOYFRIEND."
...
...IT-IT WAS JUST DIFFERENT. I DON'T KNOW.
MAYBE BECAUSE... YOU...MAYBE--'CAUSE... WHAT HAPPENED TO YOU--
SIGH AND... EVERYTHING THEY'RE SAYIN'--
ARE YOU F*#@!NG KIDDIN' ME?!

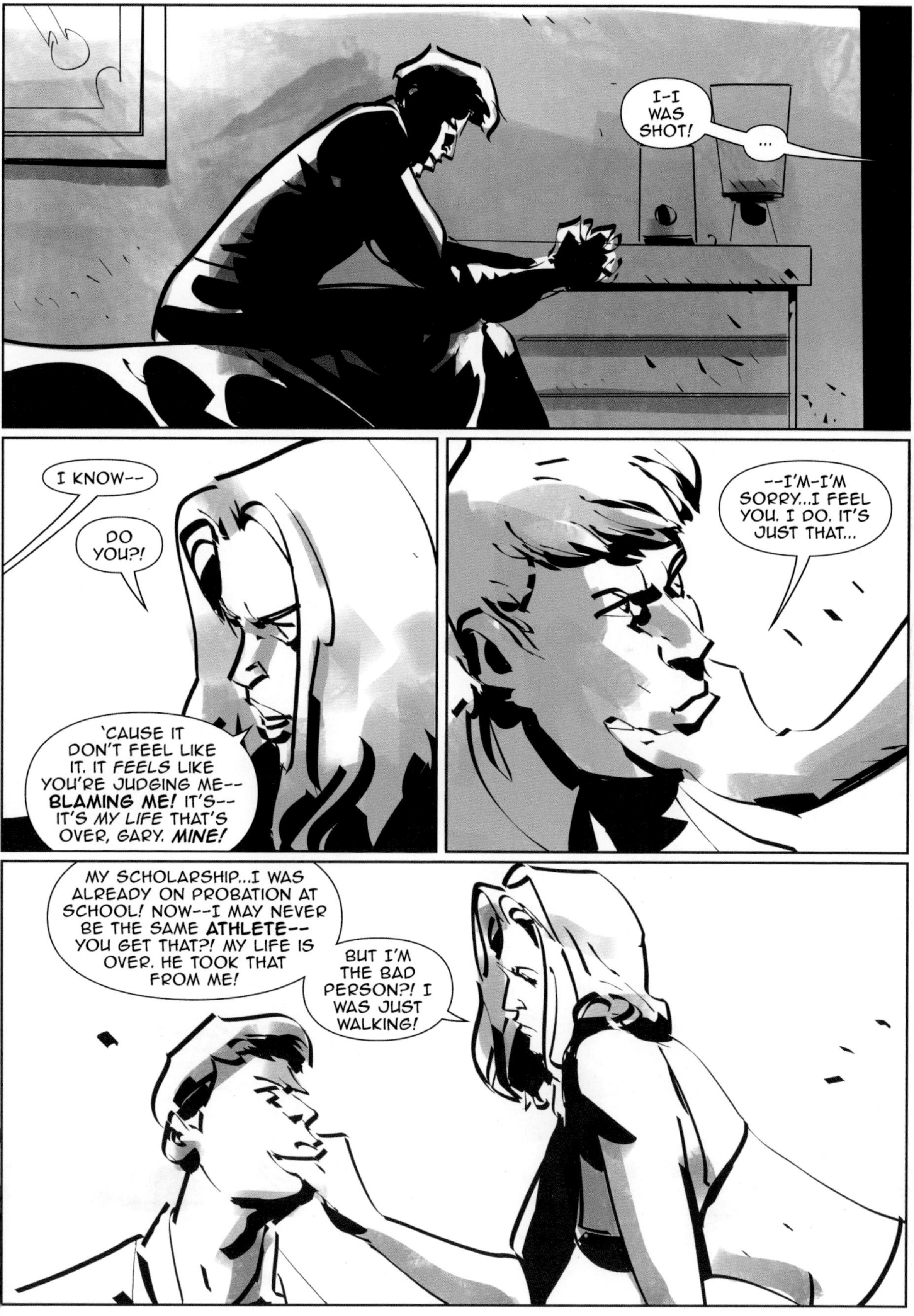
I-I WAS SHOT!
...
I KNOW--
DO YOU?!
'CAUSE IT DON'T FEEL LIKE IT. IT FEELS LIKE YOU'RE JUDGING ME-- BLAMING ME! IT'S-- IT'S MY LIFE THAT'S OVER, GARY. MINE!
--I'M-I'M SORRY...I FEEL YOU. I DO. IT'S JUST THAT...
MY SCHOLARSHIP...I WAS ALREADY ON PROBATION AT SCHOOL! NOW--I MAY NEVER BE THE SAME ATHLETE-- YOU GET THAT?! MY LIFE IS OVER. HE TOOK THAT FROM ME!
BUT I'M THE BAD PERSON?! I WAS JUST WALKING!

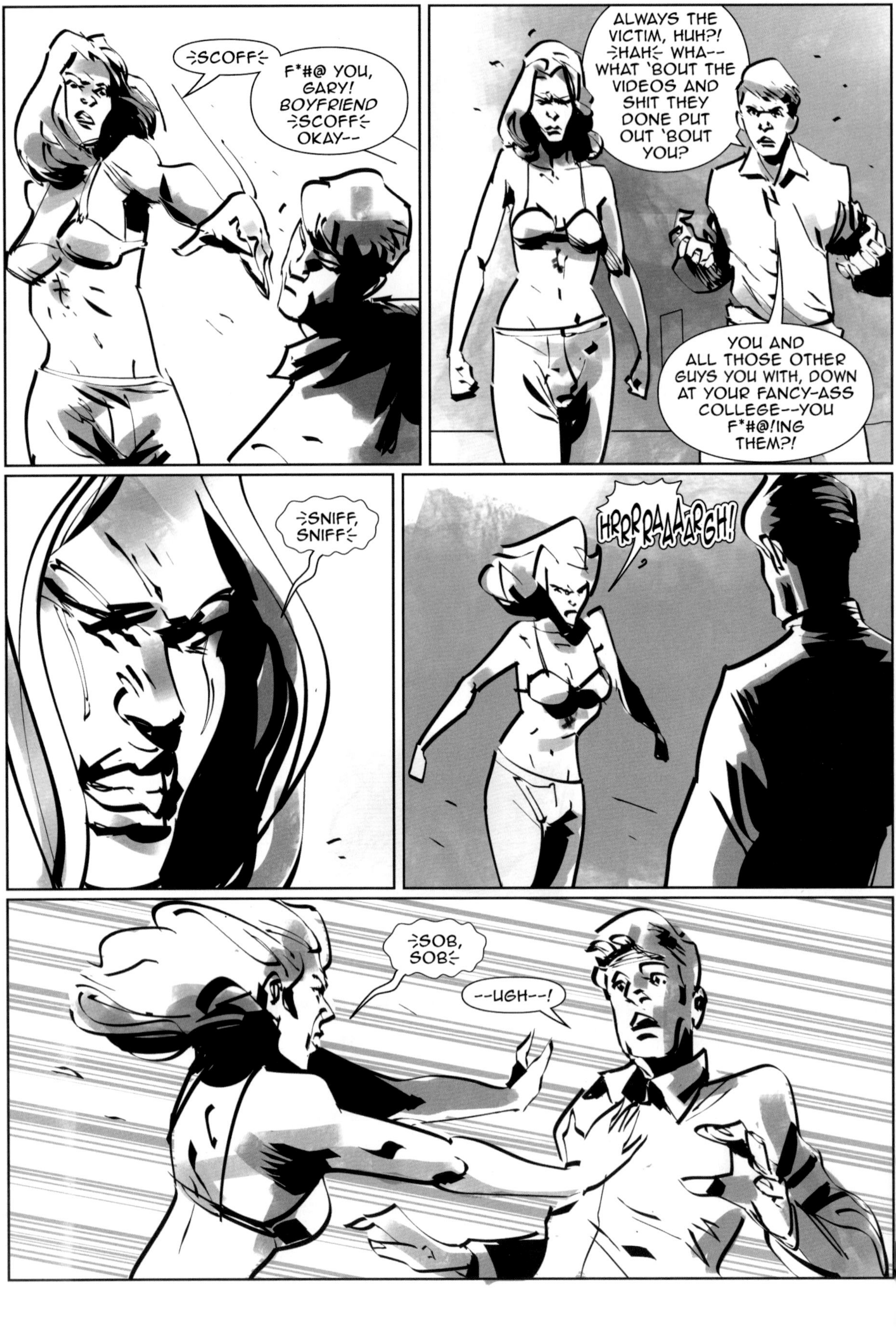

-SCOFF-
F*#@ YOU, GARY! BOYFRIEND -SCOFF- OKAY--
ALWAYS THE VICTIM, HUH?! -HAH- WHA-- WHAT 'BOUT THE VIDEOS AND SHIT THEY DONE PUT OUT 'BOUT YOU?
YOU AND ALL THOSE OTHER GUYS YOU WITH, DOWN AT YOUR FANCY-ASS COLLEGE--YOU F*#@!ING THEM?!
-SNIFF, SNIFF-
HRRRRAAAARGH!
-SOB, SOB-
--UGH--!

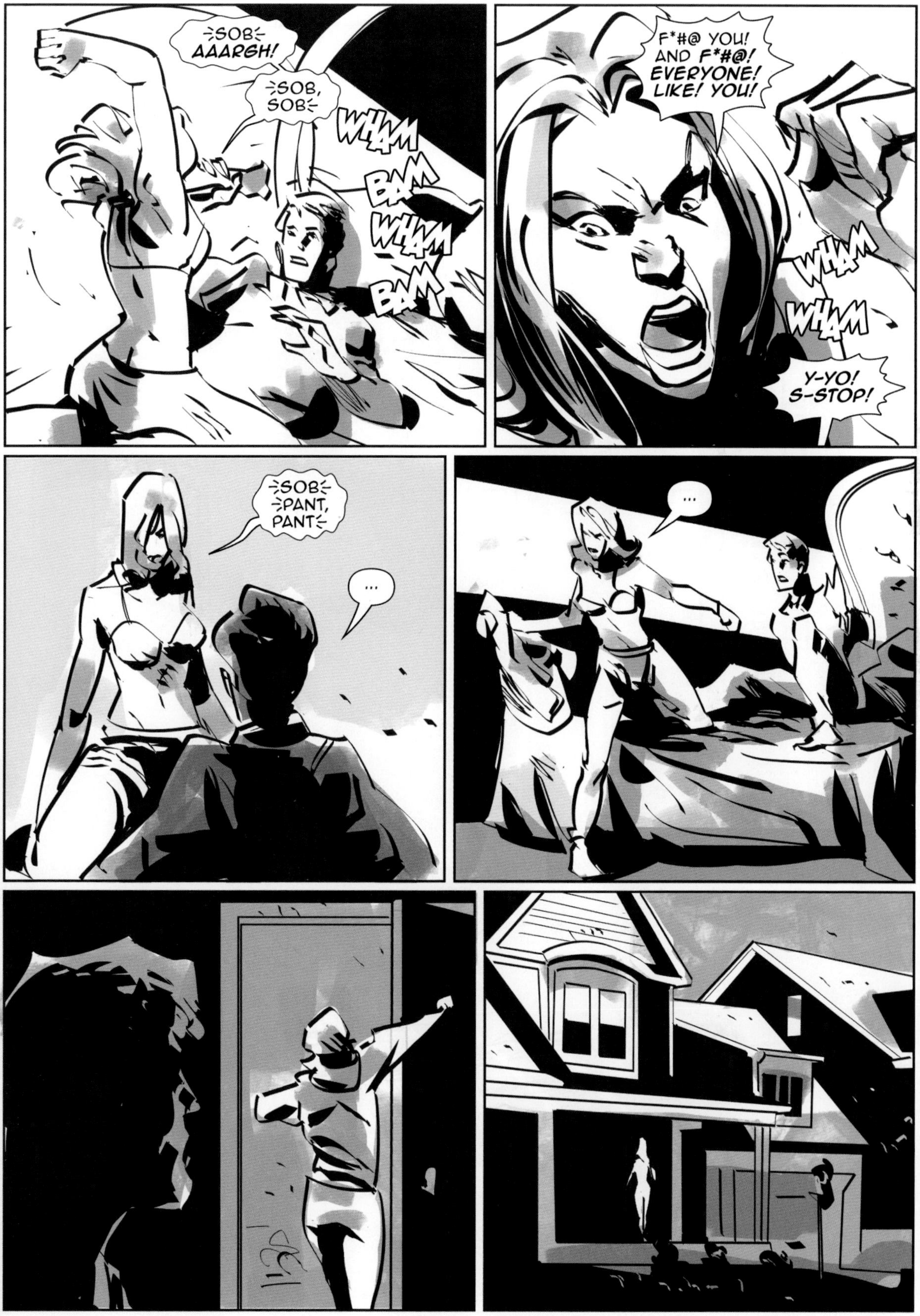

SOB AAARGH!
SOB, SOB
WHAM
BAM
WHAM
BAM
F*#@ YOU! AND F*#@! EVERYONE! LIKE! YOU!
WHAM
WHAM
Y-YO! S-STOP!
SOB PANT, PANT
...
...

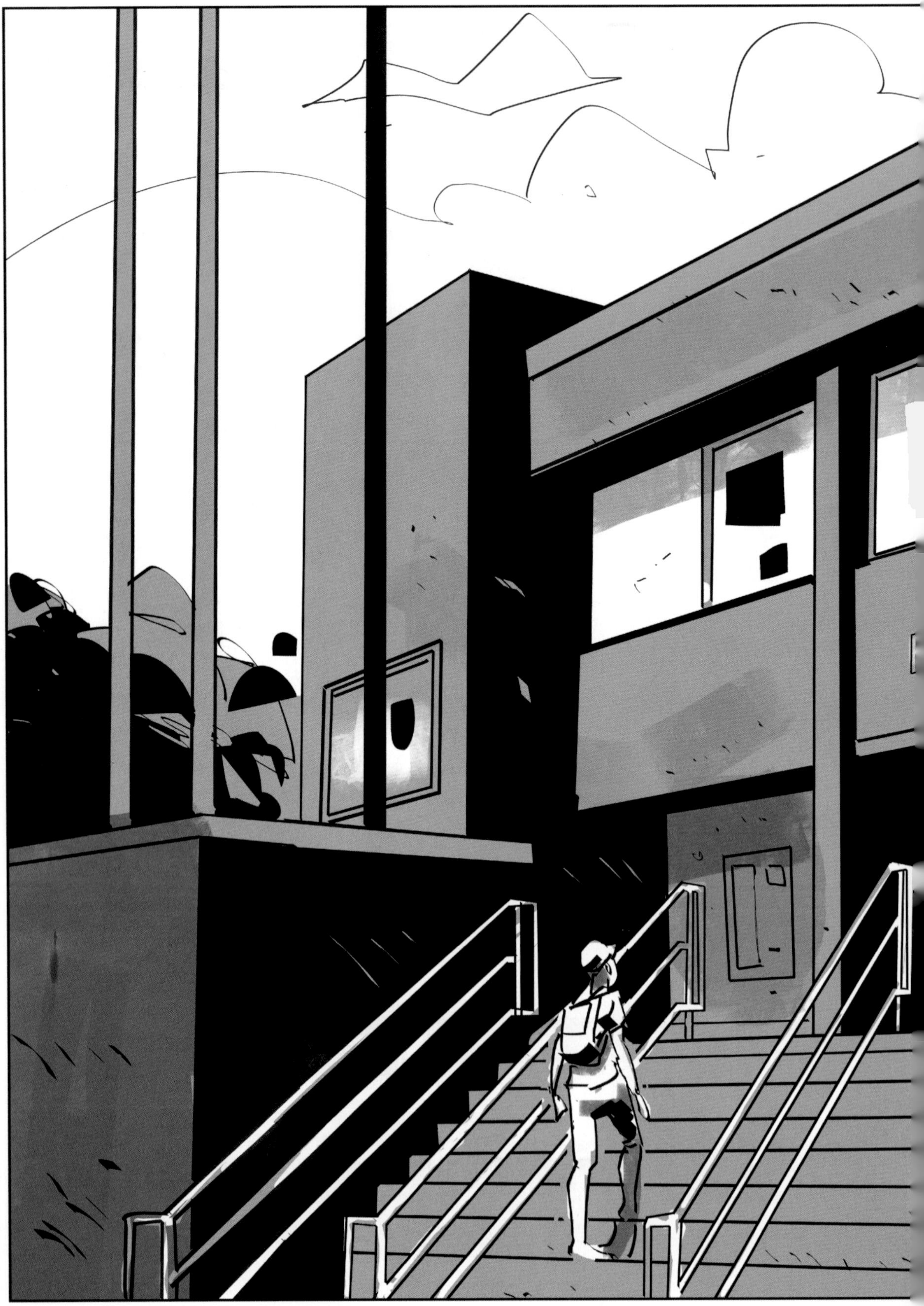

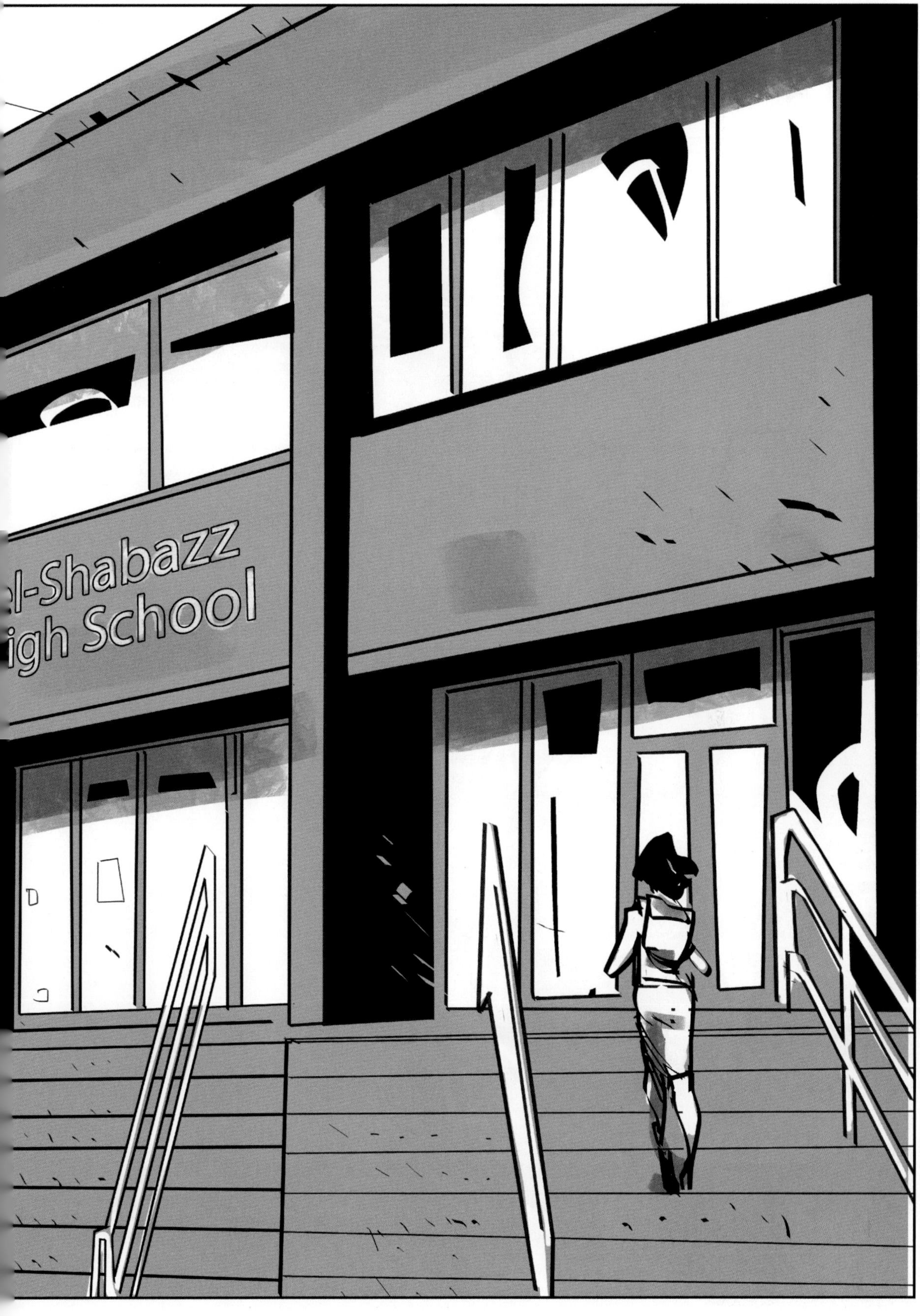
el-Shabazz
igh School

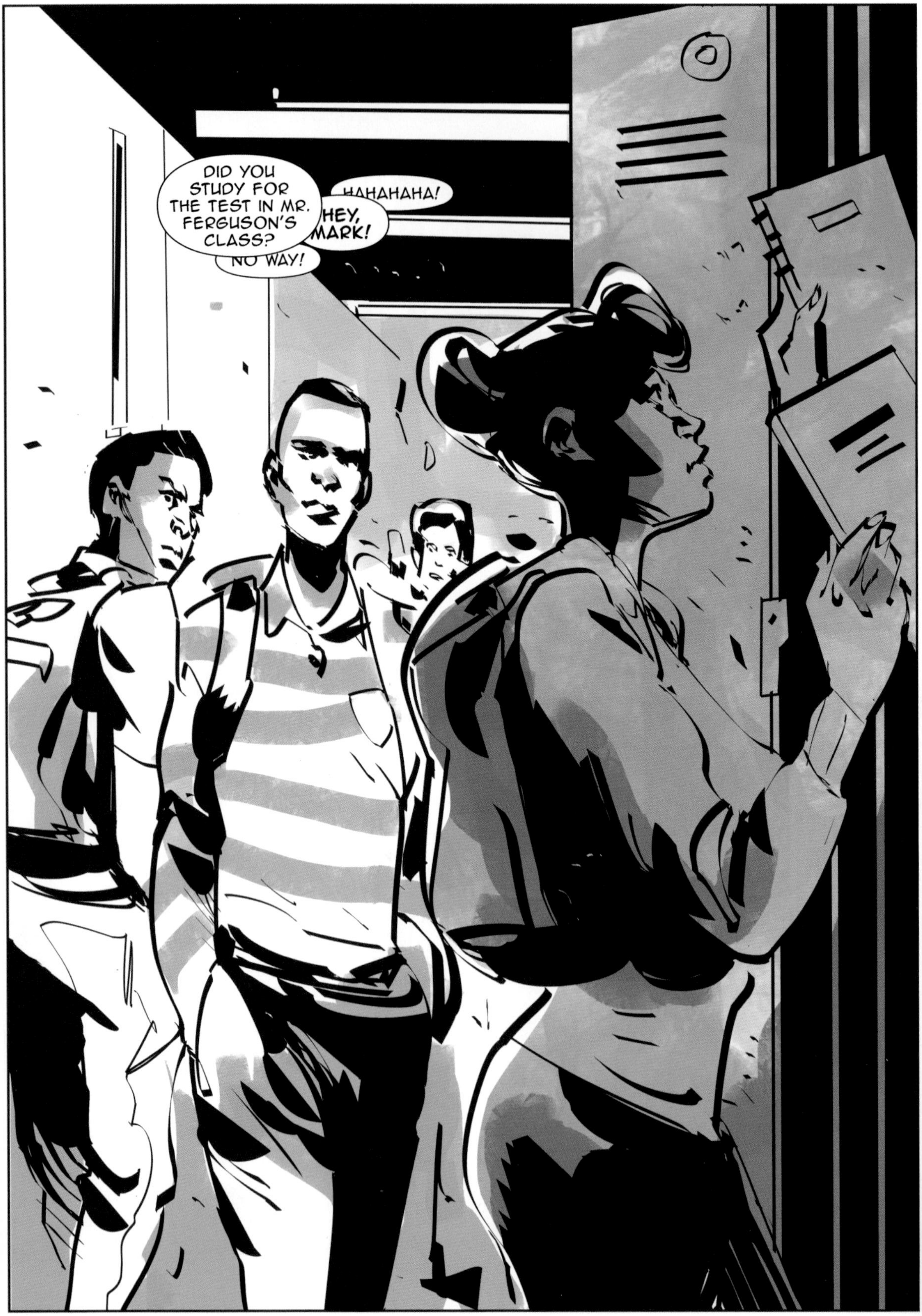
DID YOU STUDY FOR THE TEST IN MR. FERGUSON'S CLASS?
NO WAY!
HAHAHAHA!
HEY, MARK!

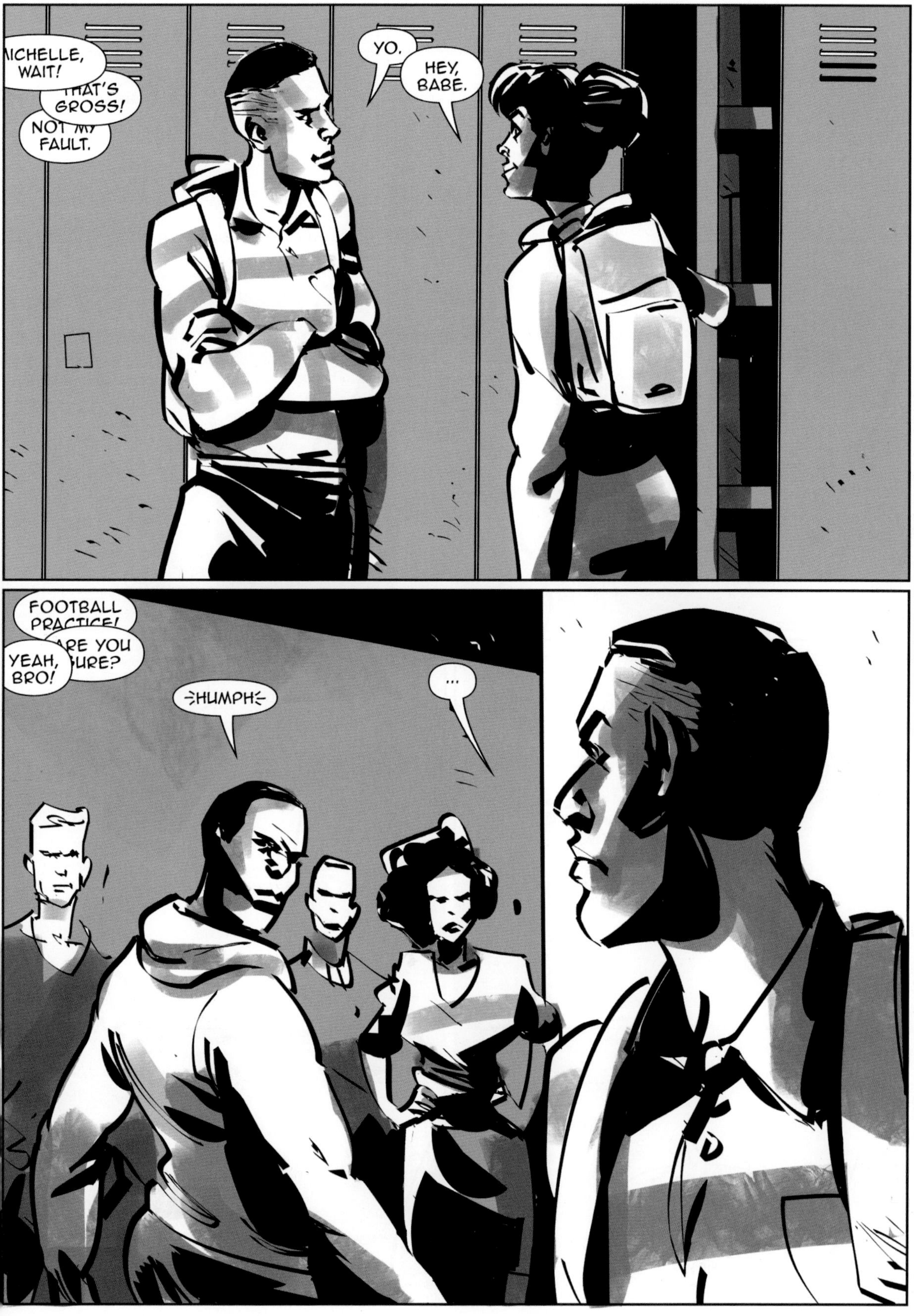
ICHELLE, WAIT!
THAT'S GROSS!
NOT MY FAULT.
YO.
HEY, BABE.
FOOTBALL PRACTICE!
ARE YOU SURE?
YEAH, BRO!
HUMPH
...

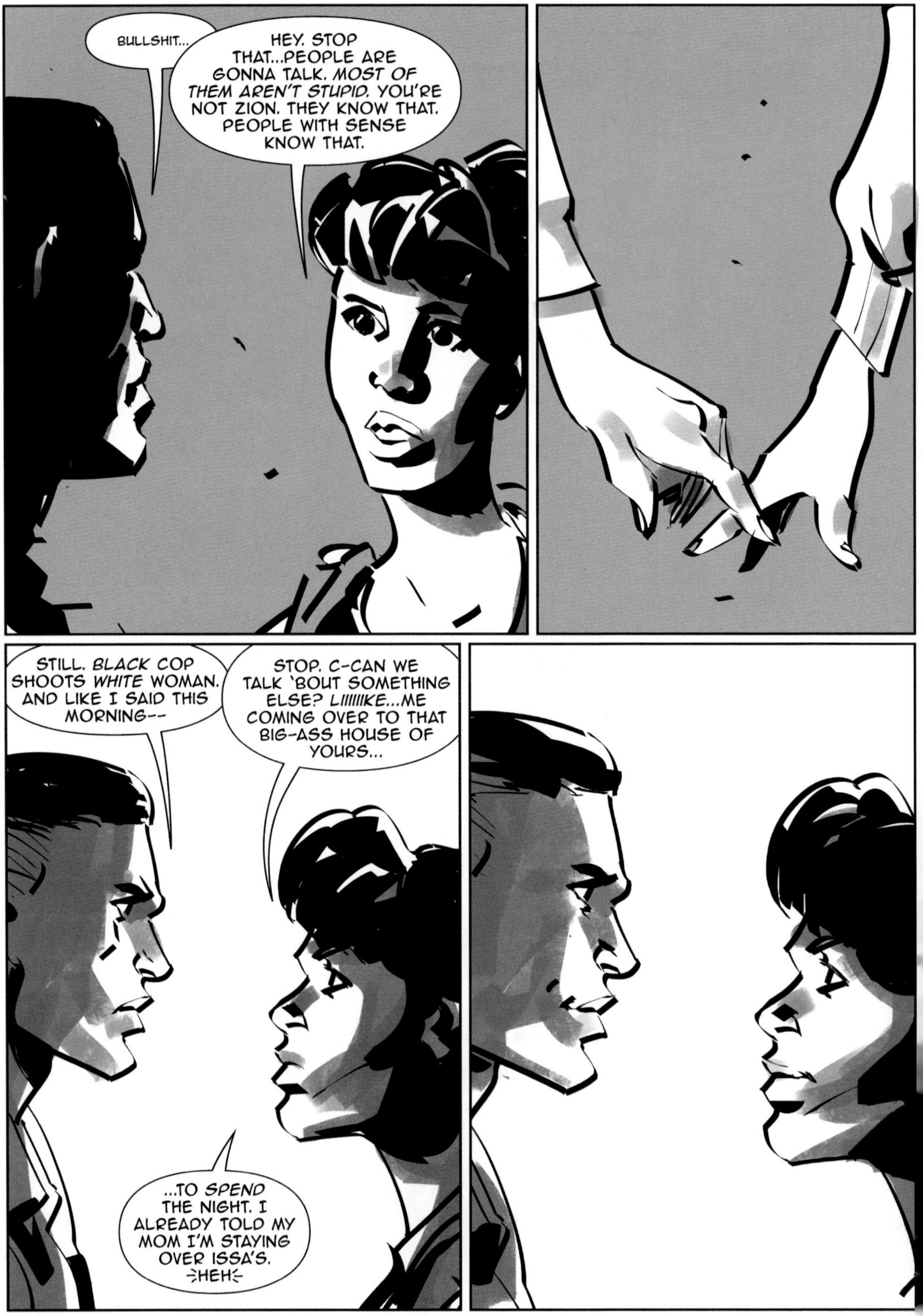
BULLSHIT...
HEY. STOP THAT...PEOPLE ARE GONNA TALK. MOST OF THEM AREN'T STUPID. YOU'RE NOT ZION. THEY KNOW THAT. PEOPLE WITH SENSE KNOW THAT.
STILL. BLACK COP SHOOTS WHITE WOMAN. AND LIKE I SAID THIS MORNING--
STOP. C-CAN WE TALK 'BOUT SOMETHING ELSE? LIIIIIIKE...ME COMING OVER TO THAT BIG-ASS HOUSE OF YOURS...
...TO SPEND THE NIGHT. I ALREADY TOLD MY MOM I'M STAYING OVER ISSA'S. HEH

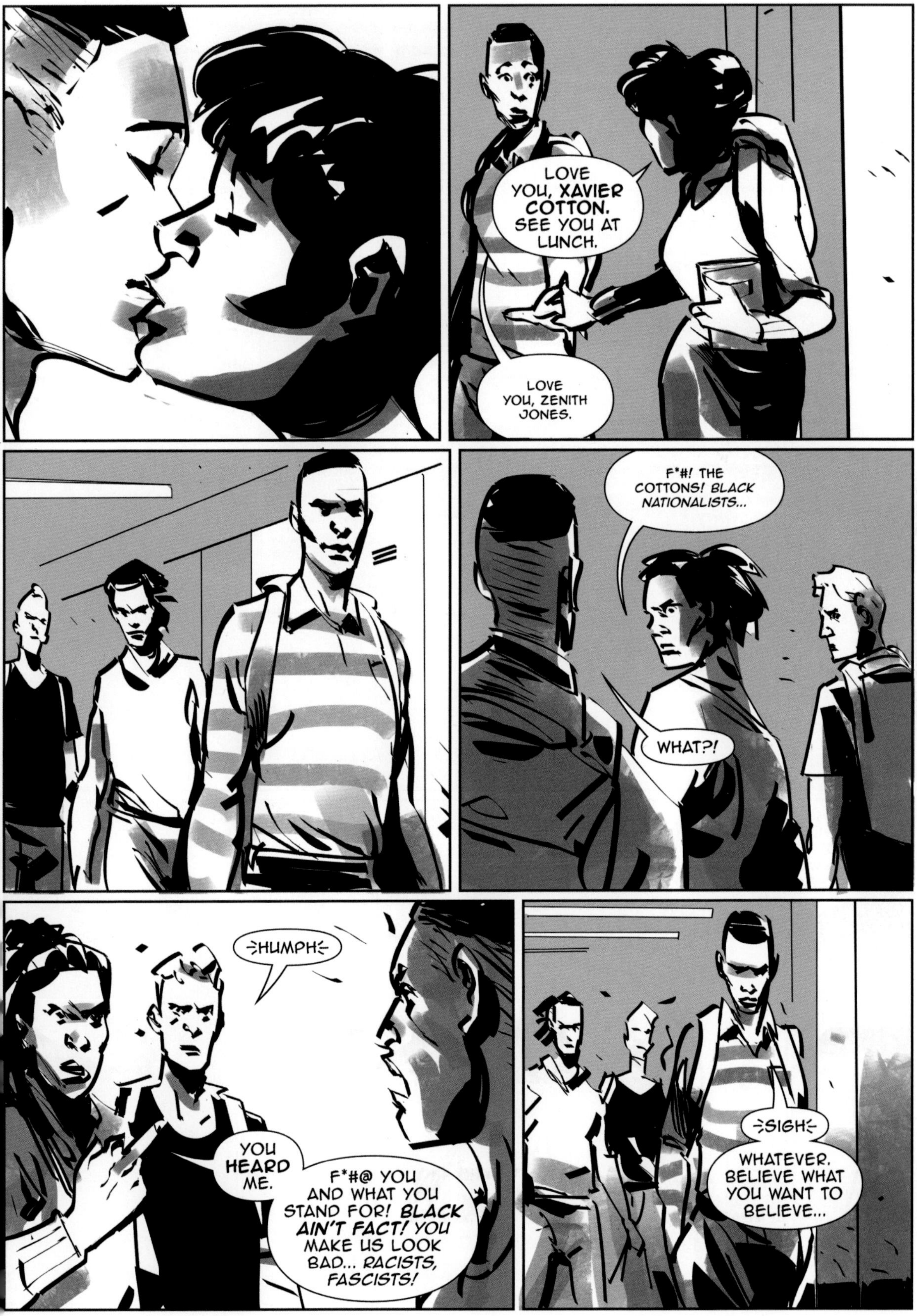
LOVE YOU, XAVIER COTTON. SEE YOU AT LUNCH.
LOVE YOU, ZENITH JONES.
F*#! THE COTTONS! BLACK NATIONALISTS...
WHAT?!
HUMPH
YOU HEARD ME.
F*#@ YOU AND WHAT YOU STAND FOR! BLACK AIN'T FACT! YOU MAKE US LOOK BAD... RACISTS, FASCISTS!
SIGH
WHATEVER. BELIEVE WHAT YOU WANT TO BELIEVE...

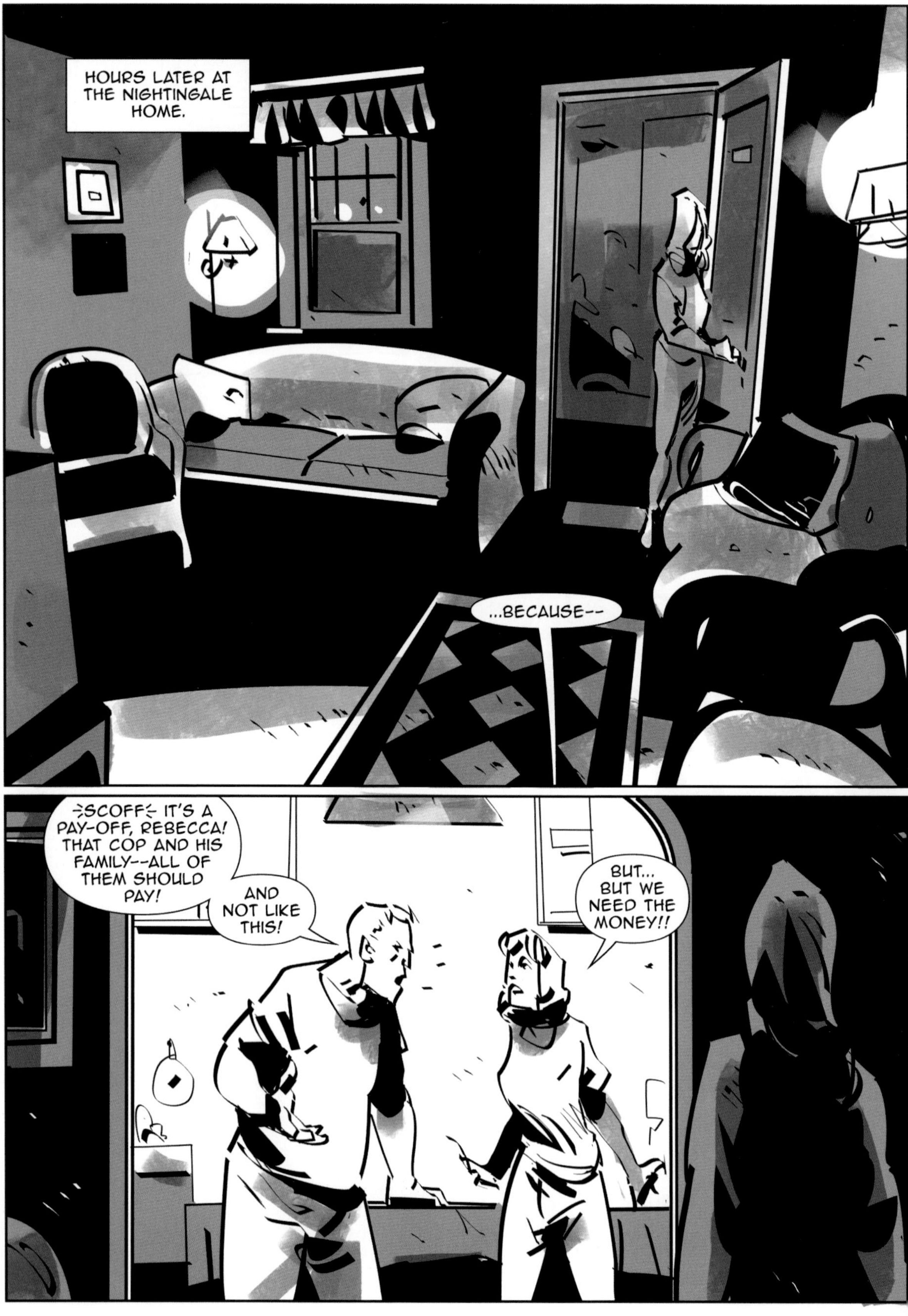
HOURS LATER AT THE NIGHTINGALE HOME.
...BECAUSE--
≈SCOFF≈ IT'S A PAY-OFF, REBECCA! THAT COP AND HIS FAMILY--ALL OF THEM SHOULD PAY!
AND NOT LIKE THIS!
BUT... BUT WE NEED THE MONEY!!

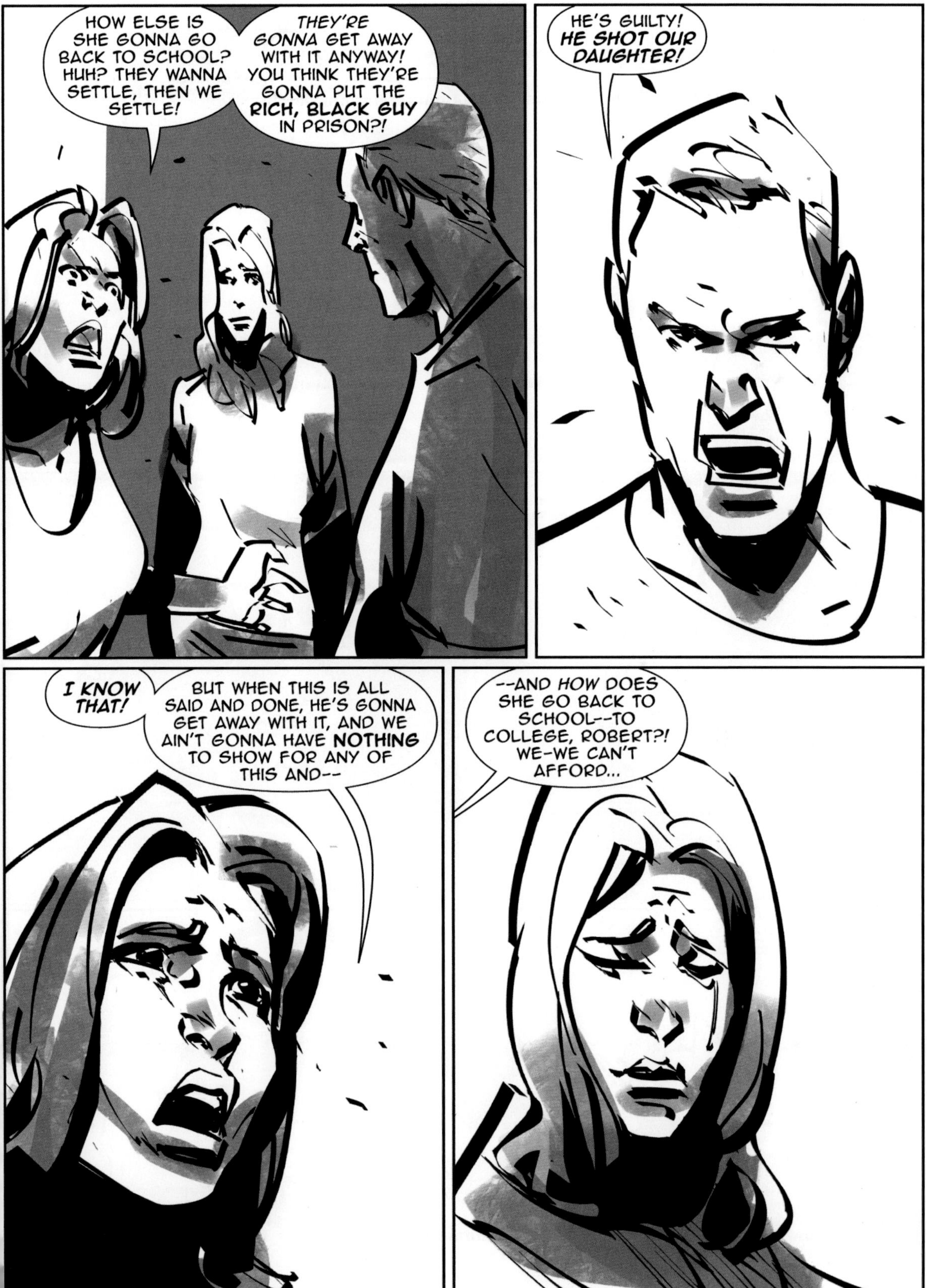
HOW ELSE IS SHE GONNA GO BACK TO SCHOOL? HUH? THEY WANNA SETTLE, THEN WE SETTLE!
THEY'RE GONNA GET AWAY WITH IT ANYWAY! YOU THINK THEY'RE GONNA PUT THE **RICH, BLACK GUY** IN PRISON?!
HE'S GUILTY! ***HE SHOT OUR DAUGHTER!***
I KNOW THAT!
BUT WHEN THIS IS ALL SAID AND DONE, HE'S GONNA GET AWAY WITH IT, AND WE AIN'T GONNA HAVE **NOTHING** TO SHOW FOR ANY OF THIS AND--
--AND *HOW* DOES SHE GO BACK TO SCHOOL--TO COLLEGE, ROBERT?! WE-WE CAN'T AFFORD...

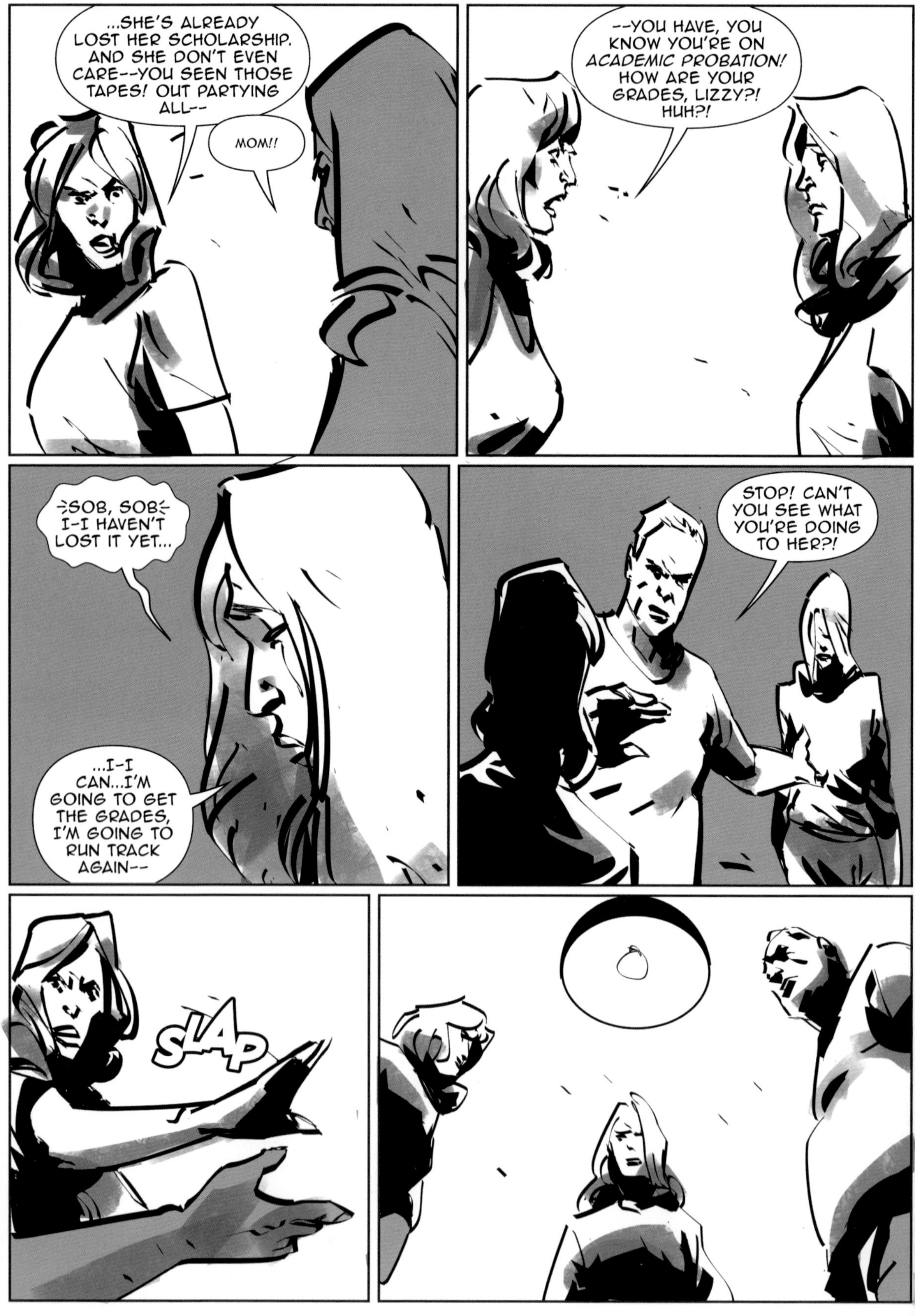
...SHE'S ALREADY LOST HER SCHOLARSHIP. AND SHE DON'T EVEN CARE--YOU SEEN THOSE TAPES! OUT PARTYING ALL--
MOM!!
--YOU HAVE, YOU KNOW YOU'RE ON ACADEMIC PROBATION! HOW ARE YOUR GRADES, LIZZY?! HUH?!
SOB, SOB I-I HAVEN'T LOST IT YET...
...I-I CAN...I'M GOING TO GET THE GRADES, I'M GOING TO RUN TRACK AGAIN--
STOP! CAN'T YOU SEE WHAT YOU'RE DOING TO HER?!
SLAP

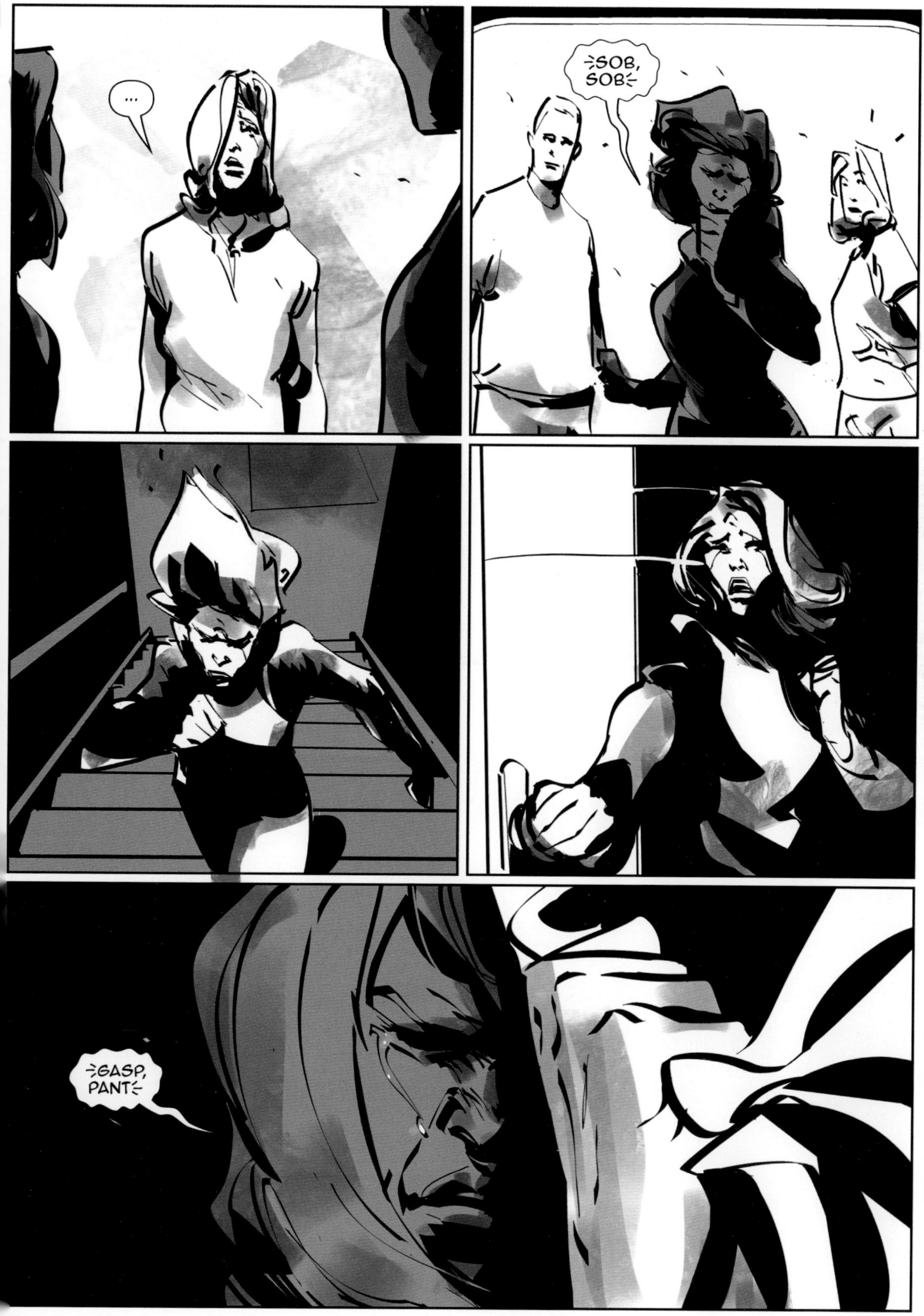
...
SOB, SOB
GASP, PANT

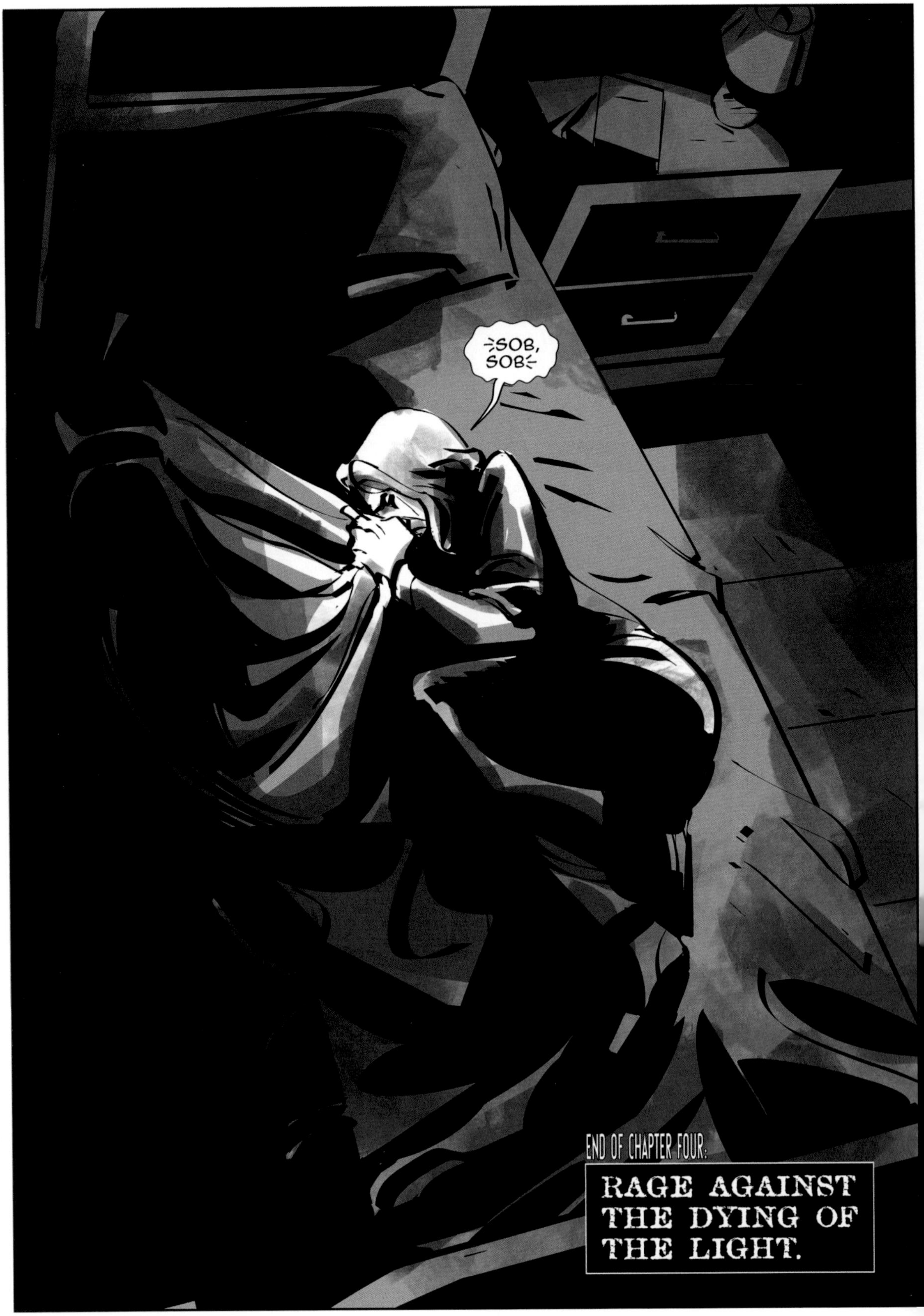
SOB, SOB
END OF CHAPTER FOUR:
RAGE AGAINST THE DYING OF THE LIGHT.

DOUBLE-SHOT/
RAGE AGAINST THE DYING OF THE LIGHT

CHAPTER
5

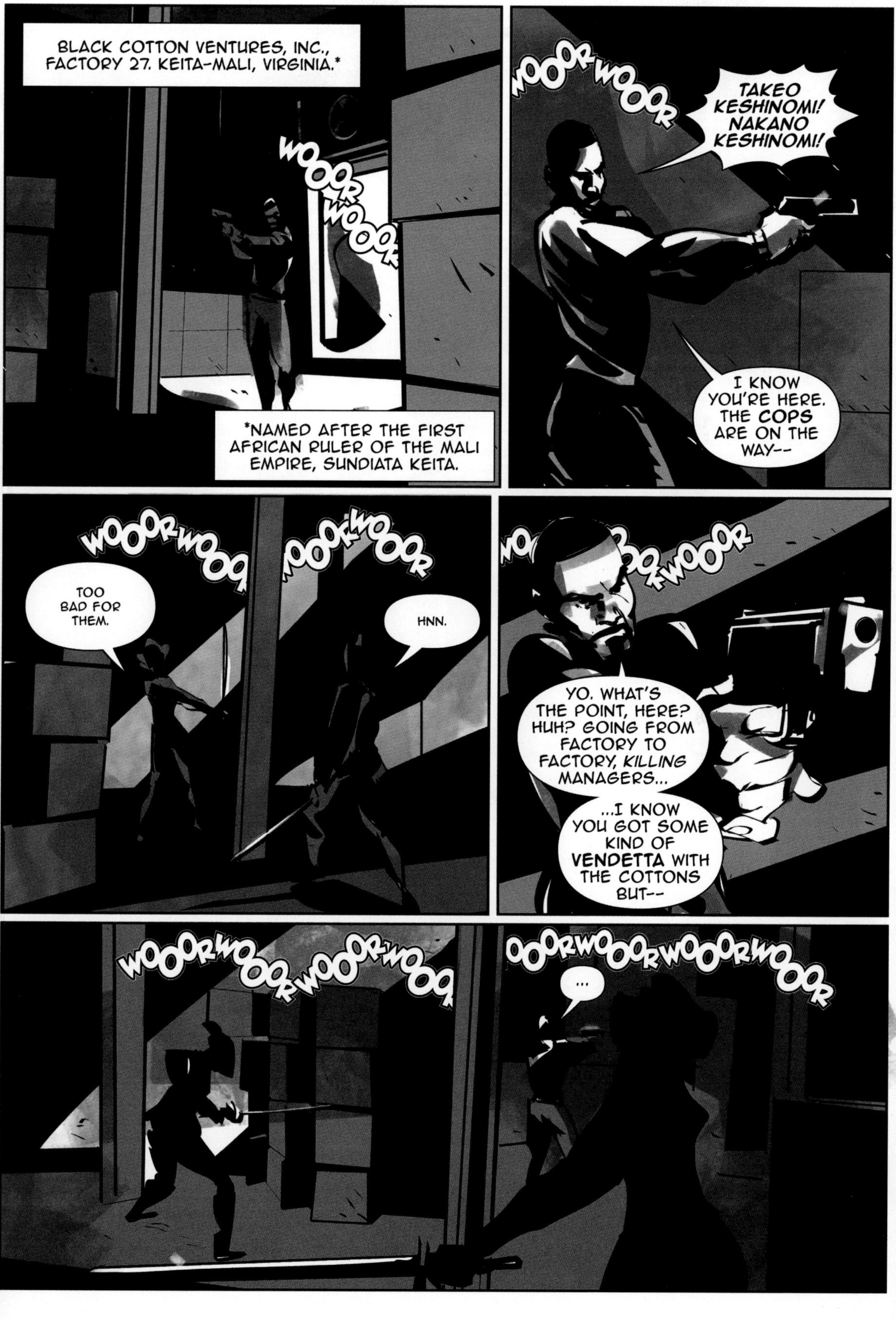

BLACK COTTON VENTURES, INC., FACTORY 27. KEITA-MALI, VIRGINIA.*
WOOOR WOOOR
*NAMED AFTER THE FIRST AFRICAN RULER OF THE MALI EMPIRE, SUNDIATA KEITA.
WOOOR WOOOR
TAKEO KESHINOMI! NAKANO KESHINOMI!
I KNOW YOU'RE HERE. THE COPS ARE ON THE WAY--
WOOORWOOOR WOOORWOOOR
TOO BAD FOR THEM.
HNN.
WOOORWOOOR
YO. WHAT'S THE POINT, HERE? HUH? GOING FROM FACTORY TO FACTORY, KILLING MANAGERS...
...I KNOW YOU GOT SOME KIND OF VENDETTA WITH THE COTTONS BUT--
WOOORWOOORWOOORWOOOR
OOORWOOORWOOORWOOOR
...

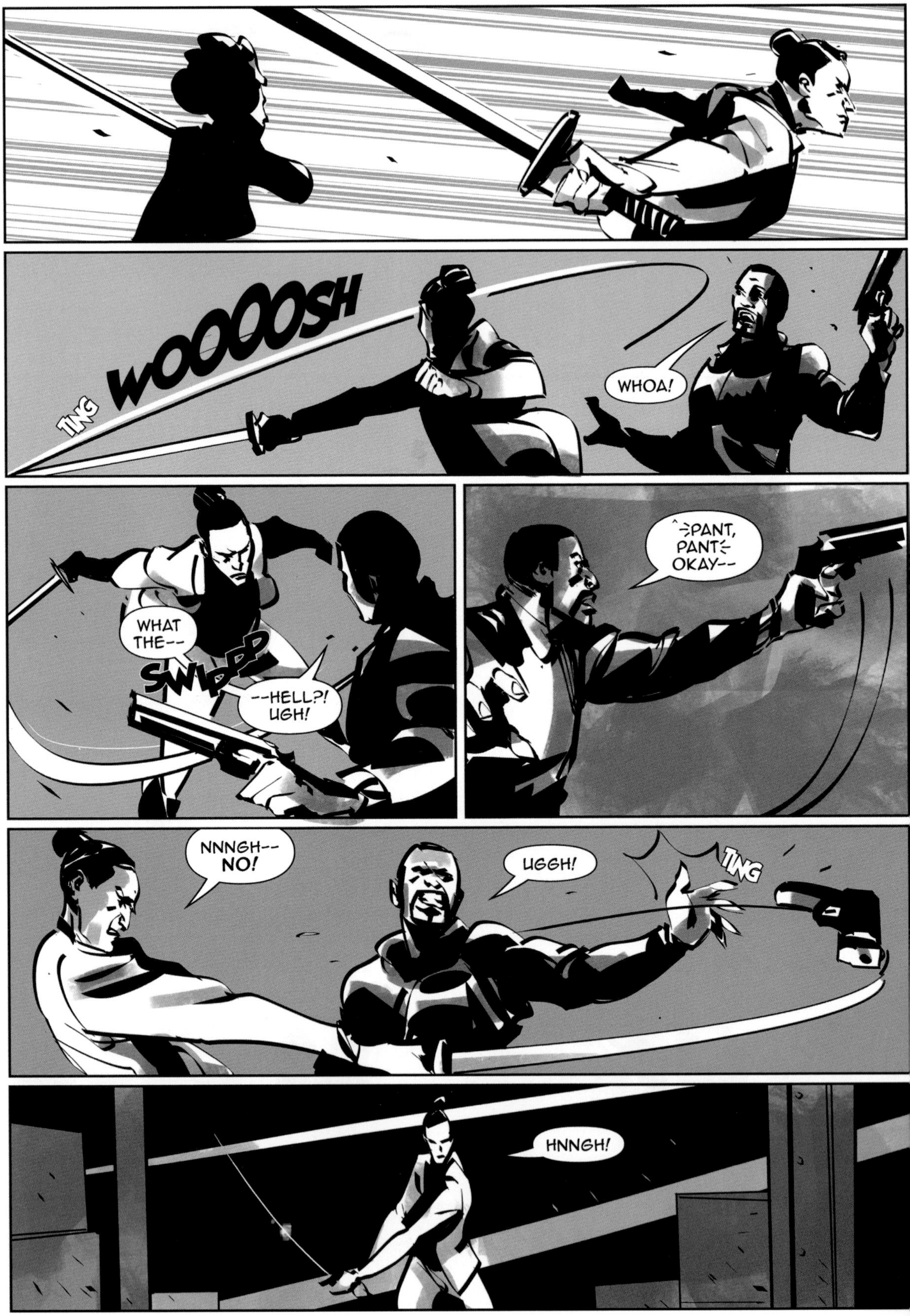
TING
WOOOOSH
WHOA!
WHAT THE--
SWIPP
--HELL?! UGH!
PANT, PANT OKAY--
NNNGH-- NO!
UGGH!
TING
HNNGH!

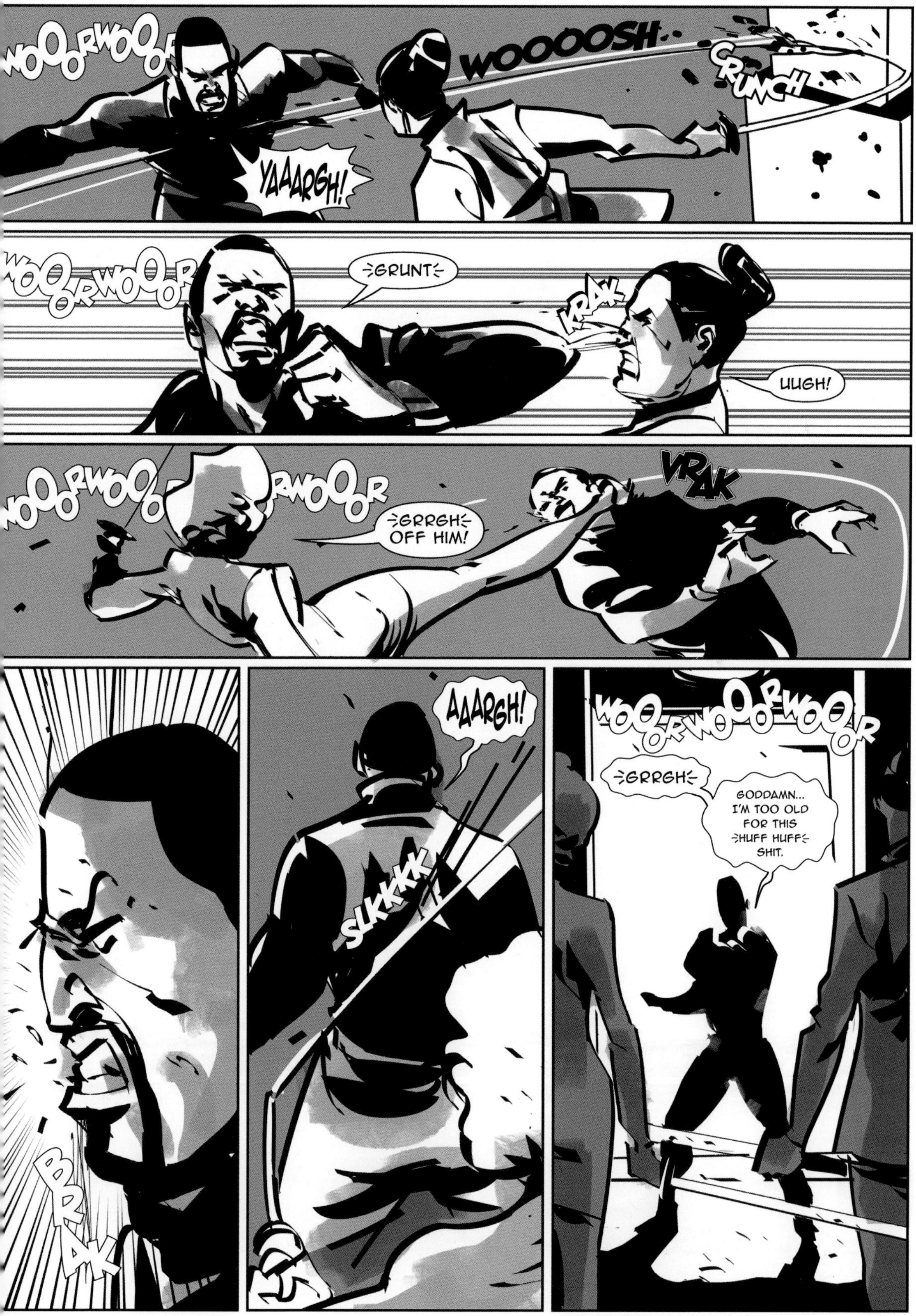
WOOORWOOOR
WOOOOSH
CRUNCH
YAAARGH!
WOOORWOOOR
GRUNT
KRAK
UUGH!
WOOORWOOOORWOOOR
VRAK
GRRGH OFF HIM!
BRAK
AAARGH!
SLKKKK
WOOORWOOORWOOOR
GRRGH
GODDAMN... I'M TOO OLD FOR THIS HUFF HUFF SHIT.

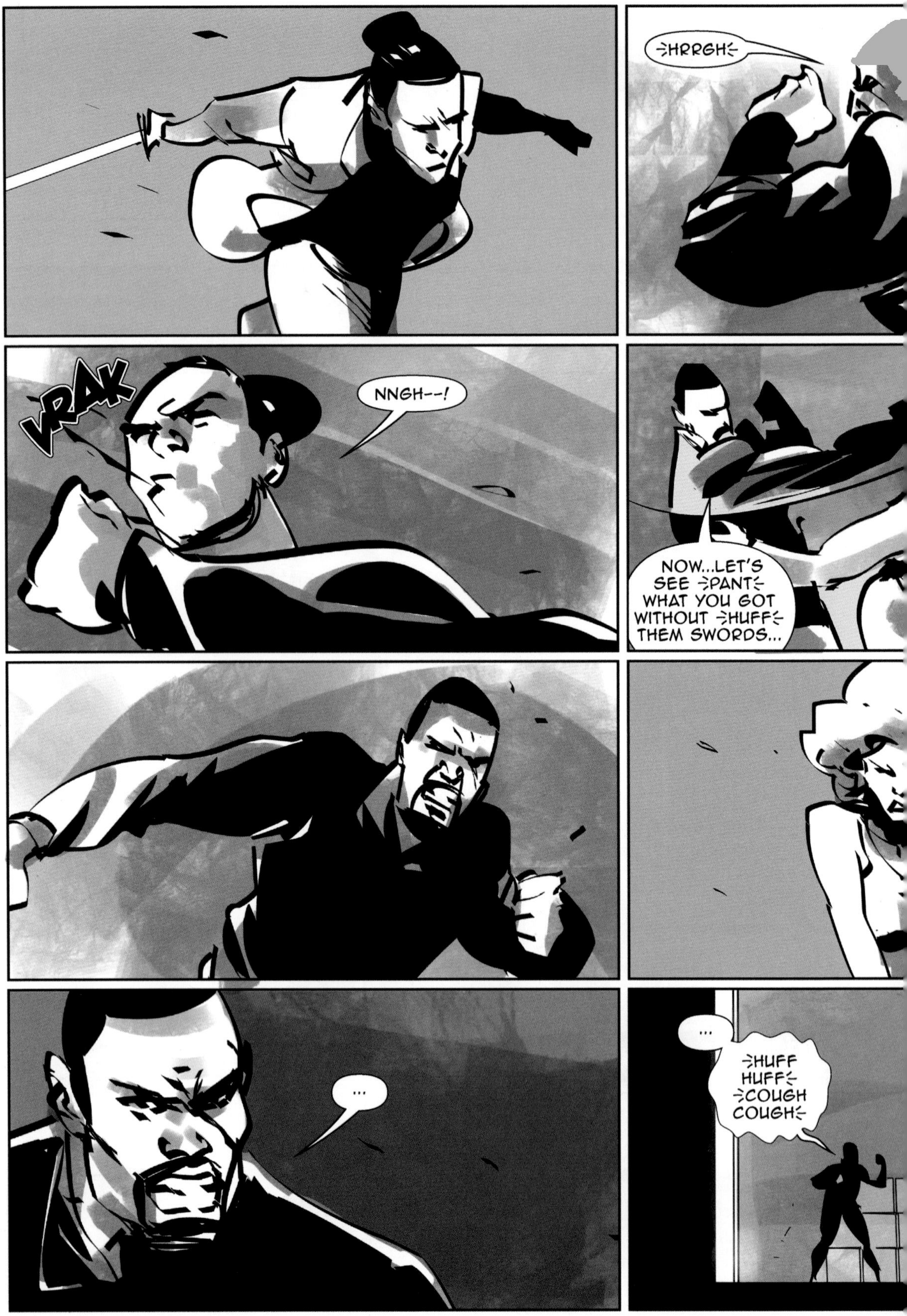

HRRGH
VRAK
NNGH--!
NOW...LET'S SEE PANT WHAT YOU GOT WITHOUT HUFF THEM SWORDS...
...
...
HUFF HUFF COUGH COUGH

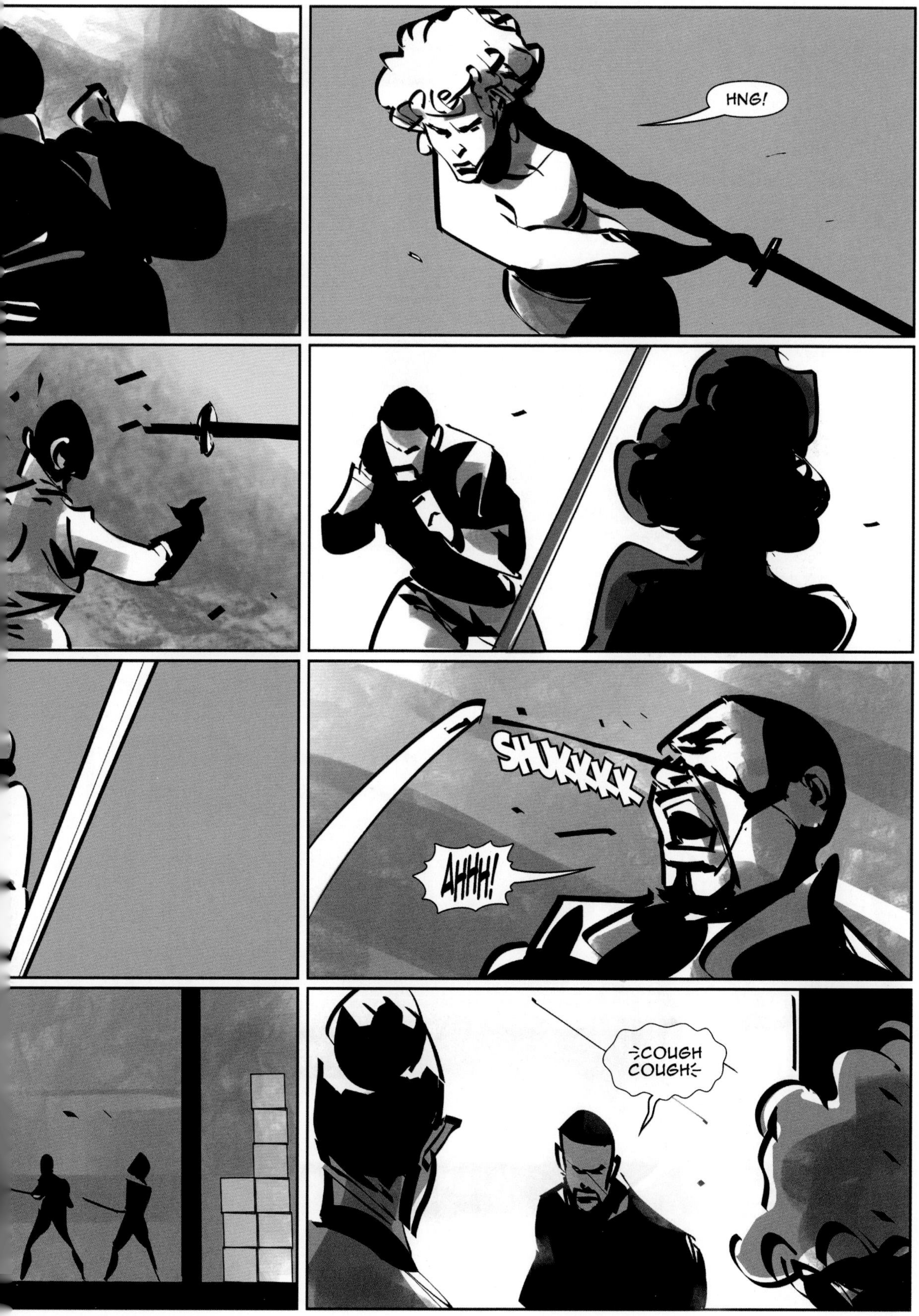
HNG!
SHUKKKK
AHHH!
COUGH COUGH

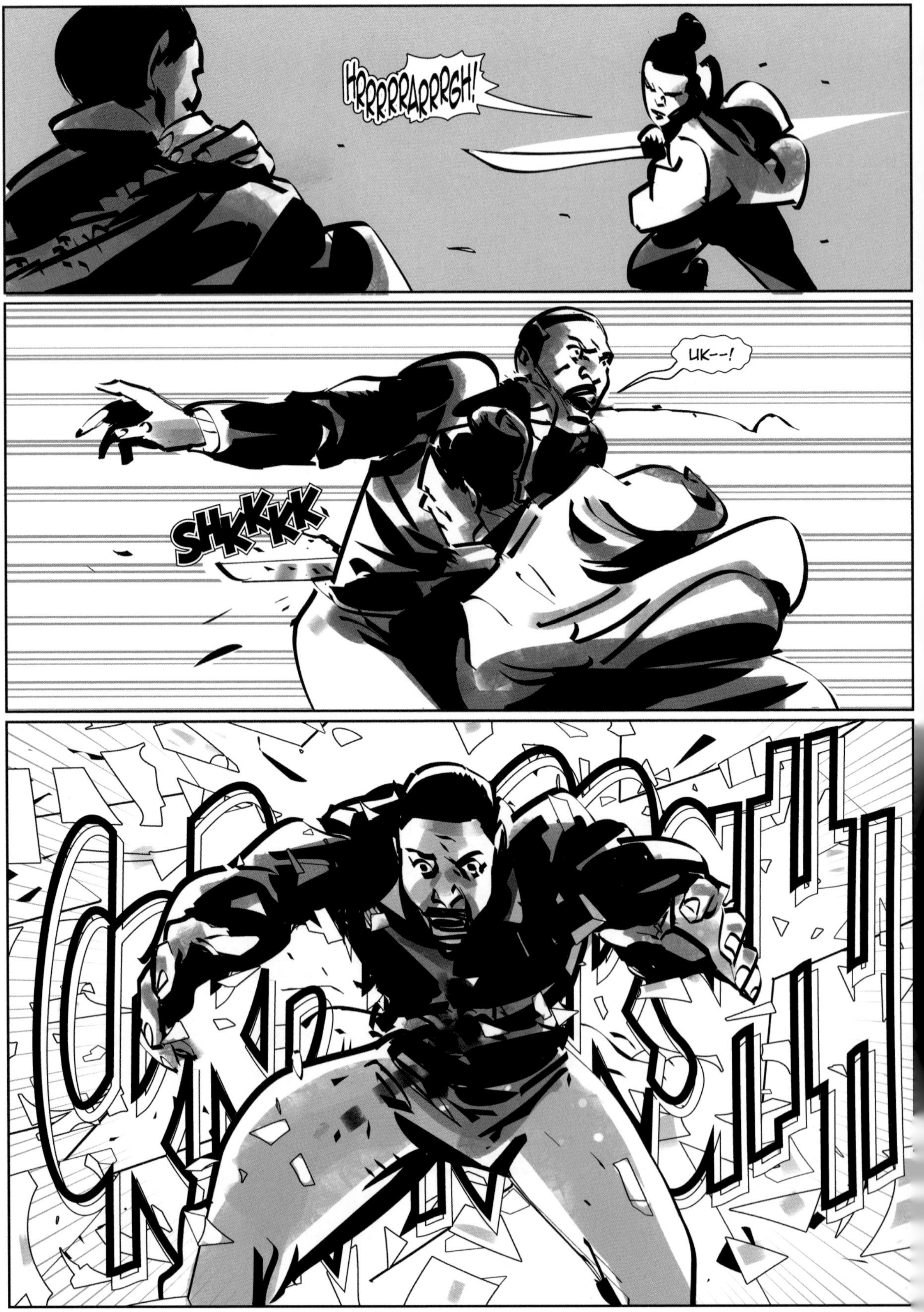
HRRRRARRRGH!
UK--!
SHKKKK

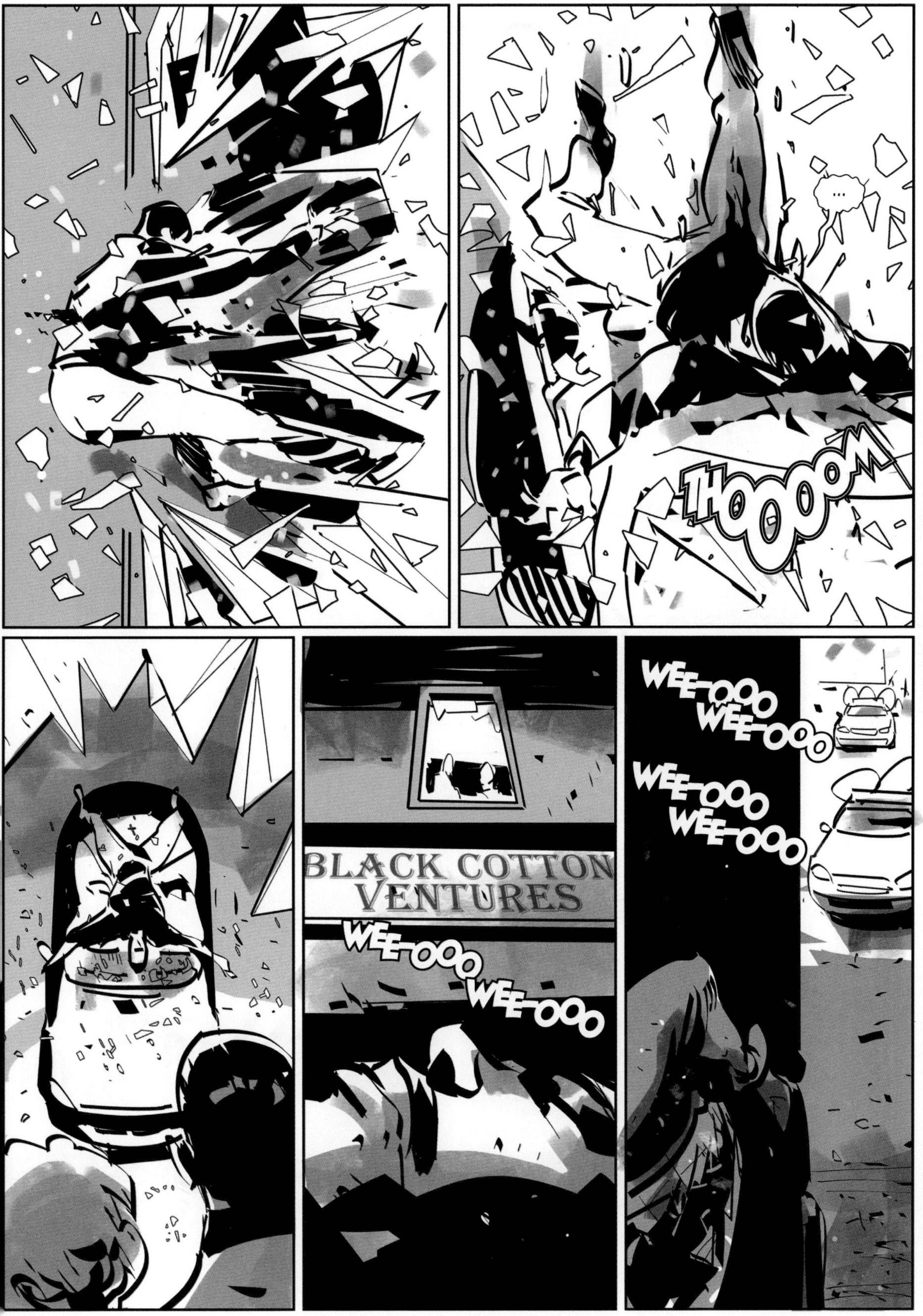
...
THOOOOOM
BLACK COTTON VENTURES
WEE-OOO WEE-OOO
WEE-OOO WEE-OOO
WEE-OOO WEE-OOO

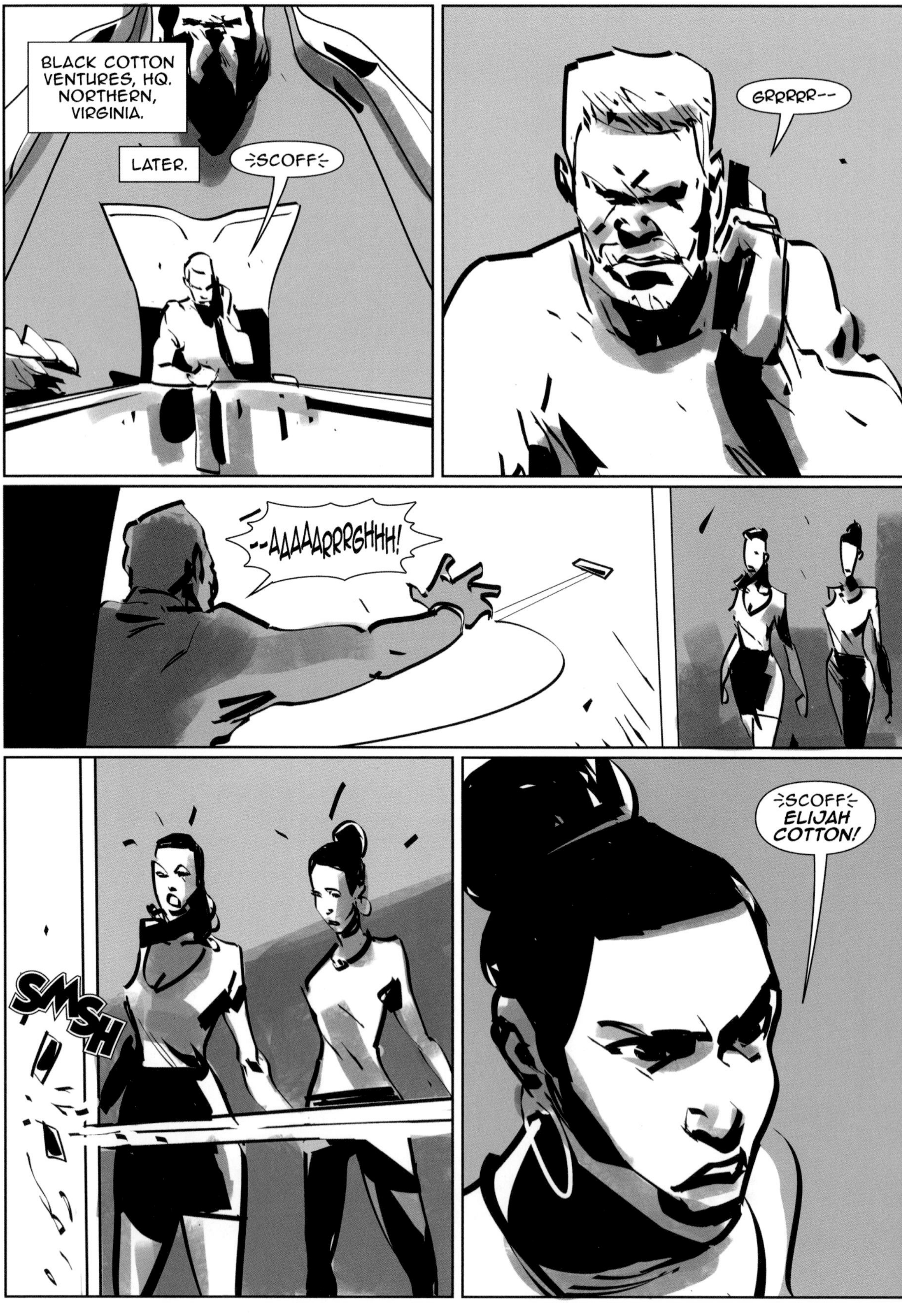
BLACK COTTON VENTURES, HQ. NORTHERN, VIRGINIA.
LATER.
SCOFF
GRRRRR--
--AAAAARRRGHHH!
SMSH
SCOFF ELIJAH COTTON!

THE PHONE LOST. YOU WON. *WHAT A VICTORY,* LOVE.

÷SIGH÷

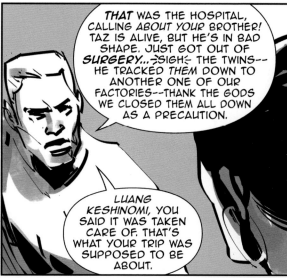

THAT WAS THE HOSPITAL, CALLING *ABOUT YOUR BROTHER!* TAZ IS ALIVE, BUT HE'S IN BAD SHAPE. JUST GOT OUT OF *SURGERY...*÷SIGH÷ THE TWINS-- HE TRACKED *THEM* DOWN TO ANOTHER ONE OF OUR FACTORIES--THANK THE GODS WE CLOSED THEM ALL DOWN AS A PRECAUTION.

LUANG KESHINOMI, YOU SAID IT WAS TAKEN CARE OF. THAT'S WHAT YOUR TRIP WAS SUPPOSED TO BE ABOUT.

BUT APPARENTLY IT ISN'T. HIS CRAZY *OFFSPRING* ARE *TERRORIZING* US--OUR COMPANY, THE *BEDROCK* OF WHO AND WHAT WE ARE, JALEESA. HAVE YOU *SEEN* THE NUMBERS? EXPORTS ARE DOWN---÷SIGH÷ AND--

--THEY'RE COMING AT US WITH *SWORDS!!* WHAT THEY DID TO OUR FACTORY MANAGER-- THE POLICE ARE STILL ASKING QUESTIONS!

TAZ...ELIJAH, I--÷SIGH÷ NO, NOW'S NOT THE TIME FOR WEAKNESS.

TAZ IS STRONG. I KNOW MY BROTHER, *HE'LL BE FINE.*

EXCUSE ME, MR. COTTON...

...UH-- UM...

NOT NOW, CAROLINA. PLEASE.

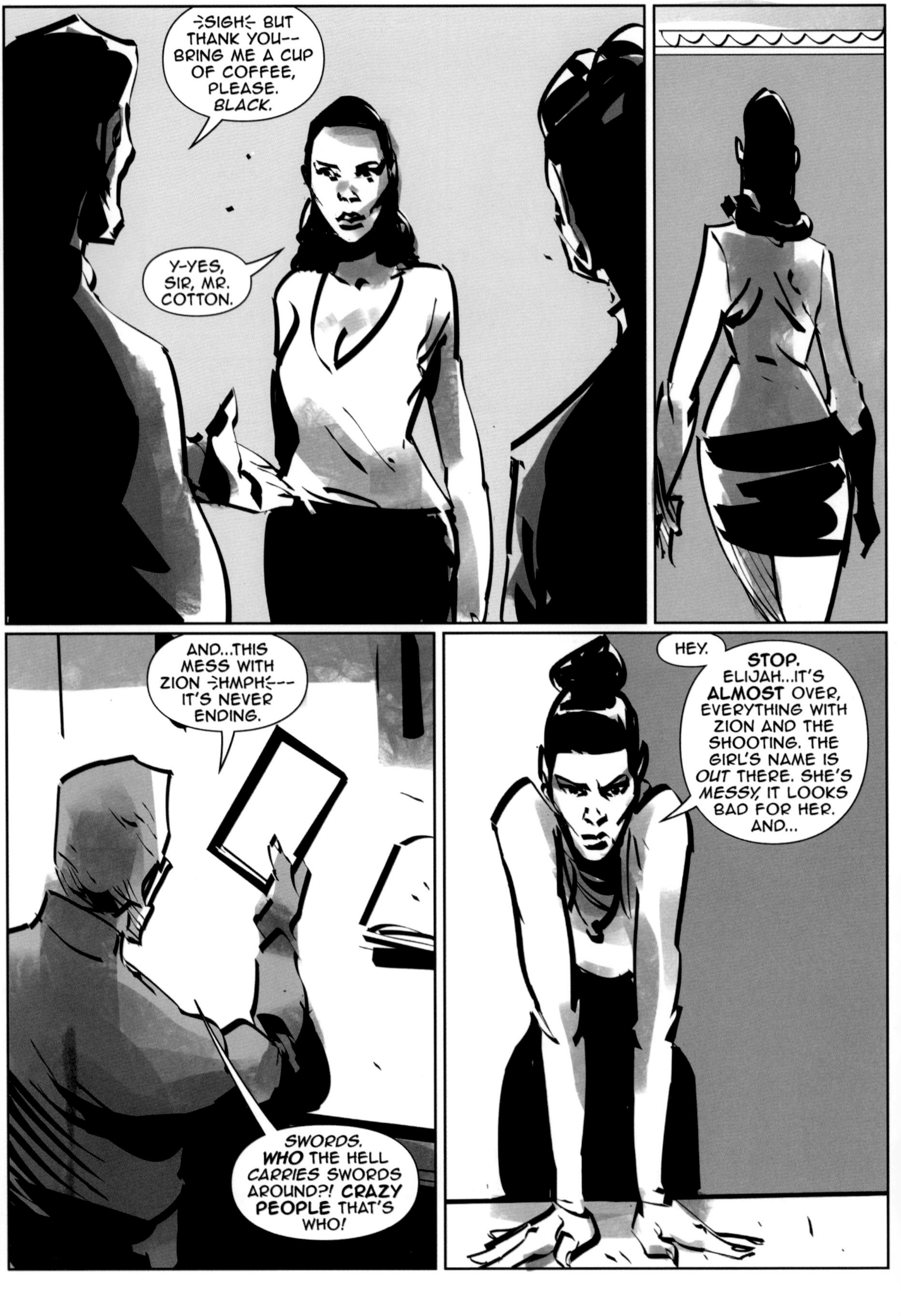

⊰SIGH⊱ BUT THANK YOU-- BRING ME A CUP OF COFFEE, PLEASE. *BLACK.*
Y-YES, SIR, MR. COTTON.
AND...THIS MESS WITH ZION ⊰HMPH⊱-- IT'S NEVER ENDING.
SWORDS. **WHO** THE HELL *CARRIES* SWORDS AROUND?! **CRAZY PEOPLE** THAT'S WHO!
HEY.
STOP. ELIJAH...IT'S **ALMOST** OVER, EVERYTHING WITH ZION AND THE SHOOTING. THE GIRL'S NAME IS *OUT* THERE. SHE'S *MESSY,* IT LOOKS BAD FOR HER. AND...

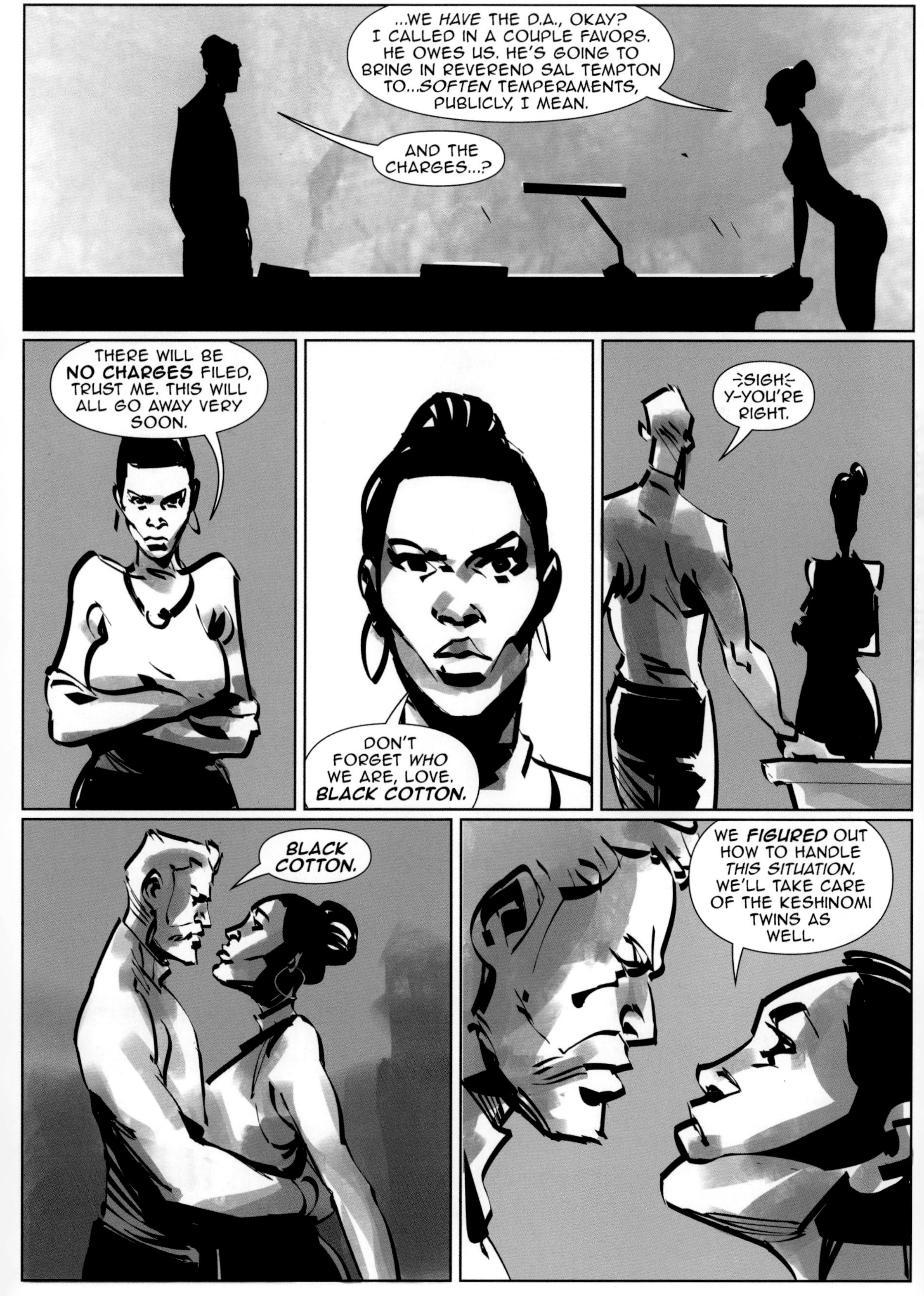
...WE HAVE THE D.A., OKAY? I CALLED IN A COUPLE FAVORS. HE OWES US. HE'S GOING TO BRING IN REVEREND SAL TEMPTON TO...SOFTEN TEMPERAMENTS, PUBLICLY, I MEAN.
AND THE CHARGES...?
THERE WILL BE NO CHARGES FILED, TRUST ME. THIS WILL ALL GO AWAY VERY SOON.
DON'T FORGET WHO WE ARE, LOVE. BLACK COTTON.
SIGH Y-YOU'RE RIGHT.
BLACK COTTON.
WE FIGURED OUT HOW TO HANDLE THIS SITUATION. WE'LL TAKE CARE OF THE KESHINOMI TWINS AS WELL.

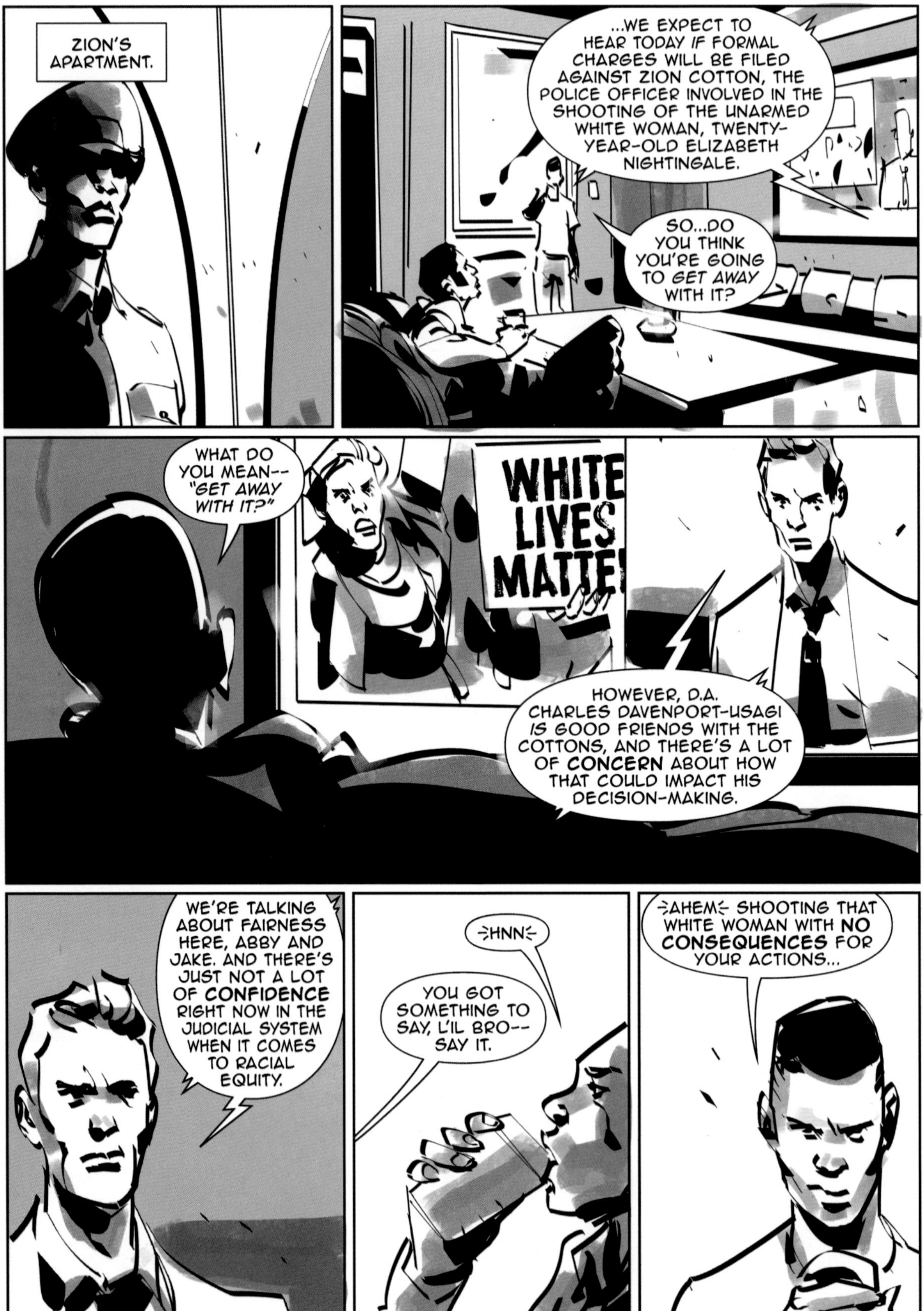
ZION'S APARTMENT.
...WE EXPECT TO HEAR TODAY *IF* FORMAL CHARGES WILL BE FILED AGAINST ZION COTTON, THE POLICE OFFICER INVOLVED IN THE SHOOTING OF THE UNARMED WHITE WOMAN, TWENTY-YEAR-OLD ELIZABETH NIGHTINGALE.
SO...DO YOU THINK YOU'RE GOING TO *GET AWAY* WITH IT?
WHAT DO YOU MEAN-- *"GET AWAY WITH IT?"*
WHITE LIVES MATTE
HOWEVER, D.A. CHARLES DAVENPORT-USAGI *IS* GOOD FRIENDS WITH THE COTTONS, AND THERE'S A LOT OF **CONCERN** ABOUT HOW THAT COULD IMPACT HIS DECISION-MAKING.
WE'RE TALKING ABOUT FAIRNESS HERE, ABBY AND JAKE. AND THERE'S JUST NOT A LOT OF **CONFIDENCE** RIGHT NOW IN THE JUDICIAL SYSTEM WHEN IT COMES TO RACIAL EQUITY.
HNN
YOU GOT SOMETHING TO SAY, L'IL BRO-- SAY IT.
AHEM SHOOTING THAT WHITE WOMAN WITH **NO CONSEQUENCES** FOR YOUR ACTIONS...

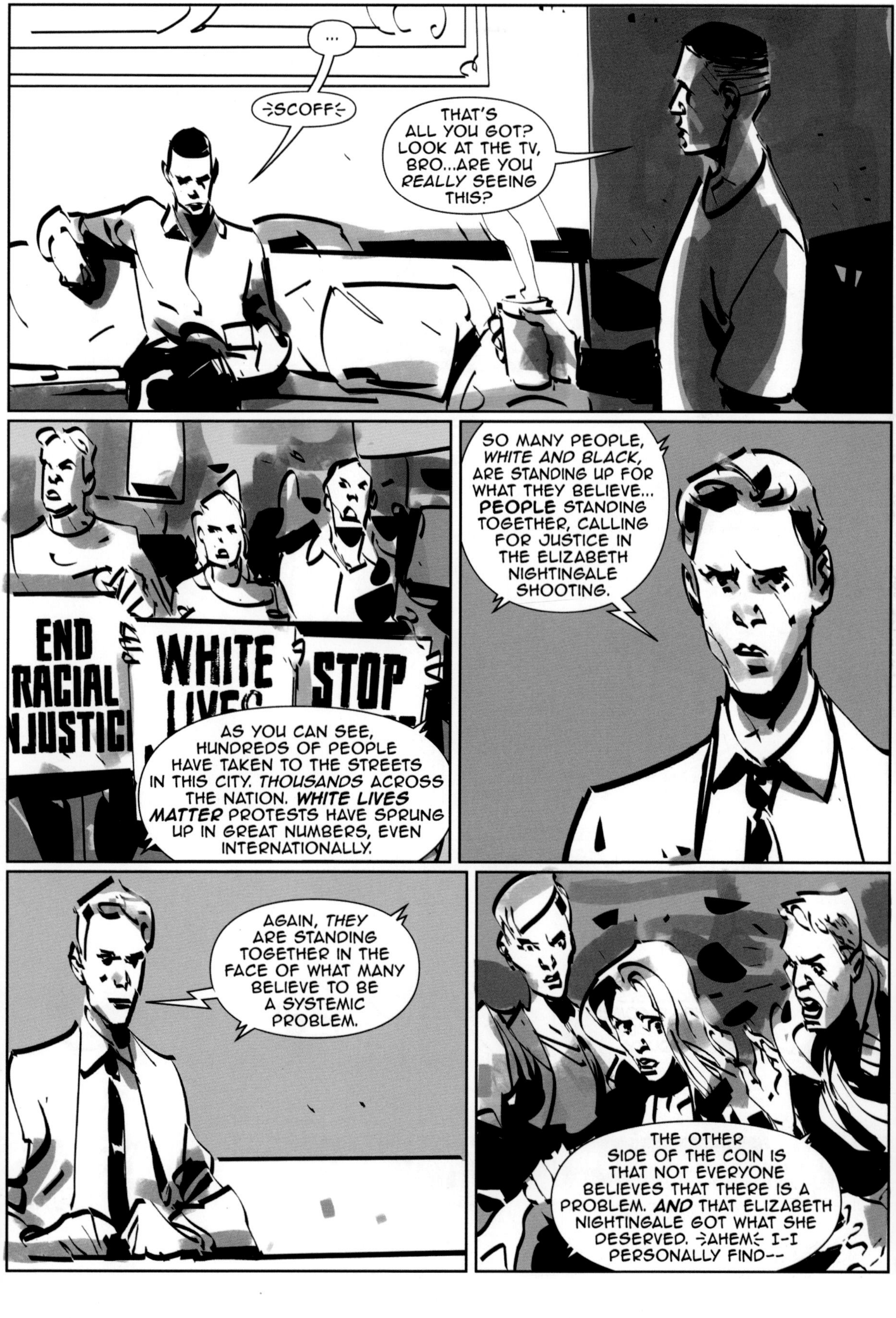

...
SCOFF
THAT'S ALL YOU GOT? LOOK AT THE TV, BRO...ARE YOU *REALLY* SEEING THIS?
END RACIAL
WHITE
STOP
AS YOU CAN SEE, HUNDREDS OF PEOPLE HAVE TAKEN TO THE STREETS IN THIS CITY. *THOUSANDS* ACROSS THE NATION. ***WHITE LIVES MATTER*** PROTESTS HAVE SPRUNG UP IN GREAT NUMBERS, EVEN INTERNATIONALLY.
SO MANY PEOPLE, *WHITE AND BLACK*, ARE STANDING UP FOR WHAT THEY BELIEVE... **PEOPLE** STANDING TOGETHER, CALLING FOR JUSTICE IN THE ELIZABETH NIGHTINGALE SHOOTING.
AGAIN, *THEY* ARE STANDING TOGETHER IN THE FACE OF WHAT MANY BELIEVE TO BE A SYSTEMIC PROBLEM.
THE OTHER SIDE OF THE COIN IS THAT NOT EVERYONE BELIEVES THAT THERE IS A PROBLEM. ***AND*** THAT ELIZABETH NIGHTINGALE GOT WHAT SHE DESERVED. AHEM I-I PERSONALLY FIND--

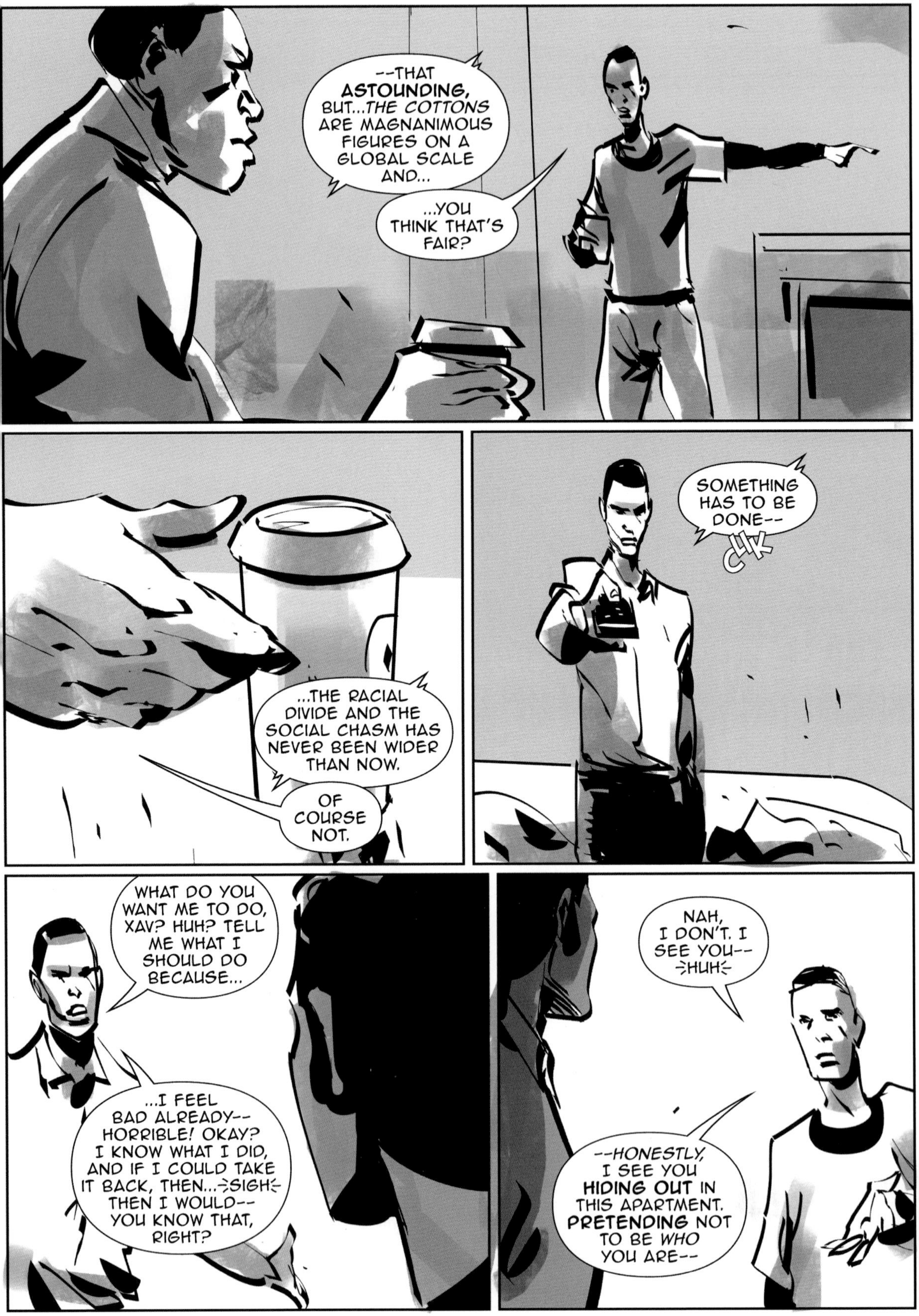
--THAT **ASTOUNDING,** BUT...*THE COTTONS* ARE MAGNANIMOUS FIGURES ON A GLOBAL SCALE AND...
...YOU THINK THAT'S FAIR?
...THE RACIAL DIVIDE AND THE SOCIAL CHASM HAS NEVER BEEN WIDER THAN NOW.
OF COURSE NOT.
SOMETHING HAS TO BE DONE--
CLIK
WHAT DO YOU WANT ME TO DO, XAV? HUH? TELL ME WHAT I SHOULD DO BECAUSE...
...I FEEL BAD ALREADY--HORRIBLE! OKAY? I KNOW WHAT I DID, AND IF I COULD TAKE IT BACK, THEN...SIGH THEN I WOULD--YOU KNOW THAT, RIGHT?
NAH, I DON'T. I SEE YOU--HUH
--*HONESTLY,* I SEE YOU **HIDING OUT** IN THIS APARTMENT. **PRETENDING** NOT TO BE *WHO* YOU ARE--

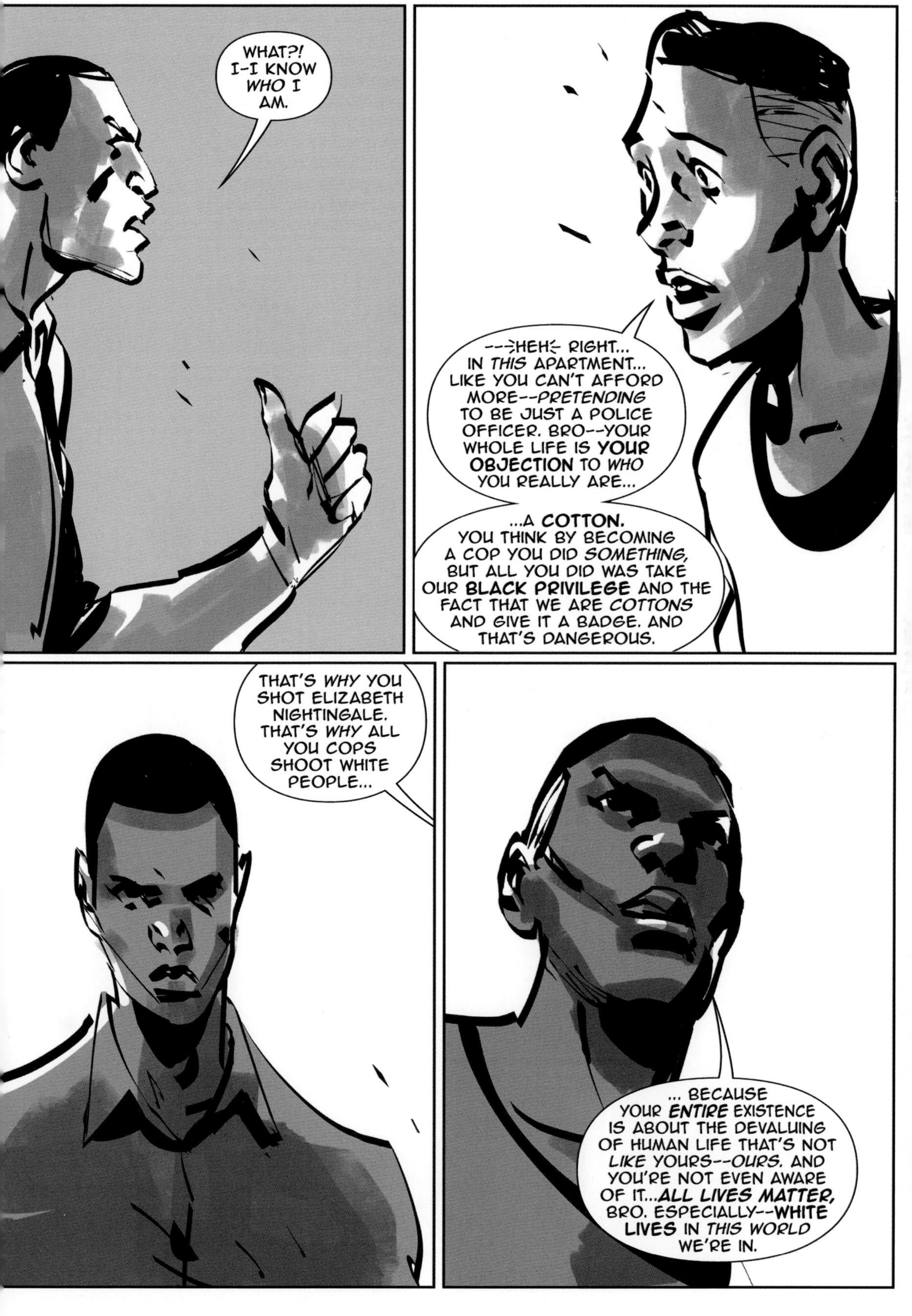
WHAT?! I-I KNOW *WHO* I AM.
--HEH-- RIGHT... IN *THIS* APARTMENT... LIKE YOU CAN'T AFFORD MORE--*PRETENDING* TO BE JUST A POLICE OFFICER. BRO--YOUR WHOLE LIFE IS **YOUR OBJECTION** TO *WHO* YOU REALLY ARE...
...A **COTTON.** YOU THINK BY BECOMING A COP YOU DID *SOMETHING,* BUT ALL YOU DID WAS TAKE OUR **BLACK PRIVILEGE** AND THE FACT THAT WE ARE *COTTONS* AND GIVE IT A BADGE. AND THAT'S DANGEROUS.
THAT'S *WHY* YOU SHOT ELIZABETH NIGHTINGALE. THAT'S *WHY* ALL YOU COPS SHOOT WHITE PEOPLE...
... BECAUSE YOUR ***ENTIRE*** EXISTENCE IS ABOUT THE DEVALUING OF HUMAN LIFE THAT'S NOT *LIKE* YOURS--*OURS.* AND YOU'RE NOT EVEN AWARE OF IT...***ALL LIVES MATTER,*** BRO. ESPECIALLY--**WHITE LIVES** IN *THIS WORLD* WE'RE IN.

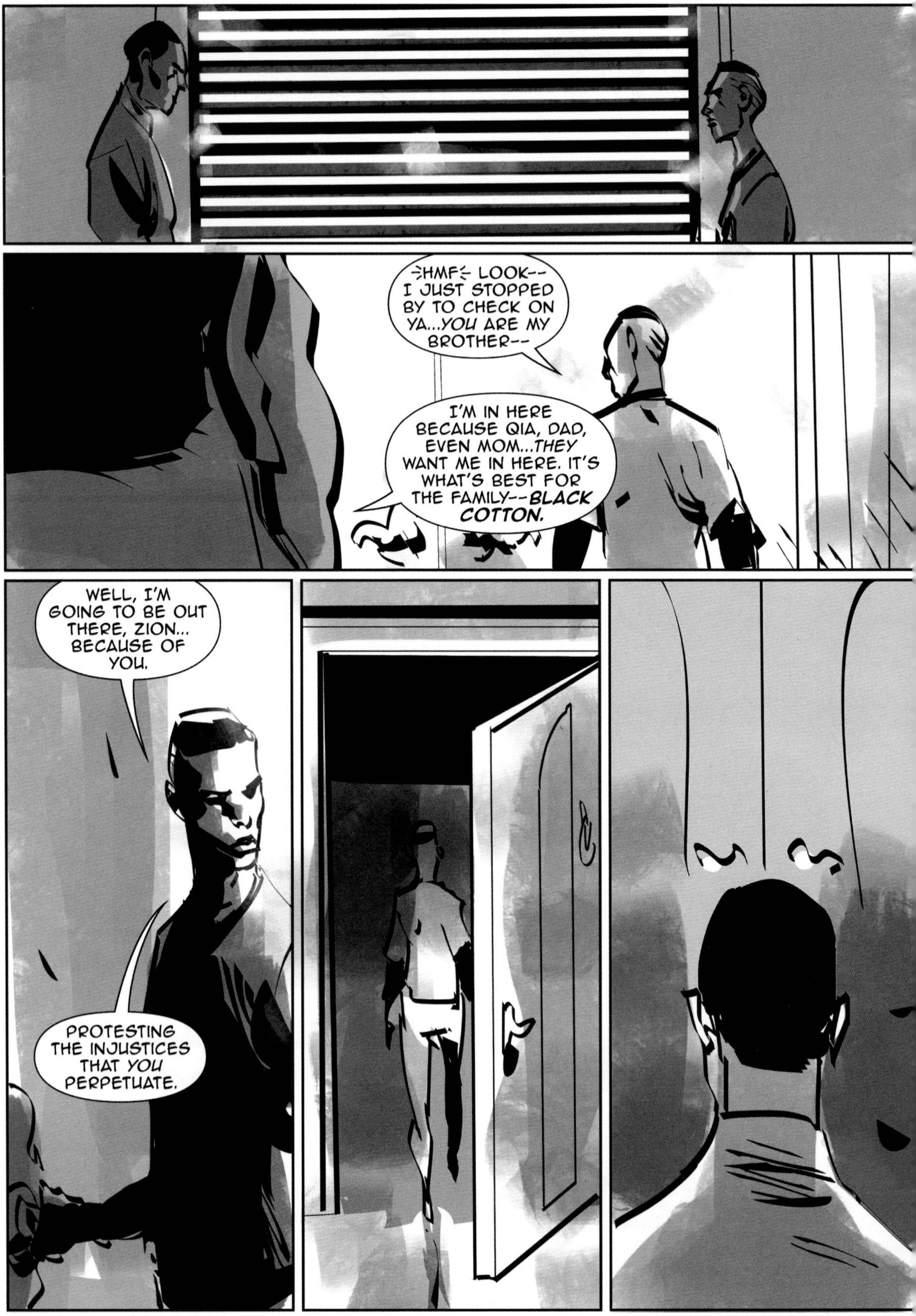
HMF LOOK-- I JUST STOPPED BY TO CHECK ON YA...YOU ARE MY BROTHER--
I'M IN HERE BECAUSE QIA, DAD, EVEN MOM...THEY WANT ME IN HERE. IT'S WHAT'S BEST FOR THE FAMILY--BLACK COTTON.
WELL, I'M GOING TO BE OUT THERE, ZION... BECAUSE OF YOU.
PROTESTING THE INJUSTICES THAT YOU PERPETUATE.

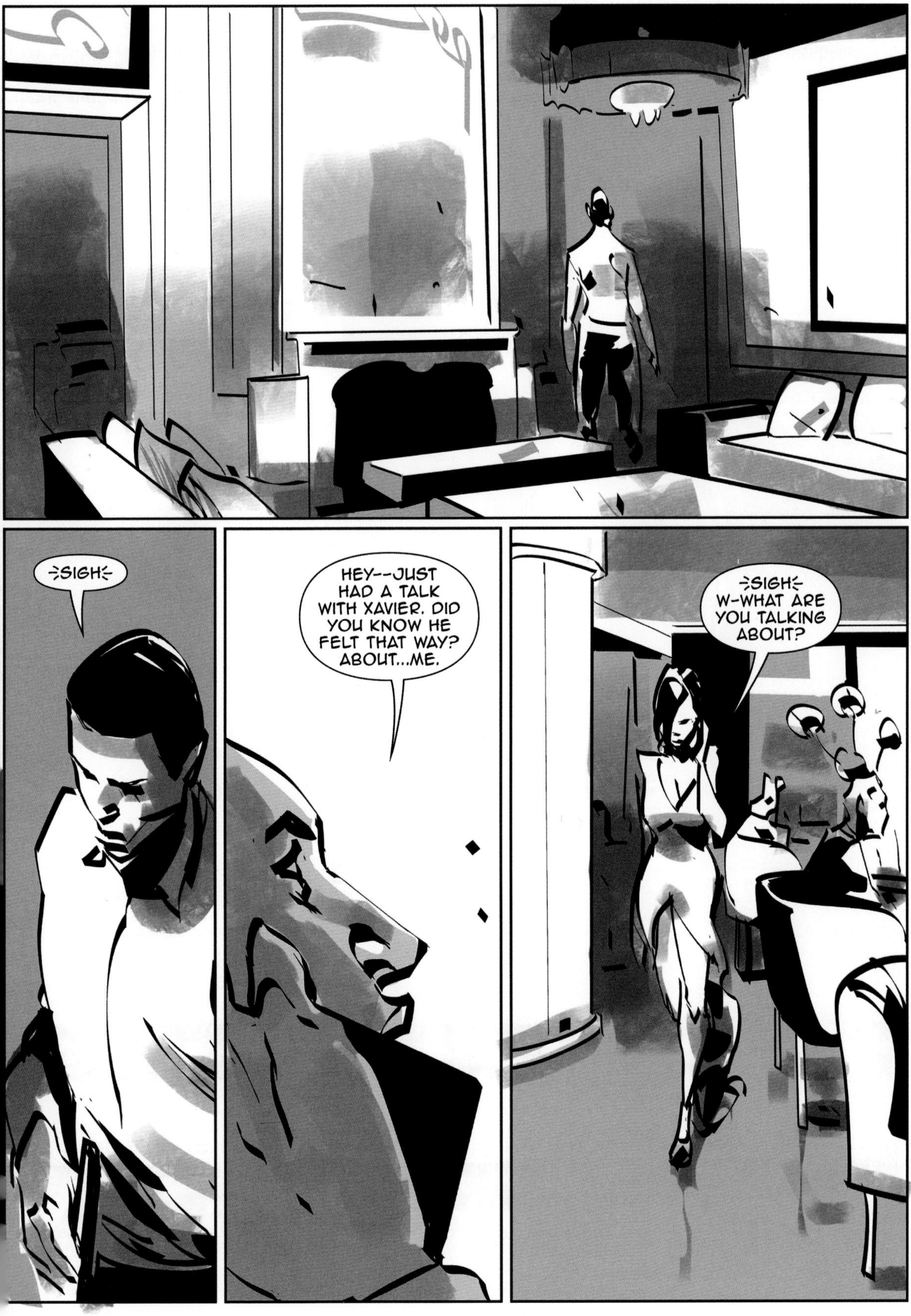

-SIGH-
HEY--JUST HAD A TALK WITH XAVIER. DID YOU KNOW HE FELT THAT WAY? ABOUT...ME.
-SIGH- W-WHAT ARE YOU TALKING ABOUT?

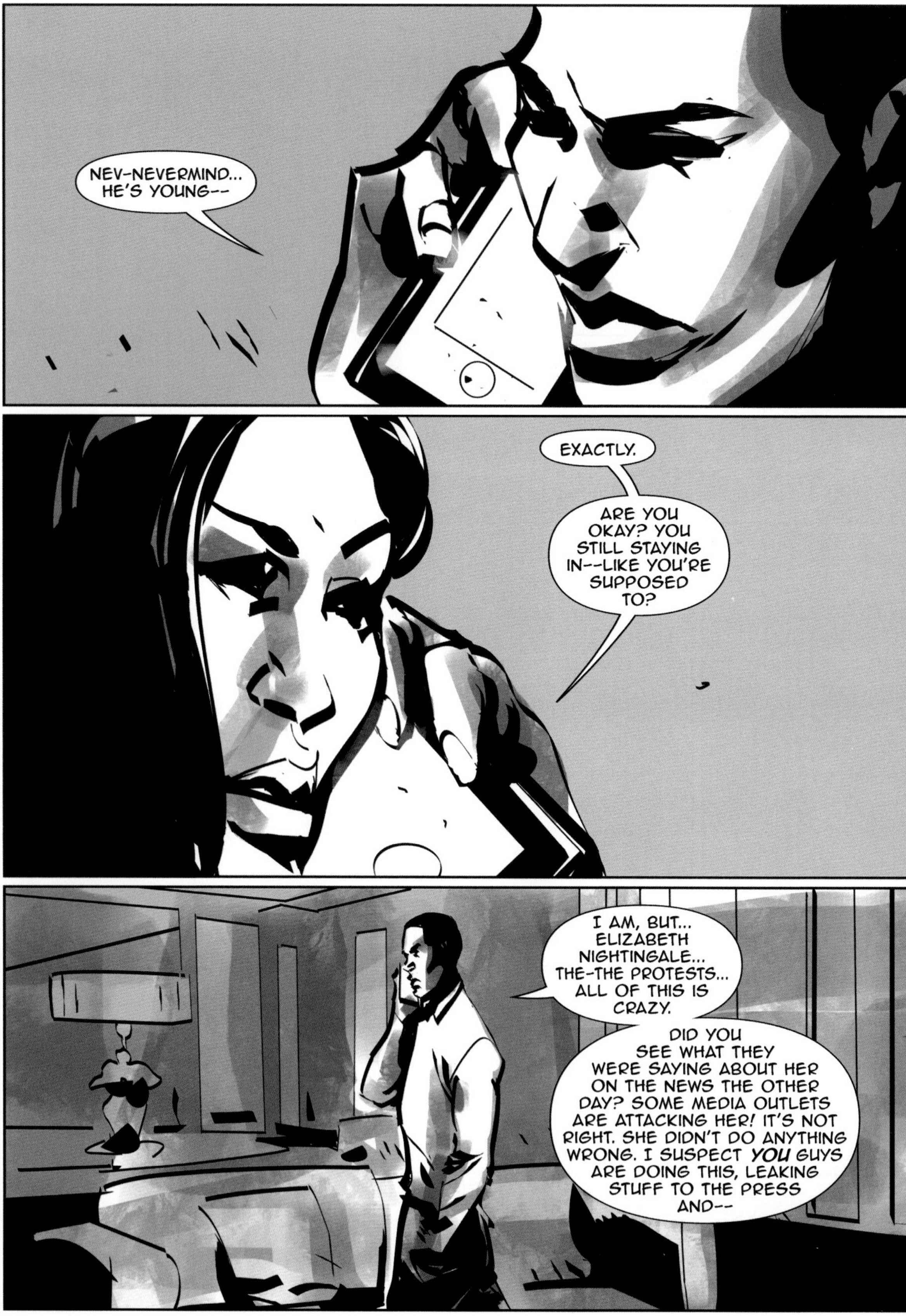
NEV-NEVERMIND... HE'S YOUNG--
EXACTLY.
ARE YOU OKAY? YOU STILL STAYING IN--LIKE YOU'RE SUPPOSED TO?
I AM, BUT... ELIZABETH NIGHTINGALE... THE-THE PROTESTS... ALL OF THIS IS CRAZY.
DID YOU SEE WHAT THEY WERE SAYING ABOUT HER ON THE NEWS THE OTHER DAY? SOME MEDIA OUTLETS ARE ATTACKING HER! IT'S NOT RIGHT. SHE DIDN'T DO ANYTHING WRONG. I SUSPECT *YOU* GUYS ARE DOING THIS, LEAKING STUFF TO THE PRESS AND--

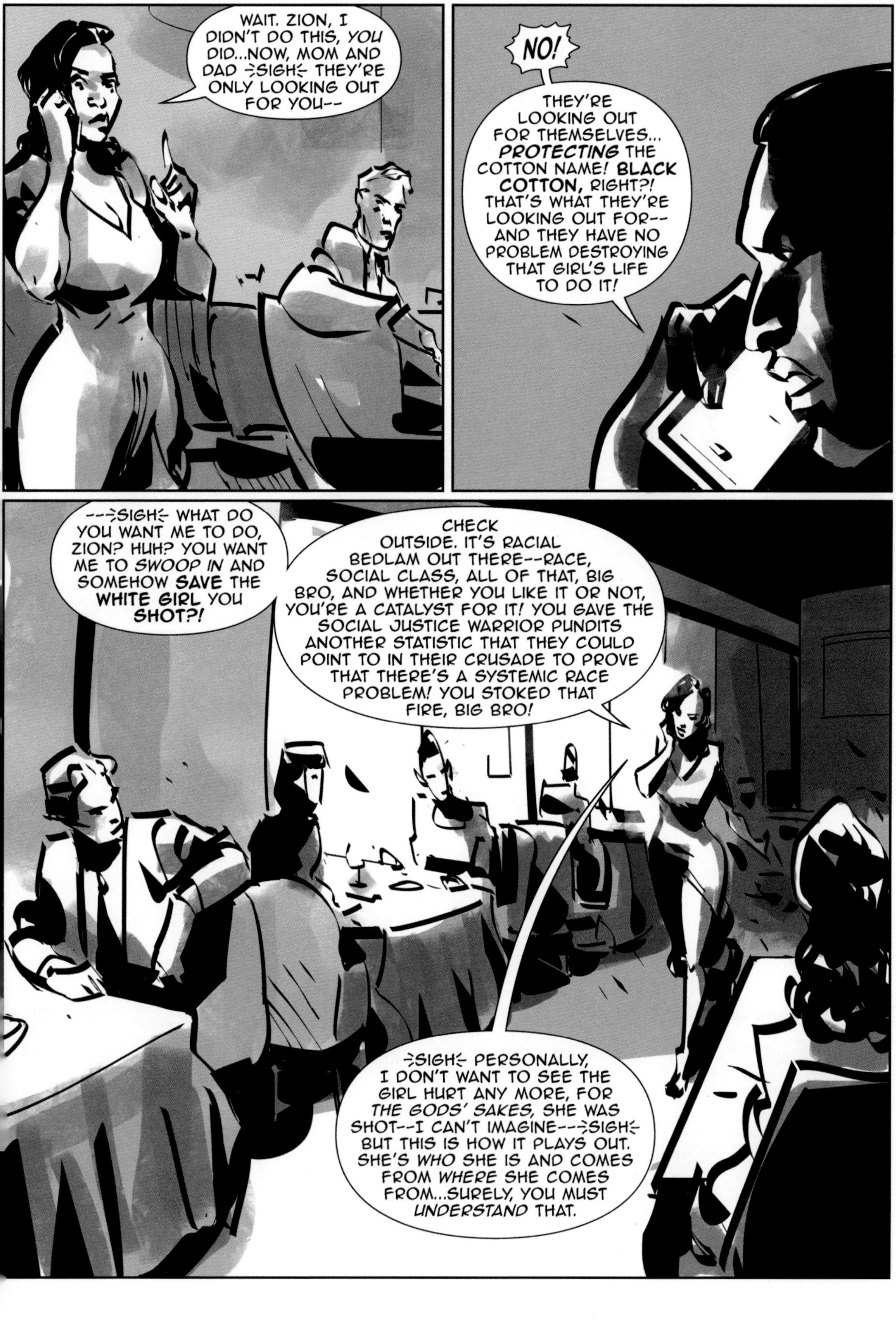
WAIT. ZION, I DIDN'T DO THIS, *YOU* DID...NOW, MOM AND DAD ~SIGH~ THEY'RE ONLY LOOKING OUT FOR YOU--
NO!
THEY'RE LOOKING OUT FOR THEMSELVES... ***PROTECTING*** THE COTTON NAME! **BLACK COTTON,** RIGHT?! THAT'S WHAT THEY'RE LOOKING OUT FOR-- AND THEY HAVE NO PROBLEM DESTROYING THAT GIRL'S LIFE TO DO IT!
--~SIGH~ WHAT DO YOU WANT ME TO DO, ZION? HUH? YOU WANT ME TO *SWOOP IN* AND SOMEHOW **SAVE** THE **WHITE GIRL** YOU **SHOT?!**
CHECK OUTSIDE. IT'S RACIAL BEDLAM OUT THERE--RACE, SOCIAL CLASS, ALL OF THAT, BIG BRO, AND WHETHER YOU LIKE IT OR NOT, YOU'RE A CATALYST FOR IT! YOU GAVE THE SOCIAL JUSTICE WARRIOR PUNDITS ANOTHER STATISTIC THAT THEY COULD POINT TO IN THEIR CRUSADE TO PROVE THAT THERE'S A SYSTEMIC RACE PROBLEM! YOU STOKED THAT FIRE, BIG BRO!
~SIGH~ PERSONALLY, I DON'T WANT TO SEE THE GIRL HURT ANY MORE, FOR *THE GODS' SAKES*, SHE WAS SHOT--I CAN'T IMAGINE--~SIGH~ BUT THIS IS HOW IT PLAYS OUT. SHE'S *WHO* SHE IS AND COMES FROM *WHERE* SHE COMES FROM...SURELY, YOU MUST *UNDERSTAND* THAT.

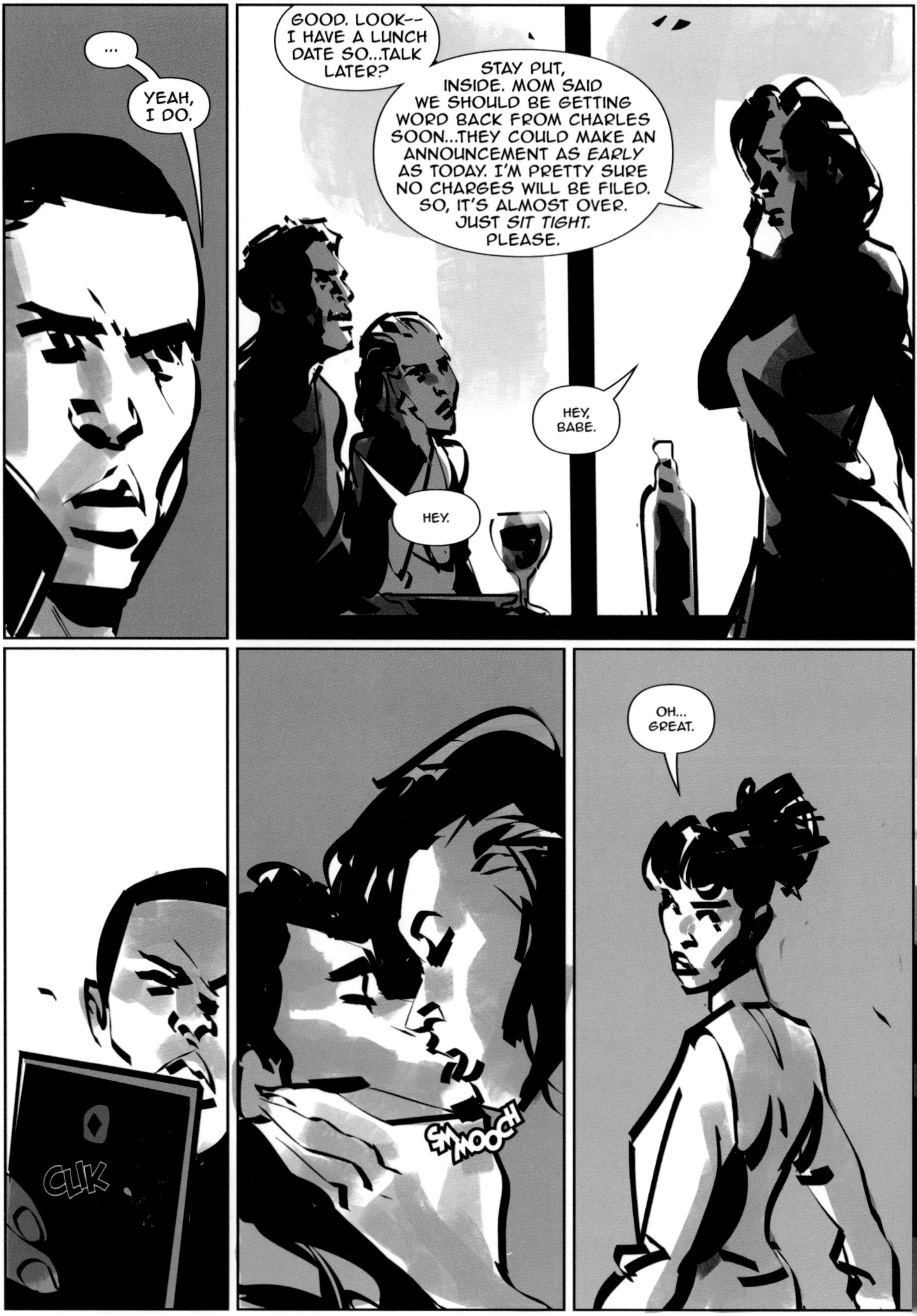
...
YEAH, I DO.
GOOD. LOOK-- I HAVE A LUNCH DATE SO...TALK LATER?
STAY PUT, INSIDE. MOM SAID WE SHOULD BE GETTING WORD BACK FROM CHARLES SOON...THEY COULD MAKE AN ANNOUNCEMENT AS *EARLY* AS TODAY. I'M PRETTY SURE NO CHARGES WILL BE FILED. SO, IT'S ALMOST OVER. JUST *SIT TIGHT.* PLEASE.
HEY, BABE.
HEY.
CLIK
SMOOCH
OH... GREAT.

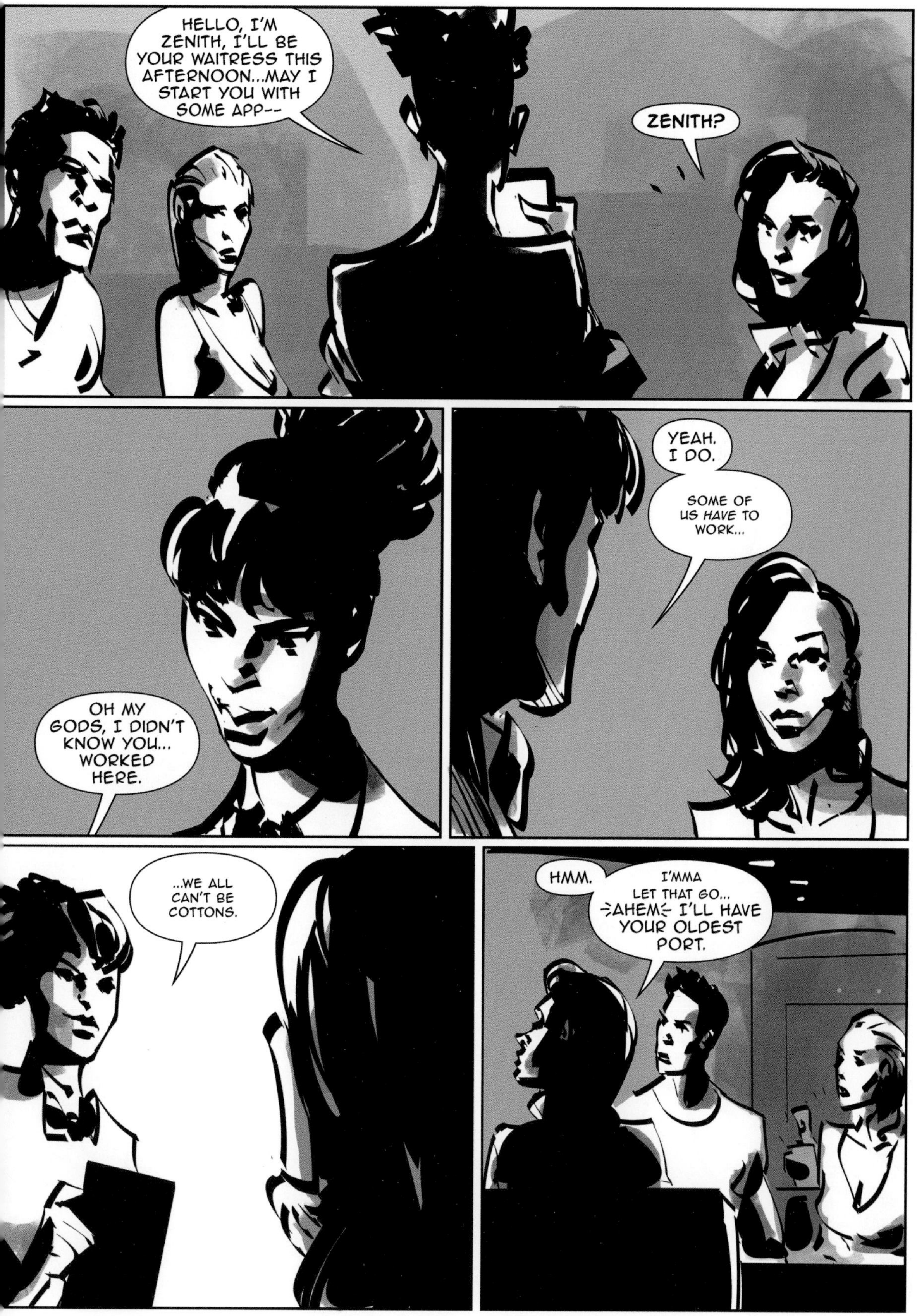
HELLO, I'M ZENITH, I'LL BE YOUR WAITRESS THIS AFTERNOON...MAY I START YOU WITH SOME APP--
ZENITH?
OH MY GODS, I DIDN'T KNOW YOU... WORKED HERE.
YEAH. I DO.
SOME OF US HAVE TO WORK...
...WE ALL CAN'T BE COTTONS.
HMM.
I'MMA LET THAT GO... AHEM I'LL HAVE YOUR OLDEST PORT.

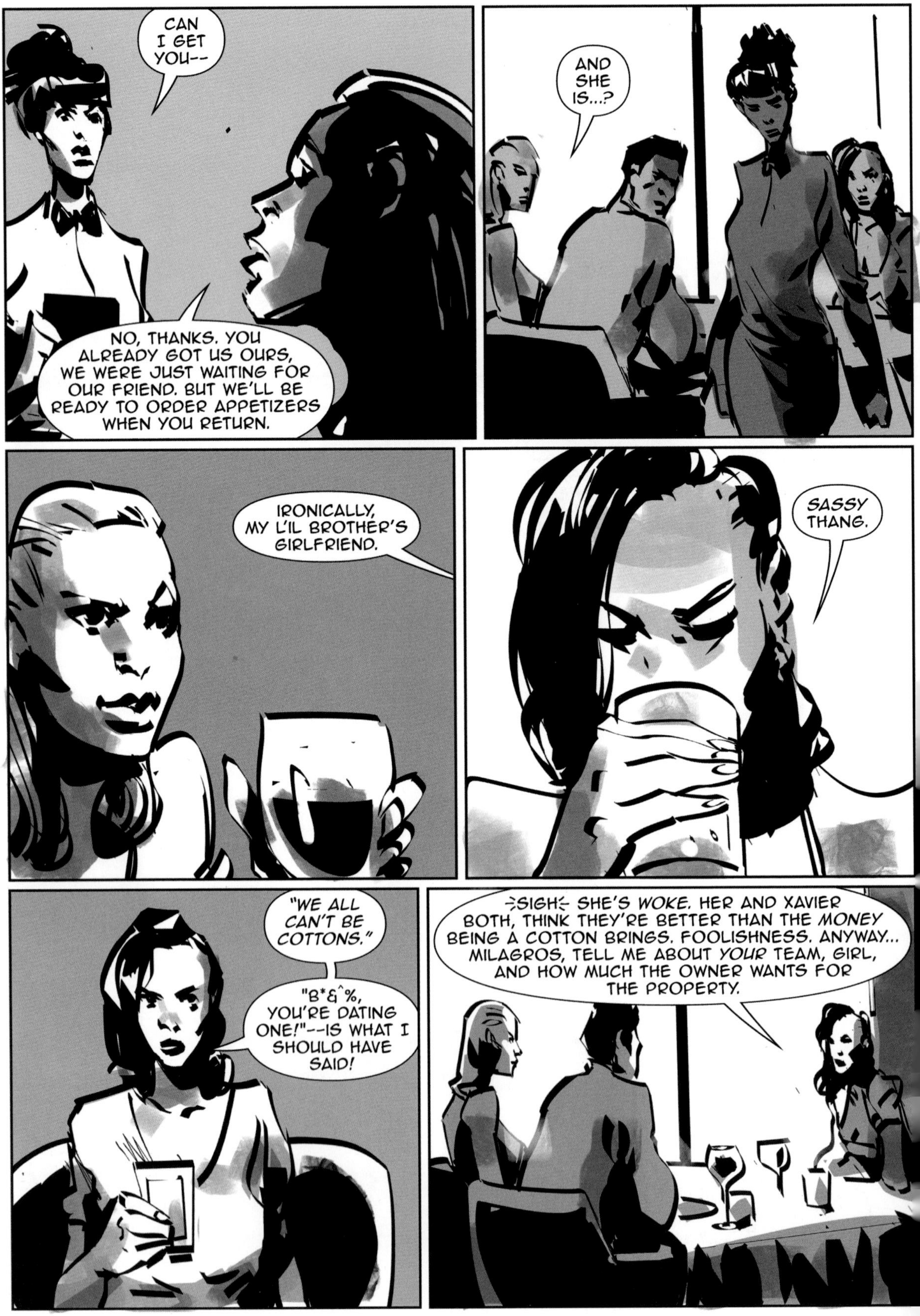
CAN I GET YOU--
NO, THANKS. YOU ALREADY GOT US OURS, WE WERE JUST WAITING FOR OUR FRIEND. BUT WE'LL BE READY TO ORDER APPETIZERS WHEN YOU RETURN.
AND SHE IS...?
IRONICALLY, MY L'IL BROTHER'S GIRLFRIEND.
SASSY THANG.
"WE ALL CAN'T BE COTTONS."
"B*&^%, YOU'RE DATING ONE!"--IS WHAT I SHOULD HAVE SAID!
SIGH SHE'S WOKE. HER AND XAVIER BOTH, THINK THEY'RE BETTER THAN THE MONEY BEING A COTTON BRINGS. FOOLISHNESS. ANYWAY... MILAGROS, TELL ME ABOUT YOUR TEAM, GIRL, AND HOW MUCH THE OWNER WANTS FOR THE PROPERTY.

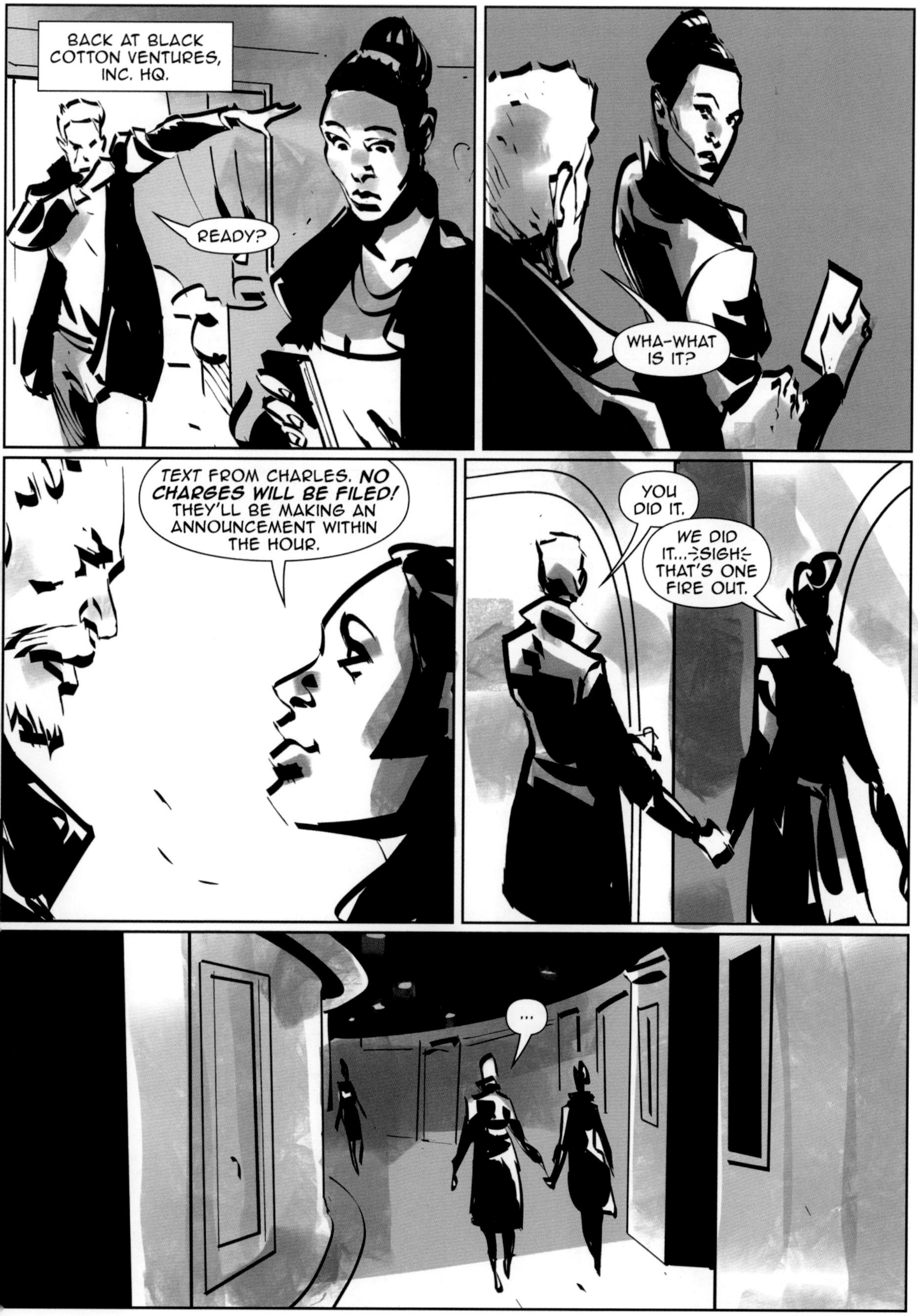
BACK AT BLACK COTTON VENTURES, INC. HQ.
READY?
WHA-WHAT IS IT?
TEXT FROM CHARLES. **NO CHARGES WILL BE FILED!** THEY'LL BE MAKING AN ANNOUNCEMENT WITHIN THE HOUR.
YOU DID IT.
WE DID IT... SIGH THAT'S ONE FIRE OUT.
...

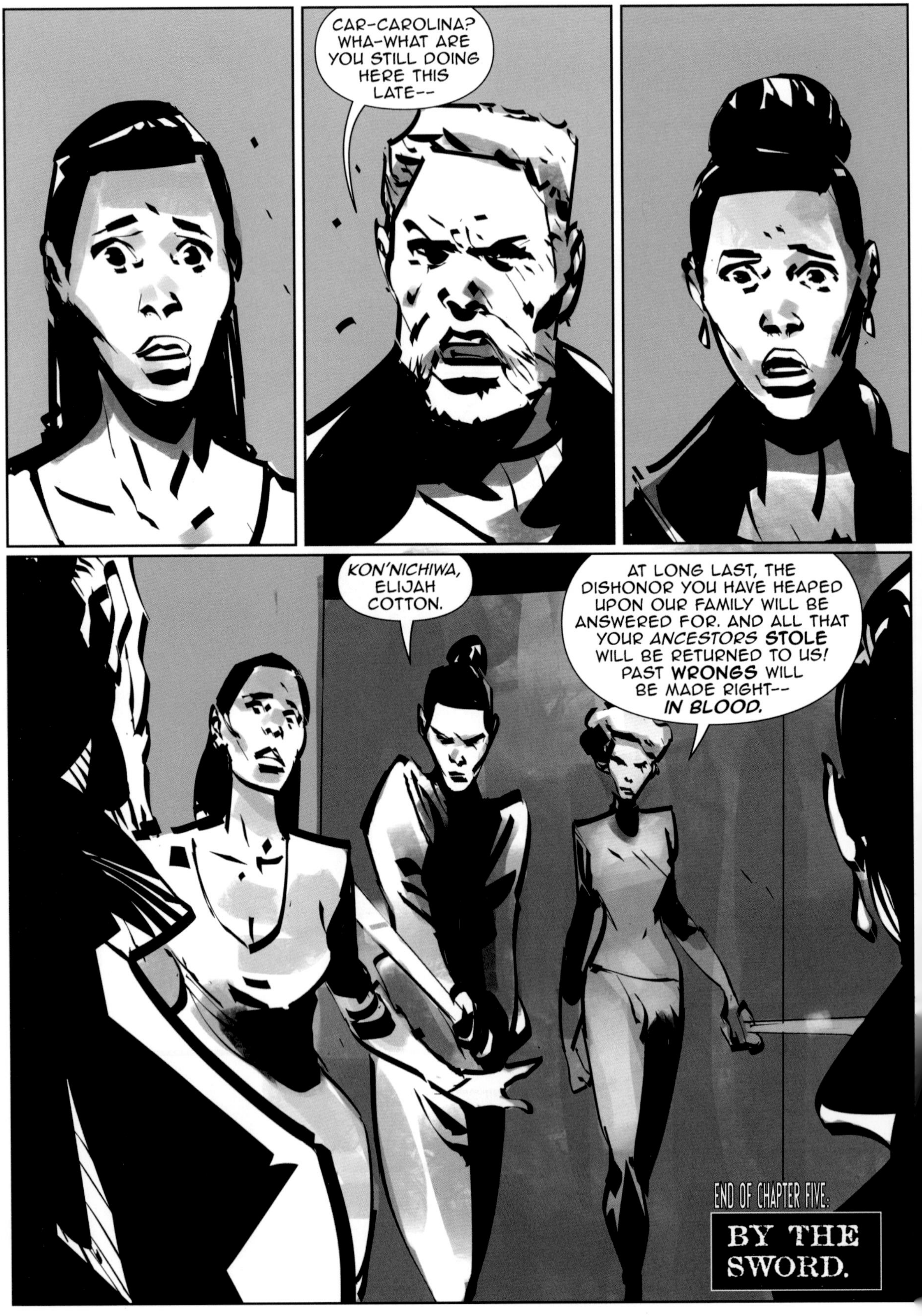

CAR-CAROLINA? WHA-WHAT ARE YOU STILL DOING HERE THIS LATE--
KON'NICHIWA, ELIJAH COTTON.
AT LONG LAST, THE DISHONOR YOU HAVE HEAPED UPON OUR FAMILY WILL BE ANSWERED FOR. AND ALL THAT YOUR ANCESTORS STOLE WILL BE RETURNED TO US! PAST WRONGS WILL BE MADE RIGHT-- IN BLOOD.
END OF CHAPTER FIVE:
BY THE SWORD.

ONLY SHOT/
BY THE SWORD

CHAPTER
6

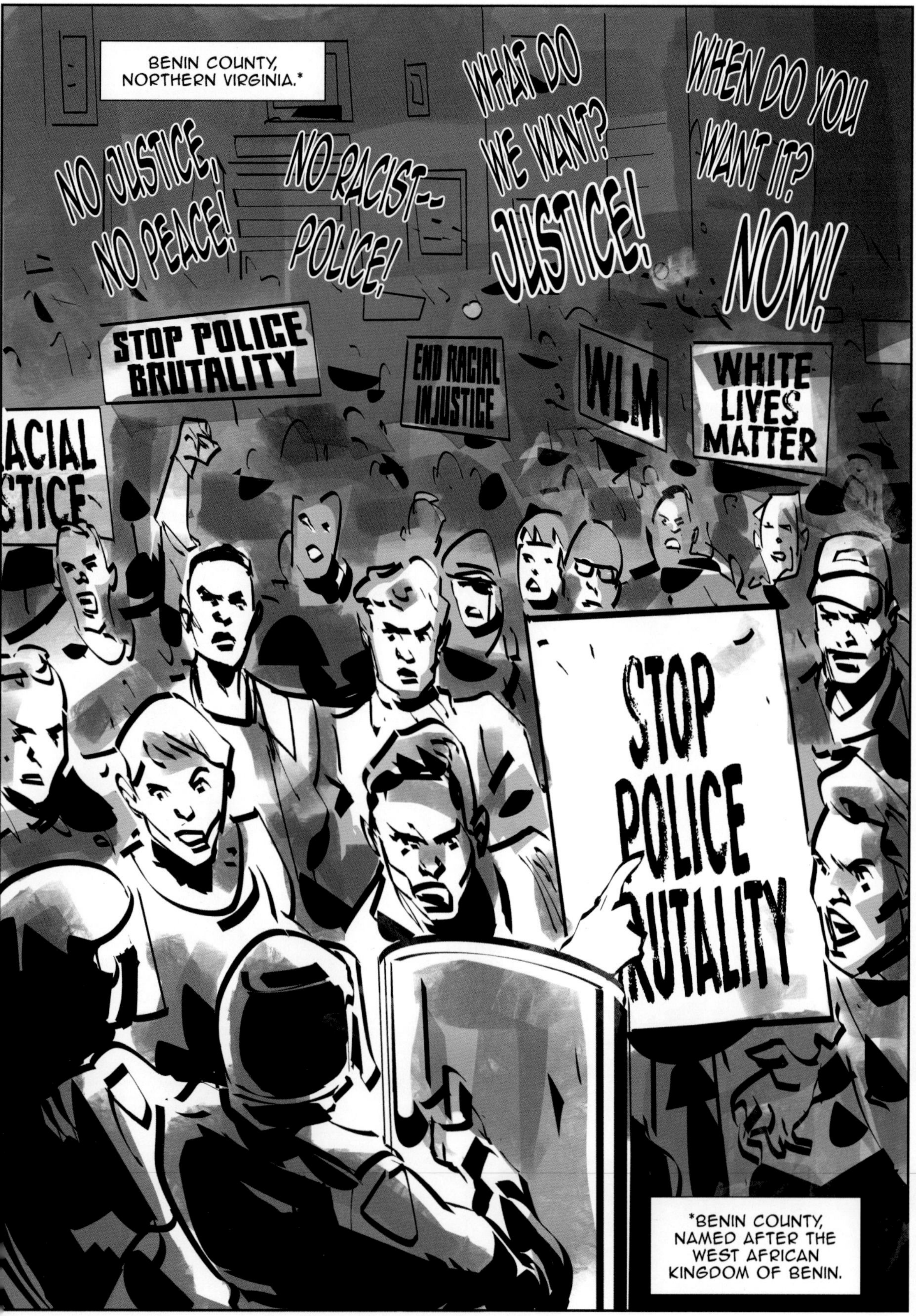
BENIN COUNTY, NORTHERN VIRGINIA.*
NO JUSTICE, NO PEACE!
NO RACIST-- POLICE!
WHAT DO WE WANT? JUSTICE!
WHEN DO YOU WANT IT? NOW!
STOP POLICE BRUTALITY
END RACIAL INJUSTICE
WLM
WHITE LIVES MATTER
STOP POLICE BRUTALITY
*BENIN COUNTY, NAMED AFTER THE WEST AFRICAN KINGDOM OF BENIN.

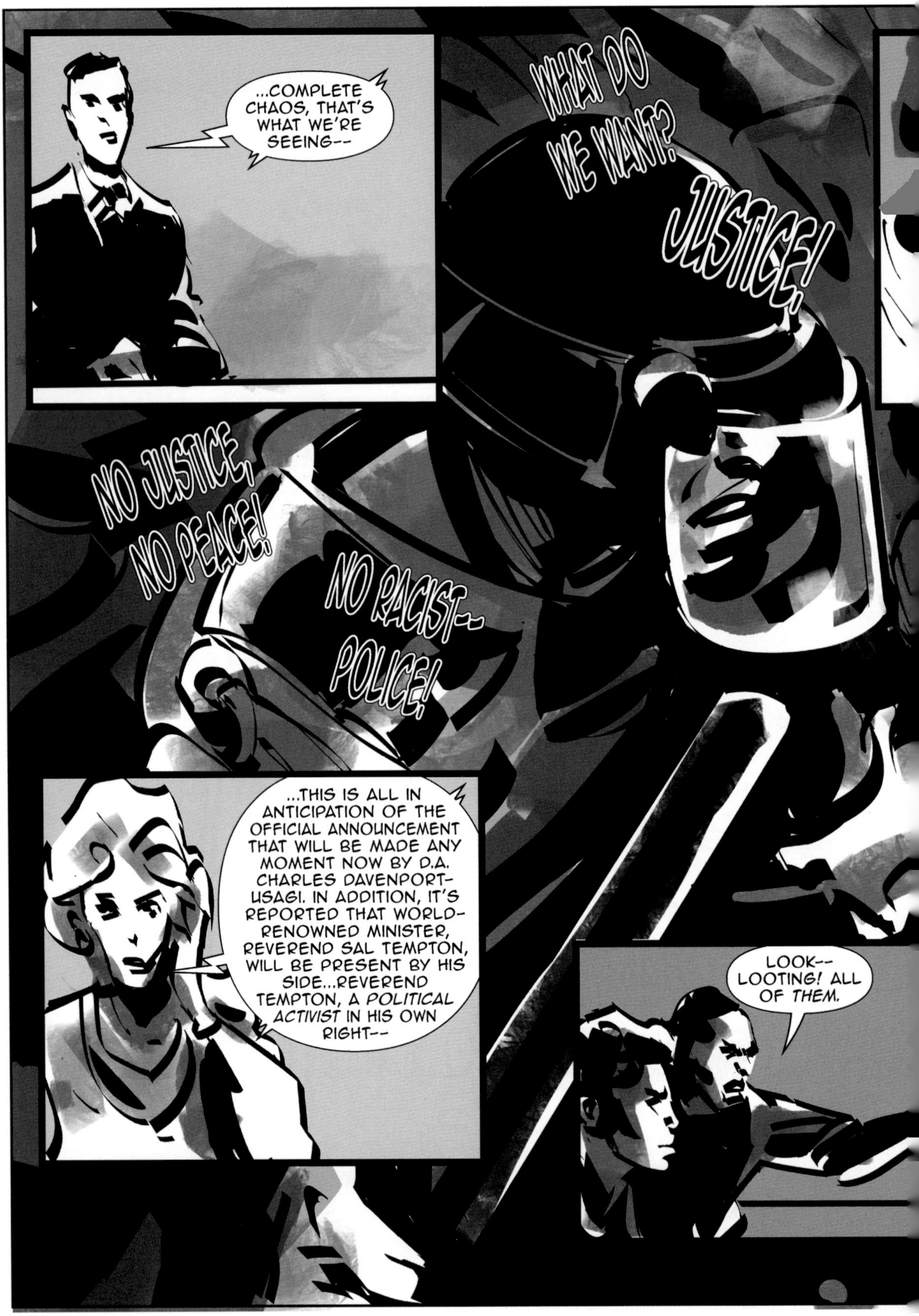
...COMPLETE CHAOS, THAT'S WHAT WE'RE SEEING--
WHAT DO WE WANT?
JUSTICE!
NO JUSTICE, NO PEACE!
NO RACIST-- POLICE!
...THIS IS ALL IN ANTICIPATION OF THE OFFICIAL ANNOUNCEMENT THAT WILL BE MADE ANY MOMENT NOW BY D.A. CHARLES DAVENPORT-USAGI. IN ADDITION, IT'S REPORTED THAT WORLD-RENOWNED MINISTER, REVEREND SAL TEMPTON, WILL BE PRESENT BY HIS SIDE...REVEREND TEMPTON, A *POLITICAL ACTIVIST* IN HIS OWN RIGHT--
LOOK-- LOOTING! ALL OF *THEM.*

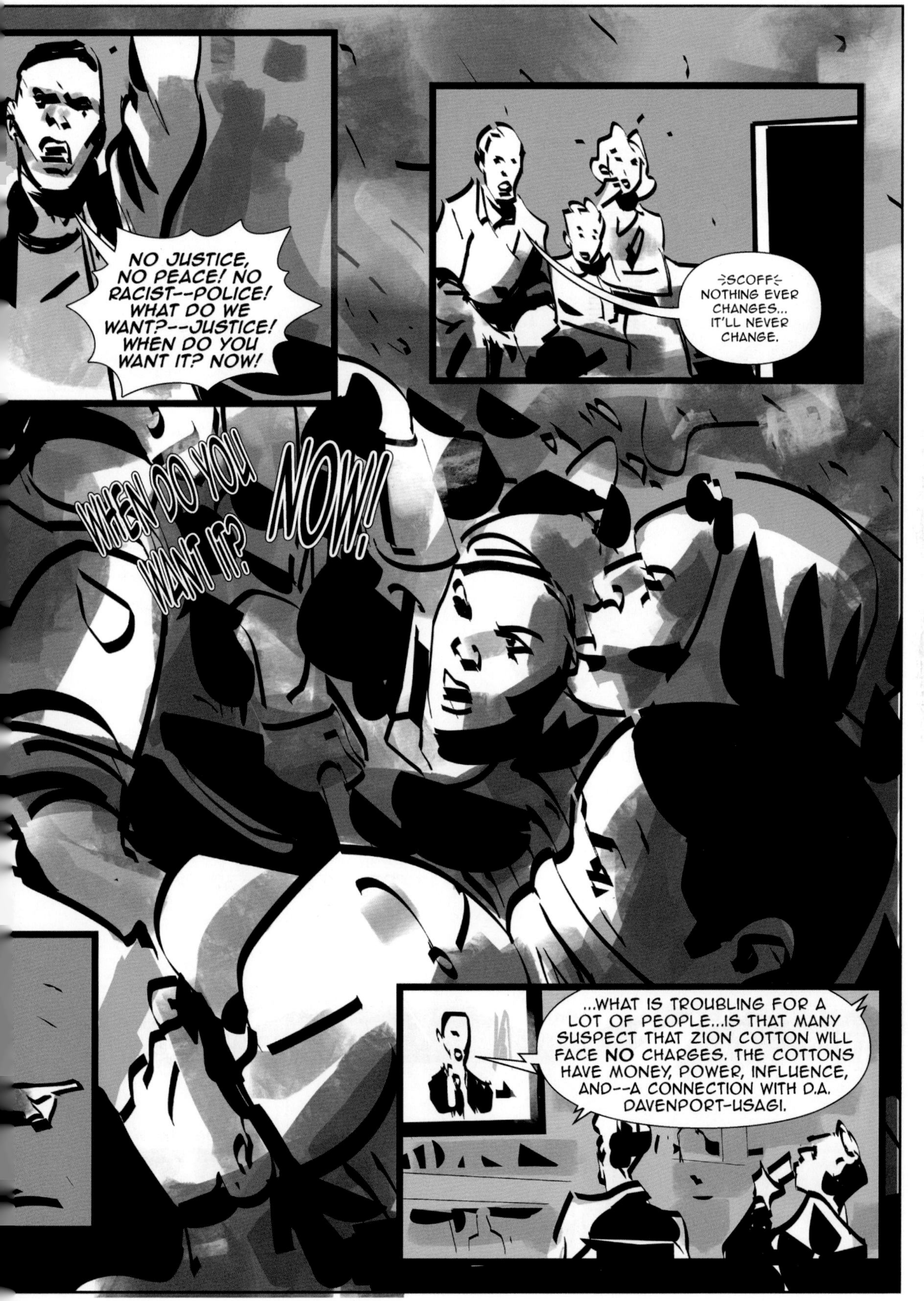
NO JUSTICE, NO PEACE! NO RACIST--POLICE! WHAT DO WE WANT?--JUSTICE! WHEN DO YOU WANT IT? NOW!
SCOFF NOTHING EVER CHANGES... IT'LL NEVER CHANGE.
WHEN DO YOU WANT IT?
NOW!
...WHAT IS TROUBLING FOR A LOT OF PEOPLE...IS THAT MANY SUSPECT THAT ZION COTTON WILL FACE NO CHARGES. THE COTTONS HAVE MONEY, POWER, INFLUENCE, AND--A CONNECTION WITH D.A. DAVENPORT-USAGI.

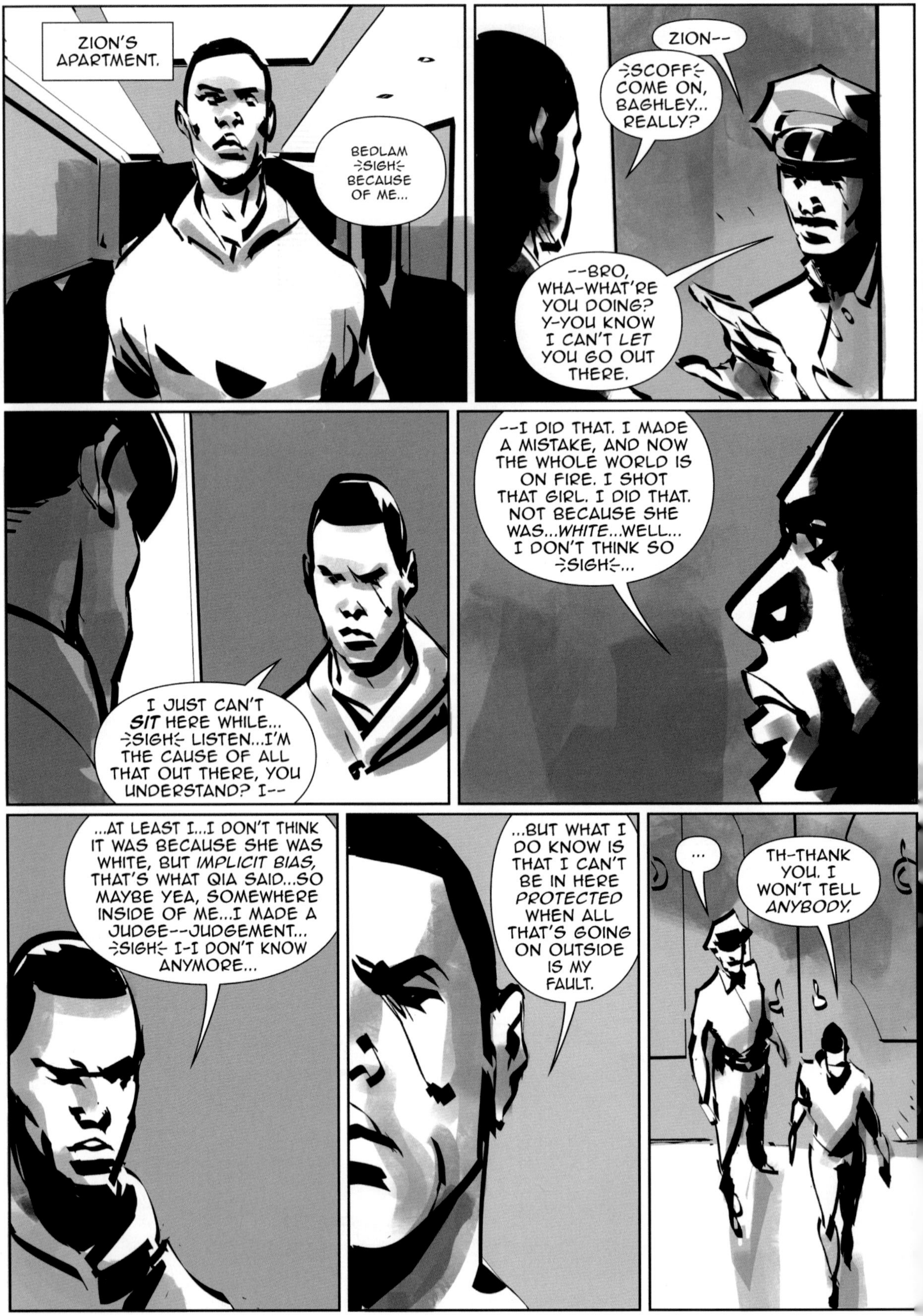
ZION'S APARTMENT.
BEDLAM ⁓SIGH⁓ BECAUSE OF ME...
ZION--
⁓SCOFF⁓ COME ON, BAGHLEY... REALLY?
--BRO, WHA-WHAT'RE YOU DOING? Y-YOU KNOW I CAN'T LET YOU GO OUT THERE.
I JUST CAN'T SIT HERE WHILE... ⁓SIGH⁓ LISTEN...I'M THE CAUSE OF ALL THAT OUT THERE, YOU UNDERSTAND? I--
--I DID THAT. I MADE A MISTAKE, AND NOW THE WHOLE WORLD IS ON FIRE. I SHOT THAT GIRL. I DID THAT. NOT BECAUSE SHE WAS...WHITE...WELL... I DON'T THINK SO ⁓SIGH⁓...
...AT LEAST I...I DON'T THINK IT WAS BECAUSE SHE WAS WHITE, BUT IMPLICIT BIAS, THAT'S WHAT QIA SAID...SO MAYBE YEA, SOMEWHERE INSIDE OF ME...I MADE A JUDGE--JUDGEMENT... ⁓SIGH⁓ I-I DON'T KNOW ANYMORE...
...BUT WHAT I DO KNOW IS THAT I CAN'T BE IN HERE PROTECTED WHEN ALL THAT'S GOING ON OUTSIDE IS MY FAULT.
...
TH-THANK YOU. I WON'T TELL ANYBODY.

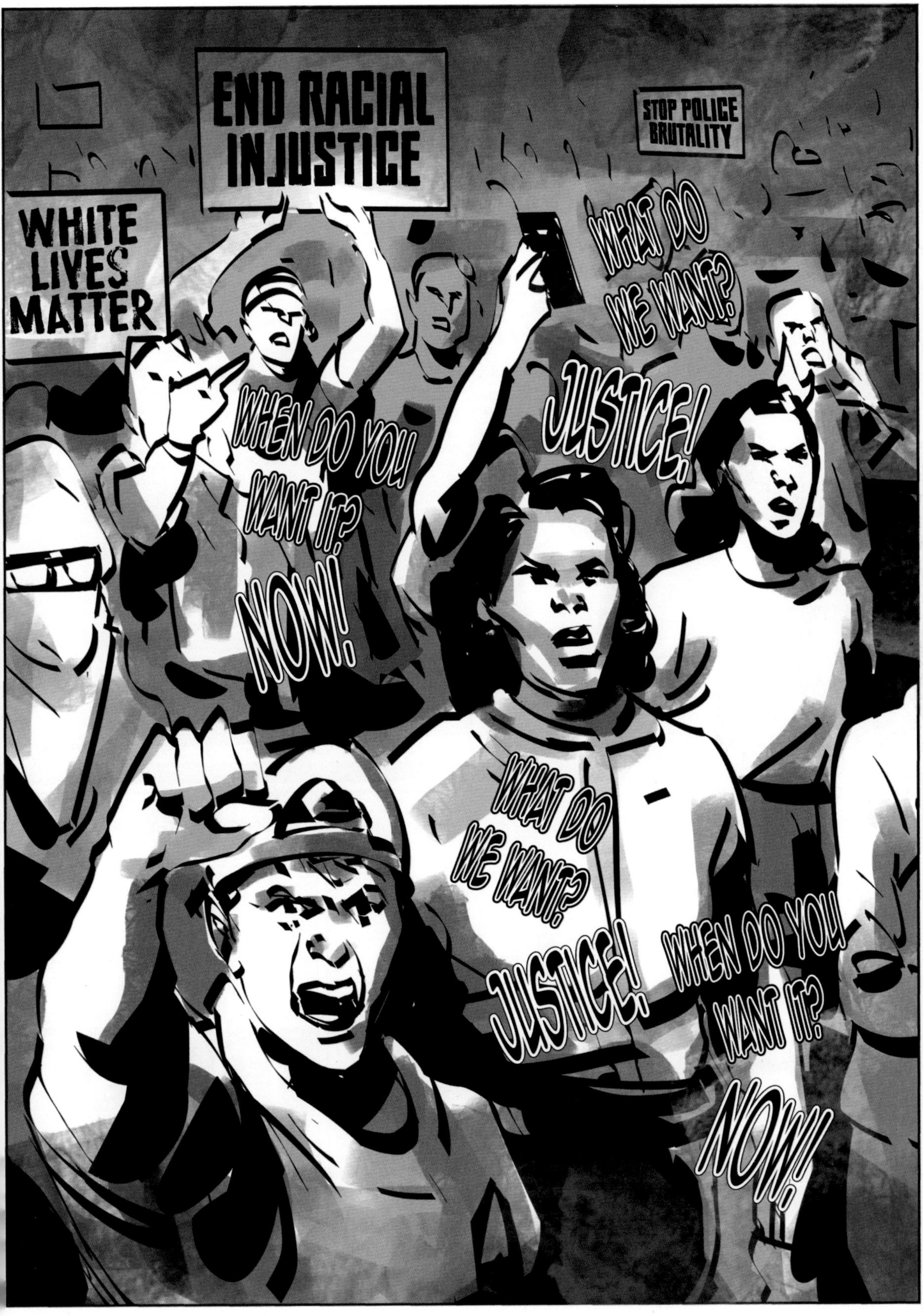
END RACIAL INJUSTICE
STOP POLICE BRUTALITY
WHITE LIVES MATTER
WHAT DO WE WANT?
JUSTICE!
WHEN DO YOU WANT IT?
NOW!
WHAT DO WE WANT?
JUSTICE!
WHEN DO YOU WANT IT?
NOW!

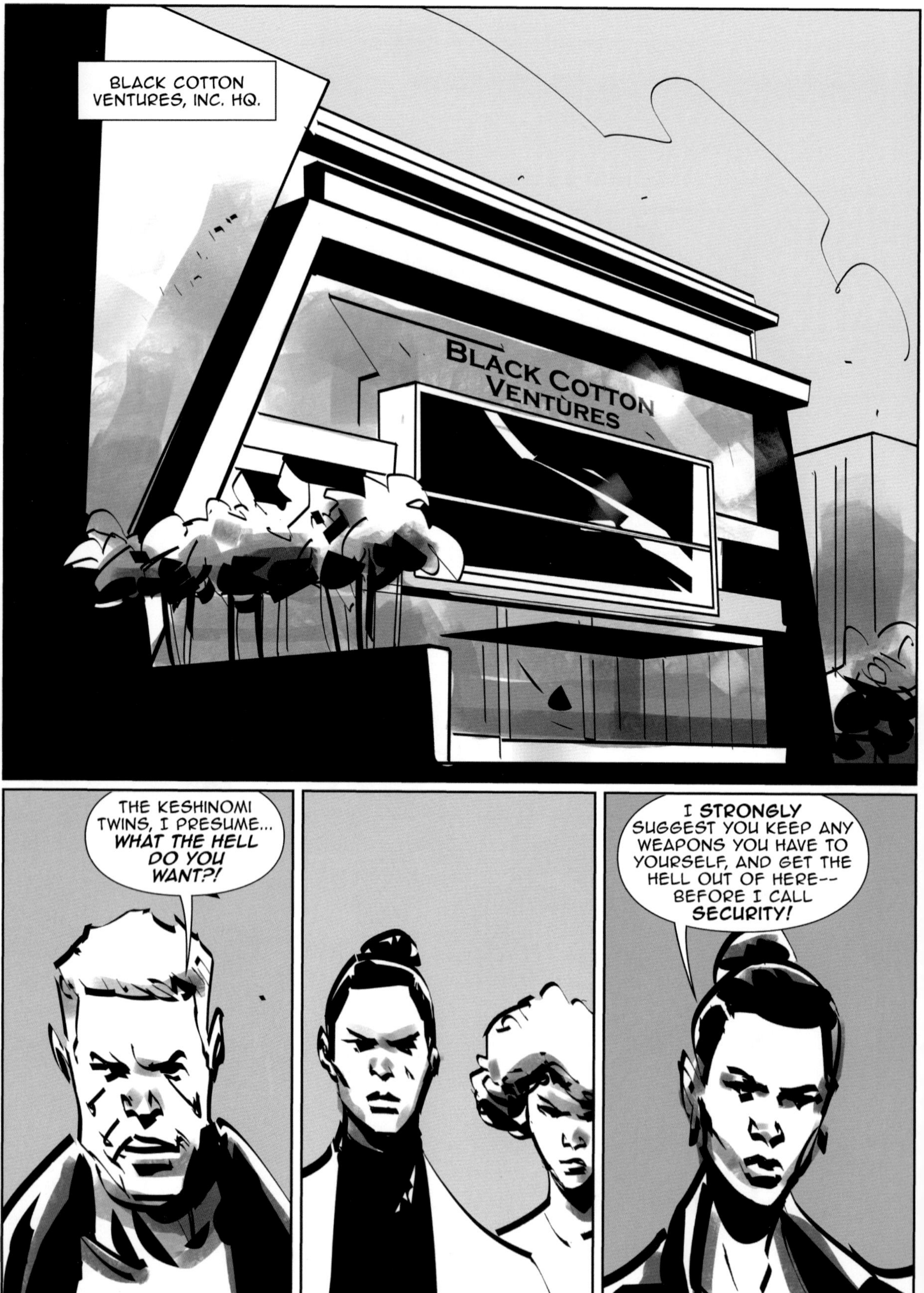
BLACK COTTON VENTURES, INC. HQ.
BLACK COTTON VENTURES
THE KESHINOMI TWINS, I PRESUME... WHAT THE HELL DO YOU WANT?!
I STRONGLY SUGGEST YOU KEEP ANY WEAPONS YOU HAVE TO YOURSELF, AND GET THE HELL OUT OF HERE-- BEFORE I CALL SECURITY!

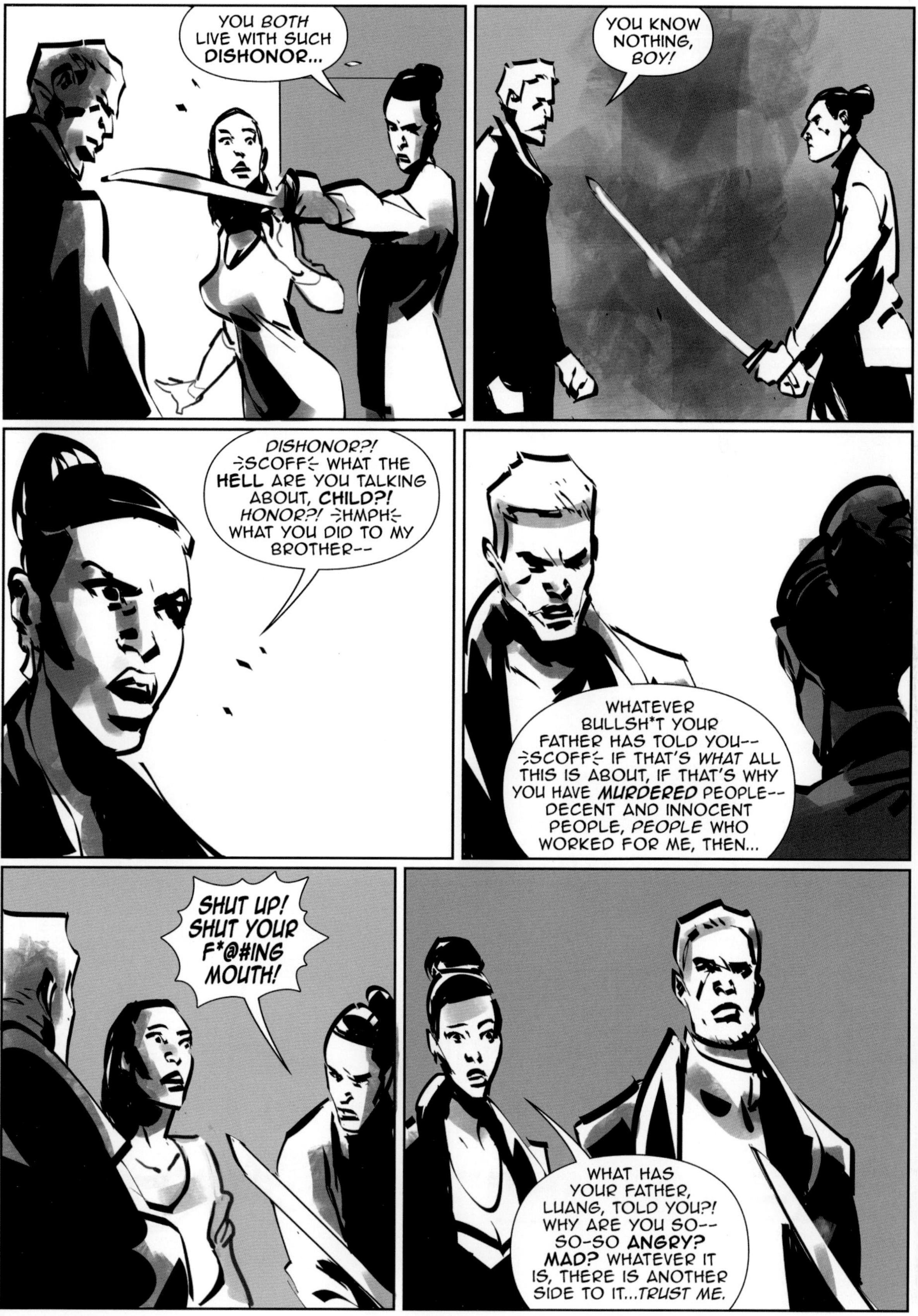
YOU BOTH LIVE WITH SUCH DISHONOR...
YOU KNOW NOTHING, BOY!
DISHONOR?! ~SCOFF~ WHAT THE HELL ARE YOU TALKING ABOUT, CHILD?! HONOR?! ~HMPH~ WHAT YOU DID TO MY BROTHER--
WHATEVER BULLSH*T YOUR FATHER HAS TOLD YOU-- ~SCOFF~ IF THAT'S WHAT ALL THIS IS ABOUT, IF THAT'S WHY YOU HAVE MURDERED PEOPLE-- DECENT AND INNOCENT PEOPLE, PEOPLE WHO WORKED FOR ME, THEN...
SHUT UP! SHUT YOUR F*@#ING MOUTH!
WHAT HAS YOUR FATHER, LUANG, TOLD YOU?! WHY ARE YOU SO-- SO-SO ANGRY? MAD? WHATEVER IT IS, THERE IS ANOTHER SIDE TO IT...TRUST ME.

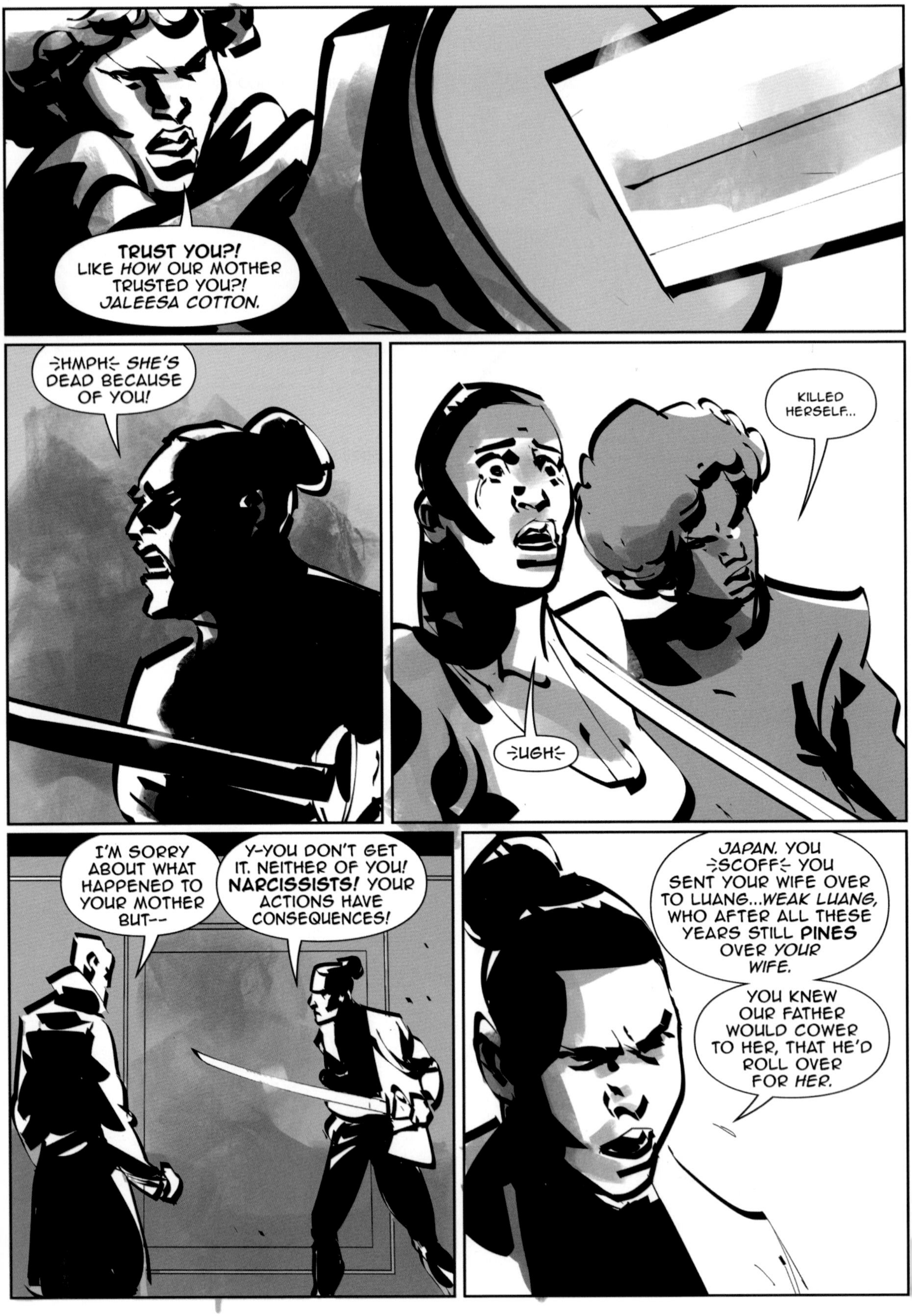
TRUST YOU?! LIKE HOW OUR MOTHER TRUSTED YOU?! JALEESA COTTON.
HMPH SHE'S DEAD BECAUSE OF YOU!
KILLED HERSELF...
UGH
I'M SORRY ABOUT WHAT HAPPENED TO YOUR MOTHER BUT--
Y-YOU DON'T GET IT. NEITHER OF YOU! NARCISSISTS! YOUR ACTIONS HAVE CONSEQUENCES!
JAPAN. YOU SCOFF YOU SENT YOUR WIFE OVER TO LUANG...WEAK LUANG, WHO AFTER ALL THESE YEARS STILL PINES OVER YOUR WIFE.
YOU KNEW OUR FATHER WOULD COWER TO HER, THAT HE'D ROLL OVER FOR HER.

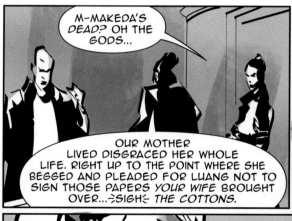

M-MAKEDA'S *DEAD?* OH THE GODS...

OUR MOTHER LIVED DISGRACED HER WHOLE LIFE, RIGHT UP TO THE POINT WHERE SHE BEGGED AND PLEADED FOR LUANG NOT TO SIGN THOSE PAPERS *YOUR WIFE BROUGHT OVER...*⋽SIGH⋽ THE COTTONS.

YOU HAVE **STOLEN, PILFERED, ABSCONDED** WITH OTHER PEOPLE'S IDEAS FOR MILLENIA! IT'S WHAT ALL *BLACK* PEOPLE DO! YOU TAKE CREDIT FOR THE WORK OF OTHERS! NONE OF THIS SHOULD BE YOURS!

⋽SCOFF⋽ BOY, YOU'RE HALF *BLACK!* ⋽HMPH⋽ AND MY FAMILY CAME HERE ON SHIPS FROM AFRICA THAT WERE BUILT BY *OUR* HANDS. BY THE GODS, BOY...THAT-THAT WAS OVER *FOUR HUNDRED* YEARS AGO!

BUT *THEY* DID NOT GET HERE ON THEIR OWN, NOT WITHOUT HELP. *MY* FAMILY--MY ANCESTORS--THEY BARTERED AND TRADED AND **INVESTED** IN YOUR PEOPLE'S EXPLORATION, DID THEY NOT? ⋽SCOFF⋽

THEN *YOUR* PEOPLE **CUT** US OUT! AND *YOU* ARE STILL *CUTTING* US OUT! YOU TOOK OUR FAMILY'S COMPANY... YOU **TOOK** OUR MOTHER FROM US!

SHE WAS YOUR BEST FRIEND, JALEESA... I WANT YOU TO *FEEL* LOSS THE WAY...⋽HNN⋽ THE WAY *WE* DID! WE'RE GOING TO TAKE **EVERYTHING** FROM YOU. PIECE BY PIECE. AND LET YOU WATCH. THOSE WORKERS WERE JUST THE BEGINNING. EVERYONE THAT EATS FROM YOUR TABLE WILL DIE BECAUSE OF YOU!

STARTING HERE...

W-WAIT, NO--!

NOOOOOO--!

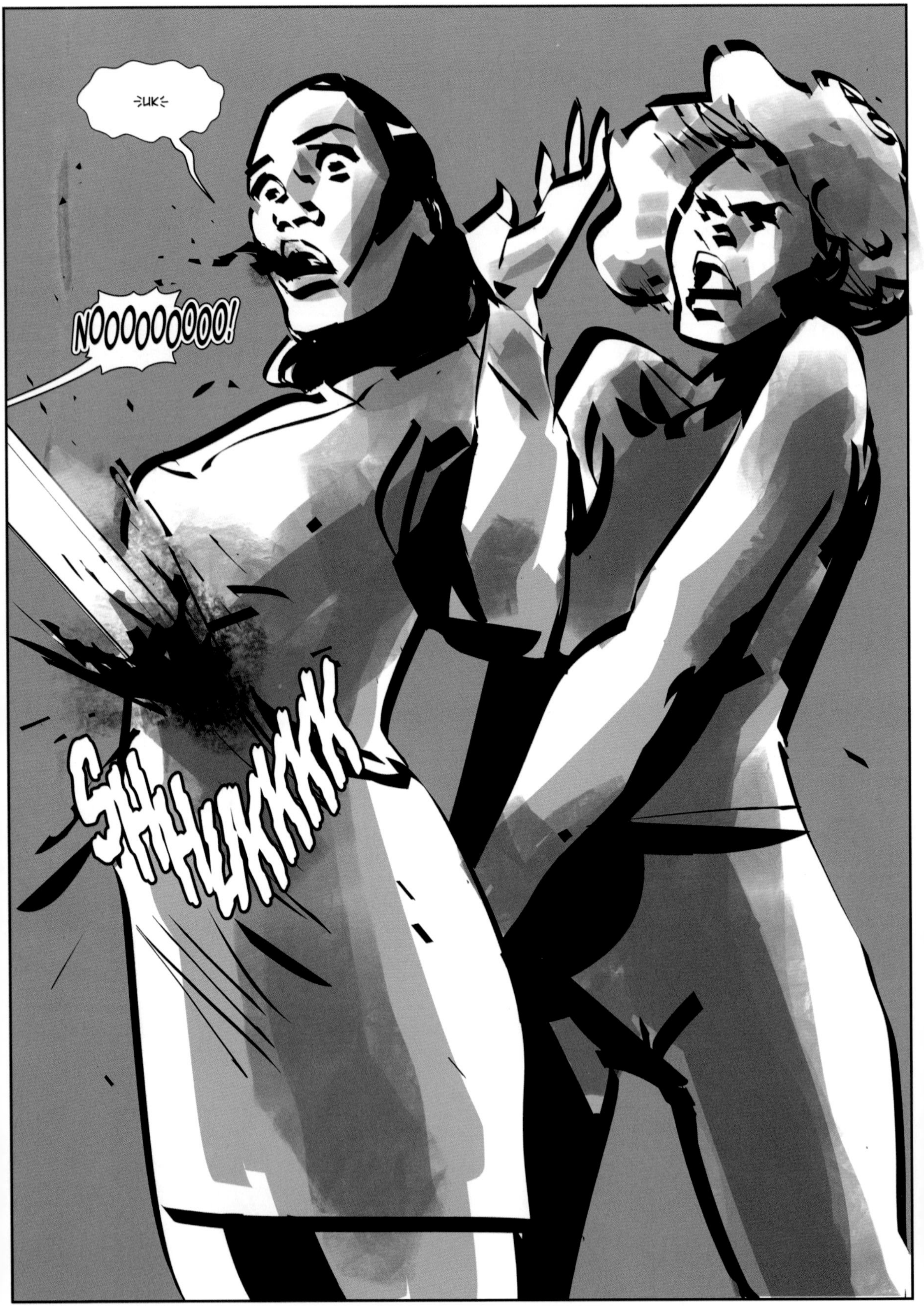

UK
NOOOOOOOOO!
SHHUKKKK

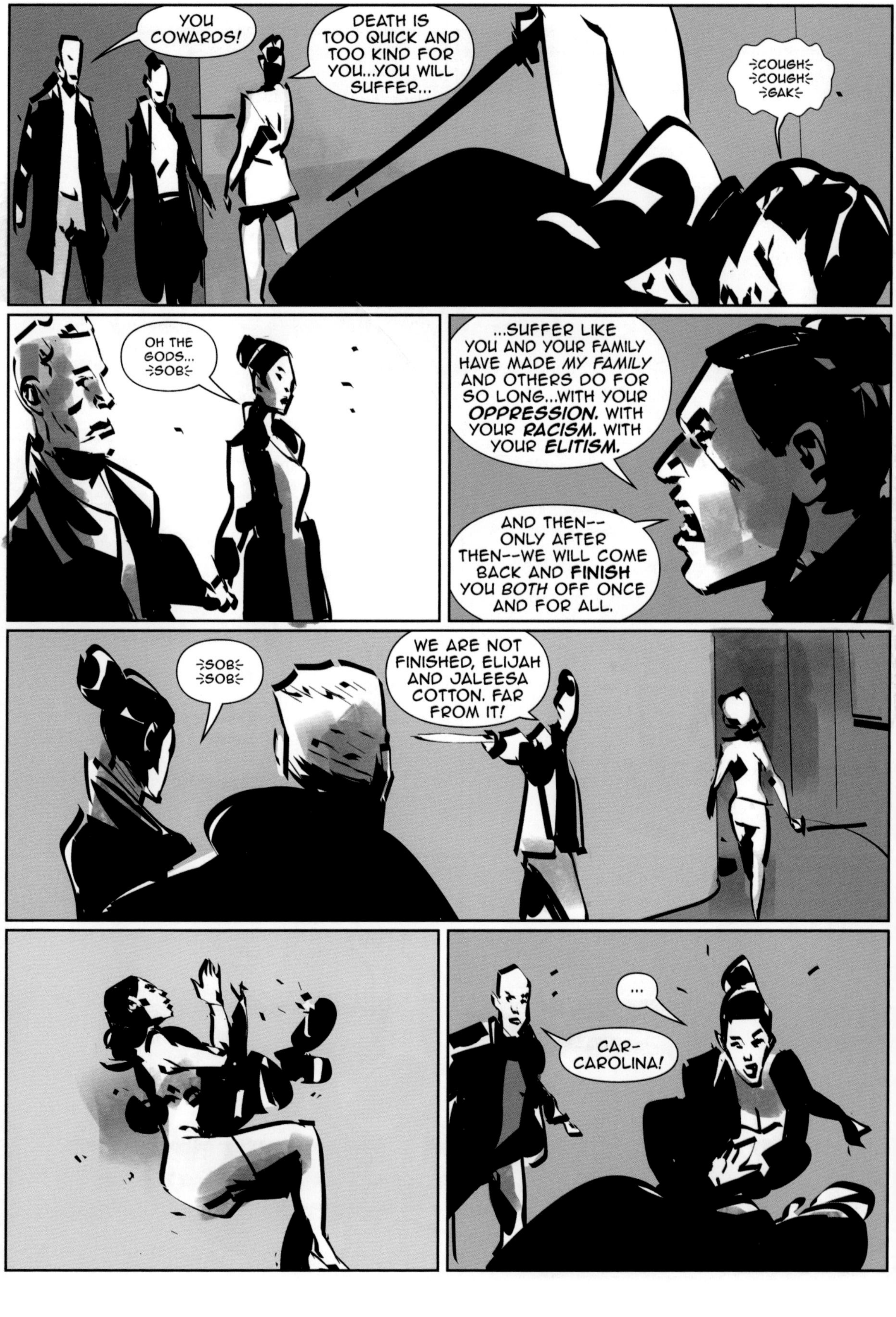
YOU COWARDS!
DEATH IS TOO QUICK AND TOO KIND FOR YOU...YOU WILL SUFFER...
COUGH COUGH GAK
OH THE GODS... SOB
...SUFFER LIKE YOU AND YOUR FAMILY HAVE MADE MY FAMILY AND OTHERS DO FOR SO LONG...WITH YOUR OPPRESSION. WITH YOUR RACISM. WITH YOUR ELITISM.
AND THEN--ONLY AFTER THEN--WE WILL COME BACK AND FINISH YOU BOTH OFF ONCE AND FOR ALL.
SOB SOB
WE ARE NOT FINISHED, ELIJAH AND JALEESA COTTON. FAR FROM IT!
...
CAR-CAROLINA!

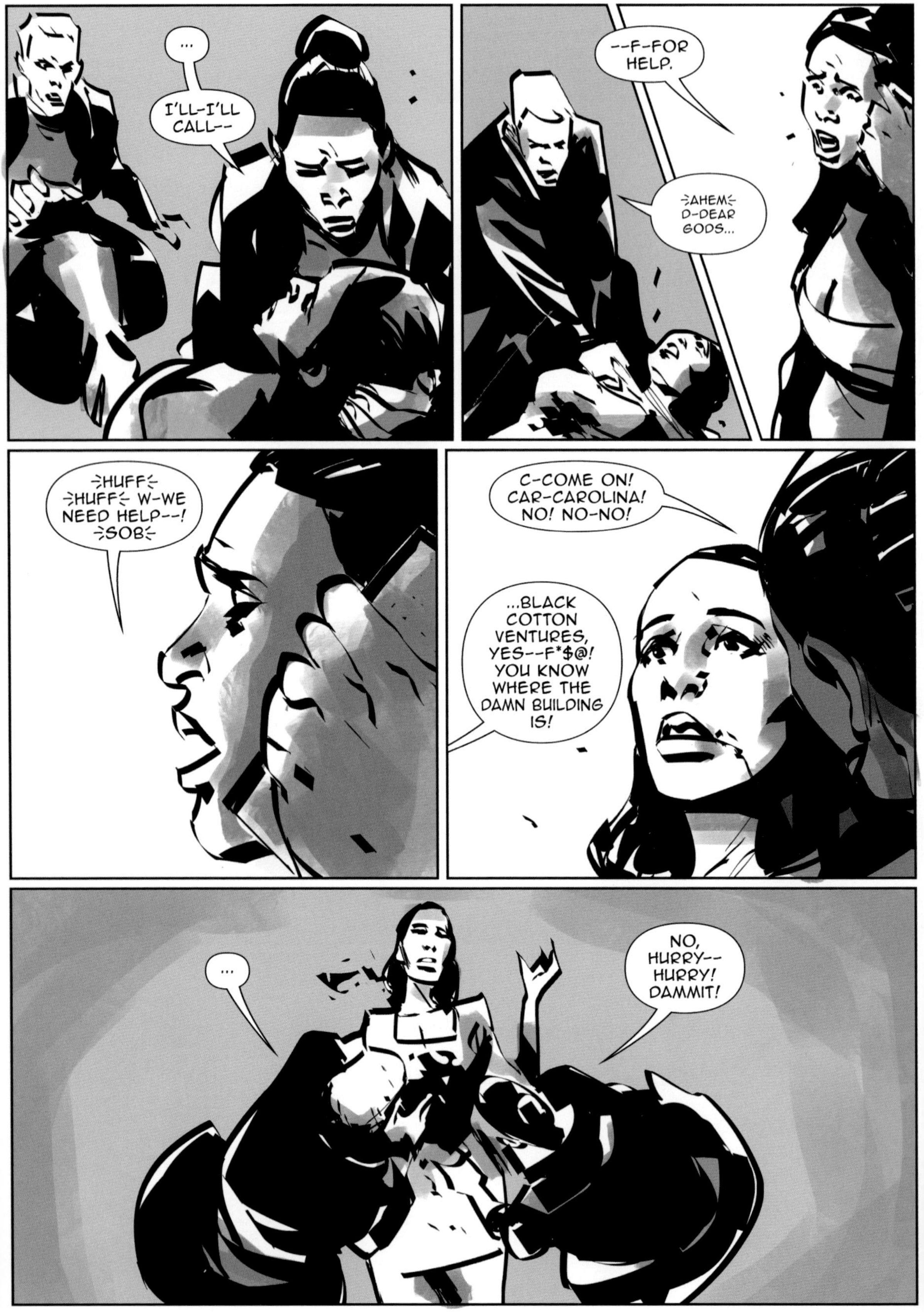
...
I'LL-I'LL CALL--
--F-FOR HELP.
AHEM D-DEAR GODS...
HUFF HUFF W-WE NEED HELP--! SOB
C-COME ON! CAR-CAROLINA! NO! NO-NO!
...BLACK COTTON VENTURES, YES--F*$@! YOU KNOW WHERE THE DAMN BUILDING IS!
...
NO, HURRY--HURRY! DAMMIT!

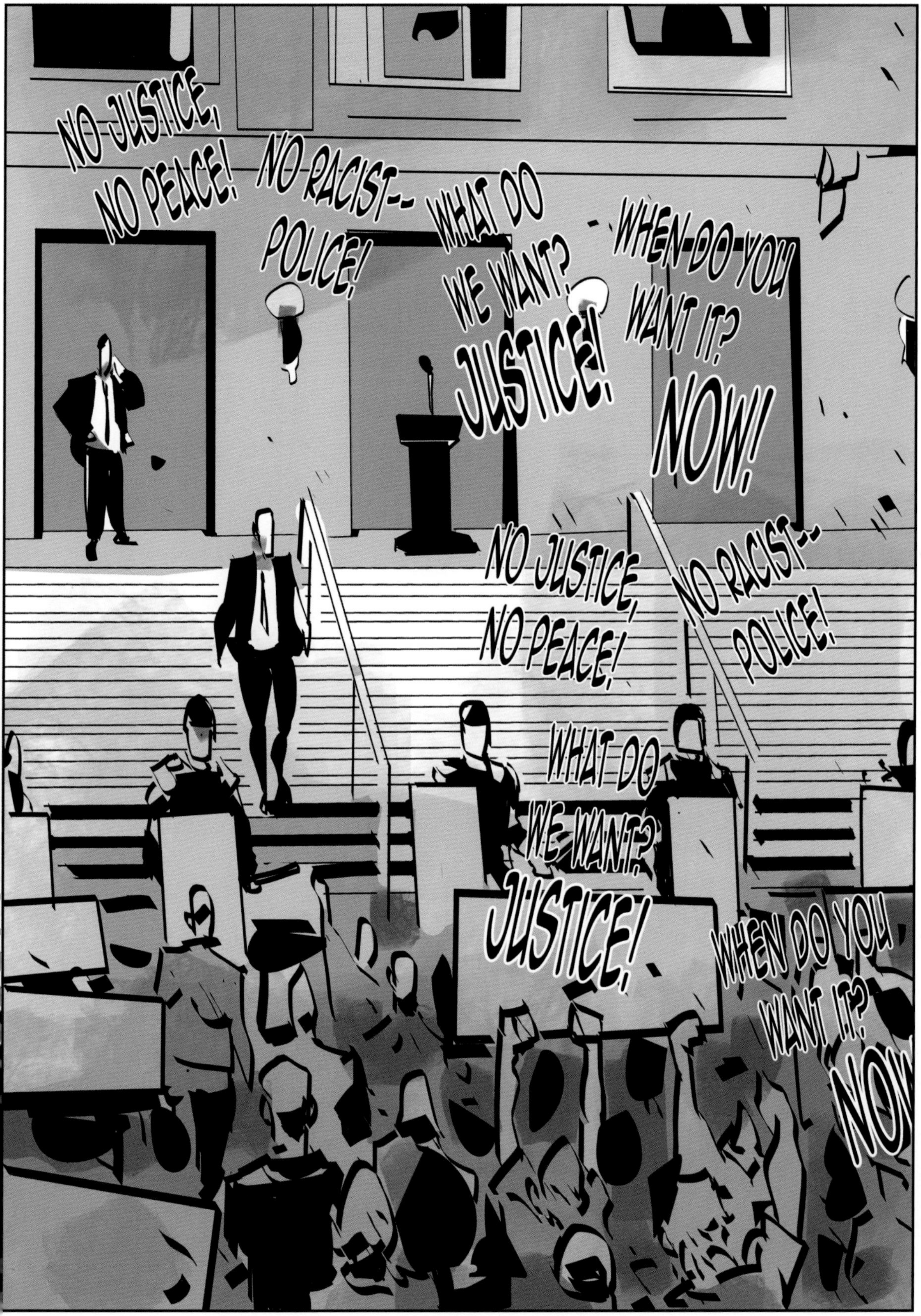
NO JUSTICE, NO PEACE!
NO RACIST-- POLICE!
WHAT DO WE WANT?
JUSTICE!
WHEN DO YOU WANT IT?
NOW!
NO JUSTICE, NO PEACE!
NO RACIST-- POLICE!
WHAT DO WE WANT?
JUSTICE!
WHEN DO YOU WANT IT?
NOW!

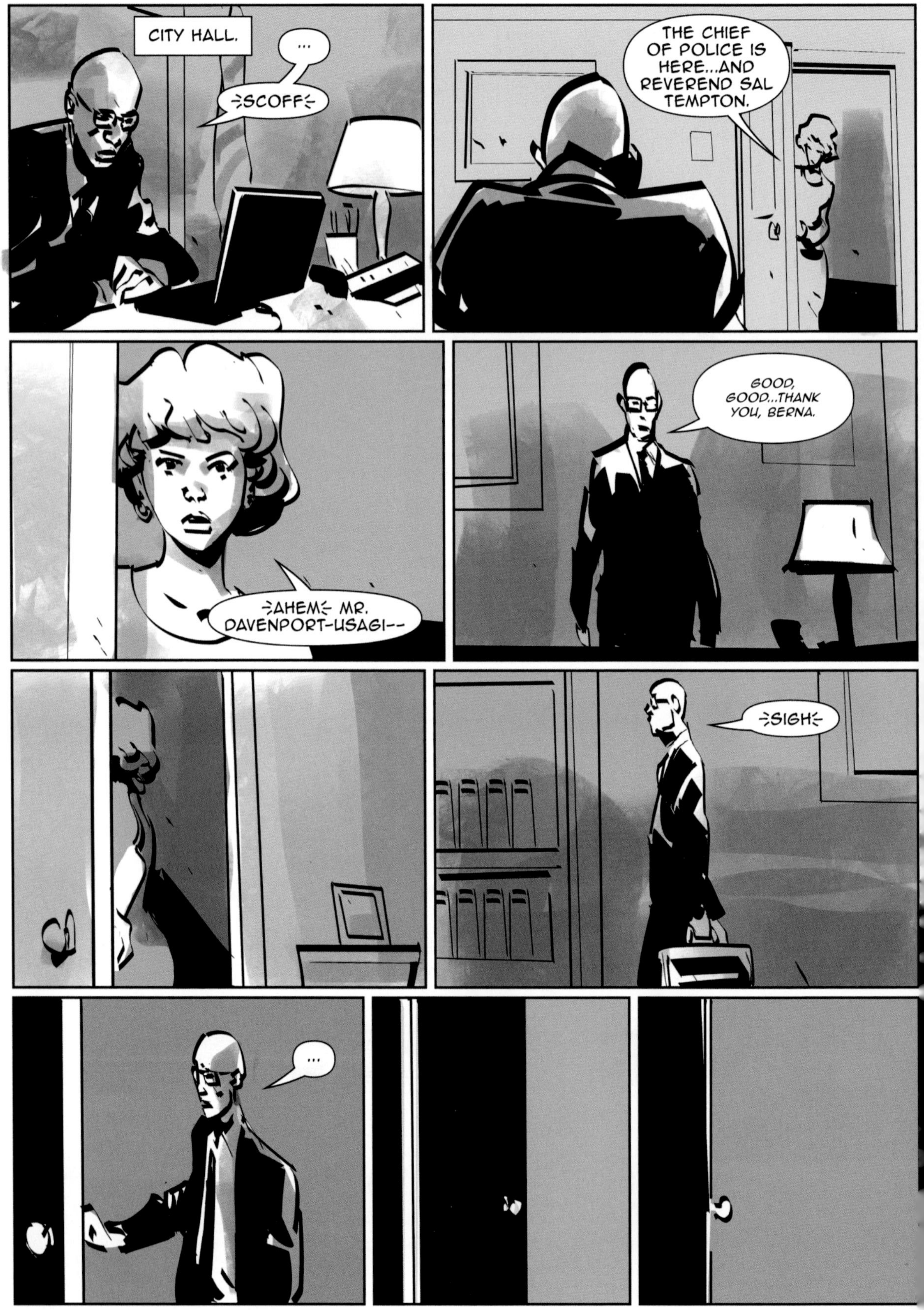
CITY HALL.
...
≈SCOFF≈
THE CHIEF OF POLICE IS HERE...AND REVEREND SAL TEMPTON.
≈AHEM≈ MR. DAVENPORT-USAGI--
GOOD, GOOD...THANK YOU, BERNA.
≈SIGH≈
...

SIGH CHIEF.

CHARLES.

REVEREND TEMPTON,

BLESSINGS, BLESSINGS.

YOU SURE ABOUT THIS?

WE HAVE TO BE...REVEREND TEMPTON--YOU KNOW WHAT TO SAY?

I DO.

GOOD. ASSUAGE THEIR OUTRAGE. HELP THEM UNDERSTAND THAT COMPLIANCE AND WORKING WITHIN THE SYSTEM WOULD BE BEST.

OPIUM FOR THE MASSES...

NO JUSTICE-- NO PEACE!

NO RACIST-- POLICE!

BRUTALITY

WLM

WHAT DO WE WANT? JUSTICE!

END RACIAL INJUSTICE

WHEN DO YOU WANT IT? NOW!

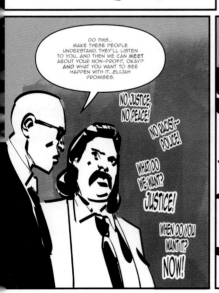

DO THIS... MAKE THESE PEOPLE UNDERSTAND. THEY'LL LISTEN TO YOU...AND THEN WE CAN MEET ABOUT YOUR NON-PROFIT, OKAY? AND WHAT YOU WANT TO SEE HAPPEN WITH IT...ELIJAH PROMISES.

NO JUSTICE, NO PEACE!

NO RACIST-- POLICE!

WHAT DO WE WANT? JUSTICE!

WHEN DO YOU WANT IT? NOW!

NO JUSTICE, NO PEACE!

NO RACIST-- POLICE!

WHAT DO WE WANT? JUSTICE!

WHEN DO YOU WANT IT? NOW!

AHEM

...

NO JUSTICE, NO PEACE!

NO RACIST-- POLICE!

WHAT DO WE WANT? JUSTICE!

WHAT DO YOU

SPLITTT

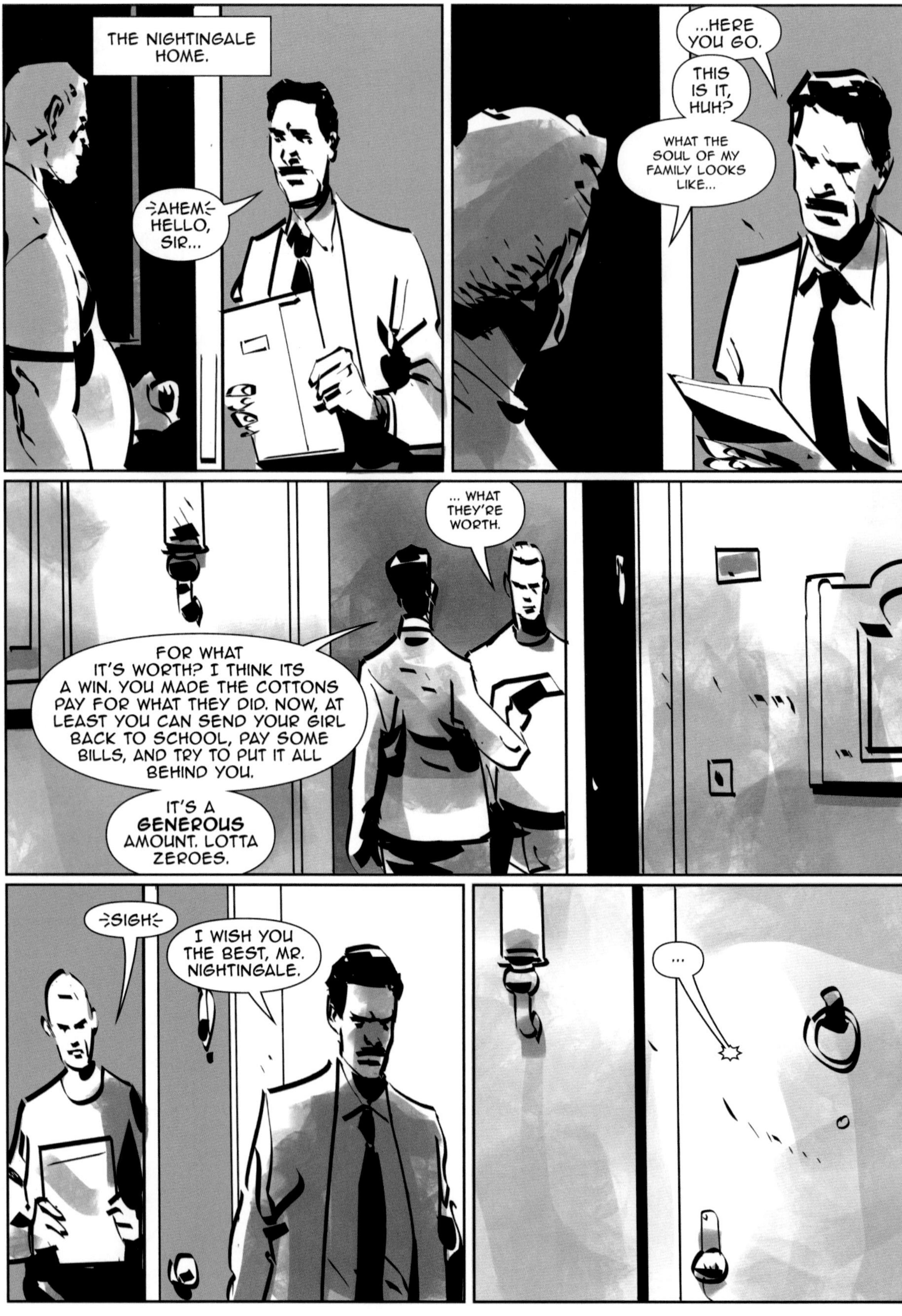
THE NIGHTINGALE HOME.
AHEM HELLO, SIR...
...HERE YOU GO.
THIS IS IT, HUH?
WHAT THE SOUL OF MY FAMILY LOOKS LIKE...
... WHAT THEY'RE WORTH.
FOR WHAT IT'S WORTH? I THINK ITS A WIN. YOU MADE THE COTTONS PAY FOR WHAT THEY DID. NOW, AT LEAST YOU CAN SEND YOUR GIRL BACK TO SCHOOL, PAY SOME BILLS, AND TRY TO PUT IT ALL BEHIND YOU.
IT'S A **GENEROUS** AMOUNT. LOTTA ZEROES.
SIGH
I WISH YOU THE BEST, MR. NIGHTINGALE.
...

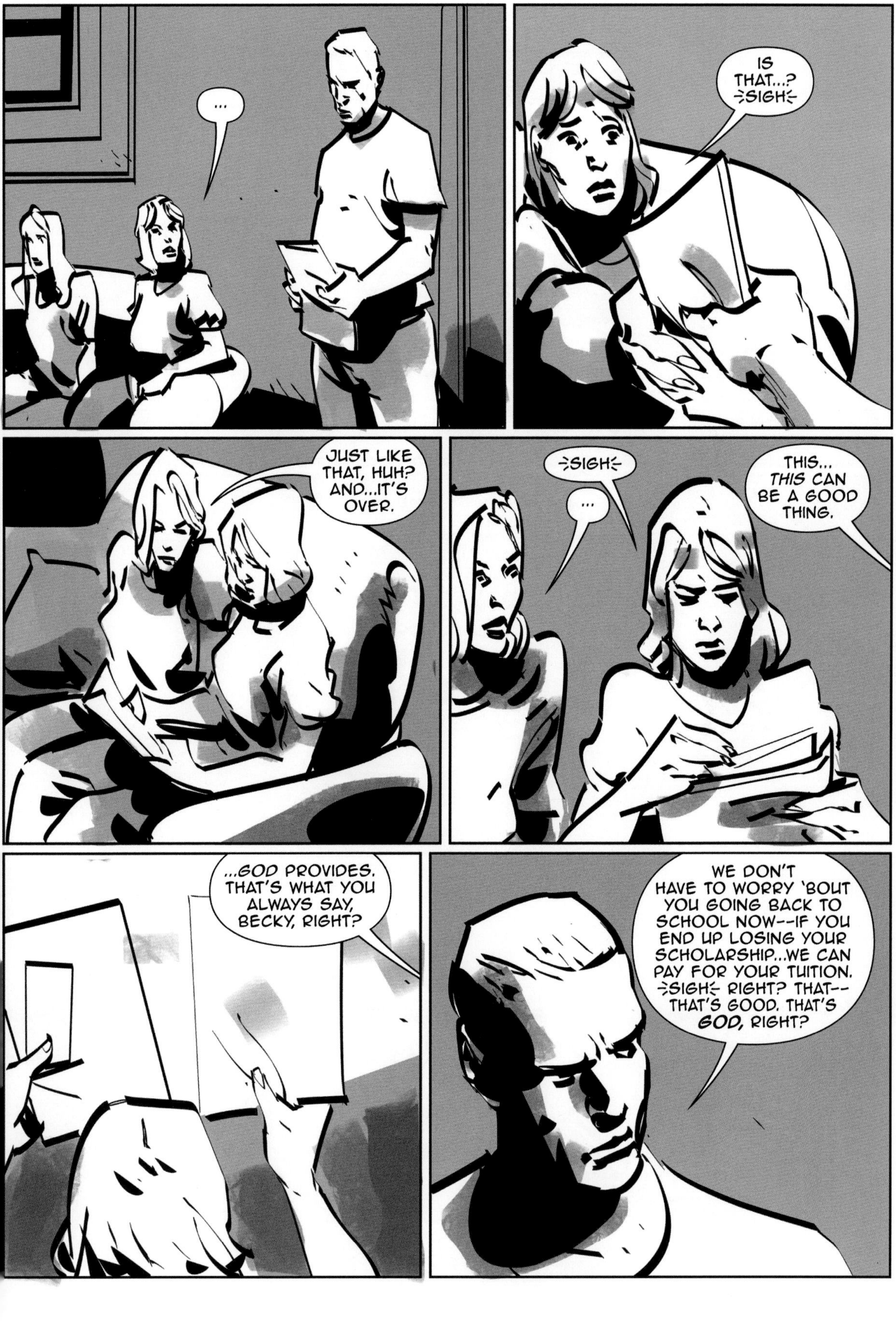
...
IS THAT...? ⊰SIGH⊱
JUST LIKE THAT, HUH? AND...IT'S OVER.
⊰SIGH⊱
...
THIS... *THIS* CAN BE A GOOD THING.
...*GOD* PROVIDES. THAT'S WHAT YOU ALWAYS SAY, BECKY, RIGHT?
WE DON'T HAVE TO WORRY 'BOUT YOU GOING BACK TO SCHOOL NOW--IF YOU END UP LOSING YOUR SCHOLARSHIP...WE CAN PAY FOR YOUR TUITION. ⊰SIGH⊱ RIGHT? THAT--THAT'S GOOD. THAT'S *GOD*, RIGHT?

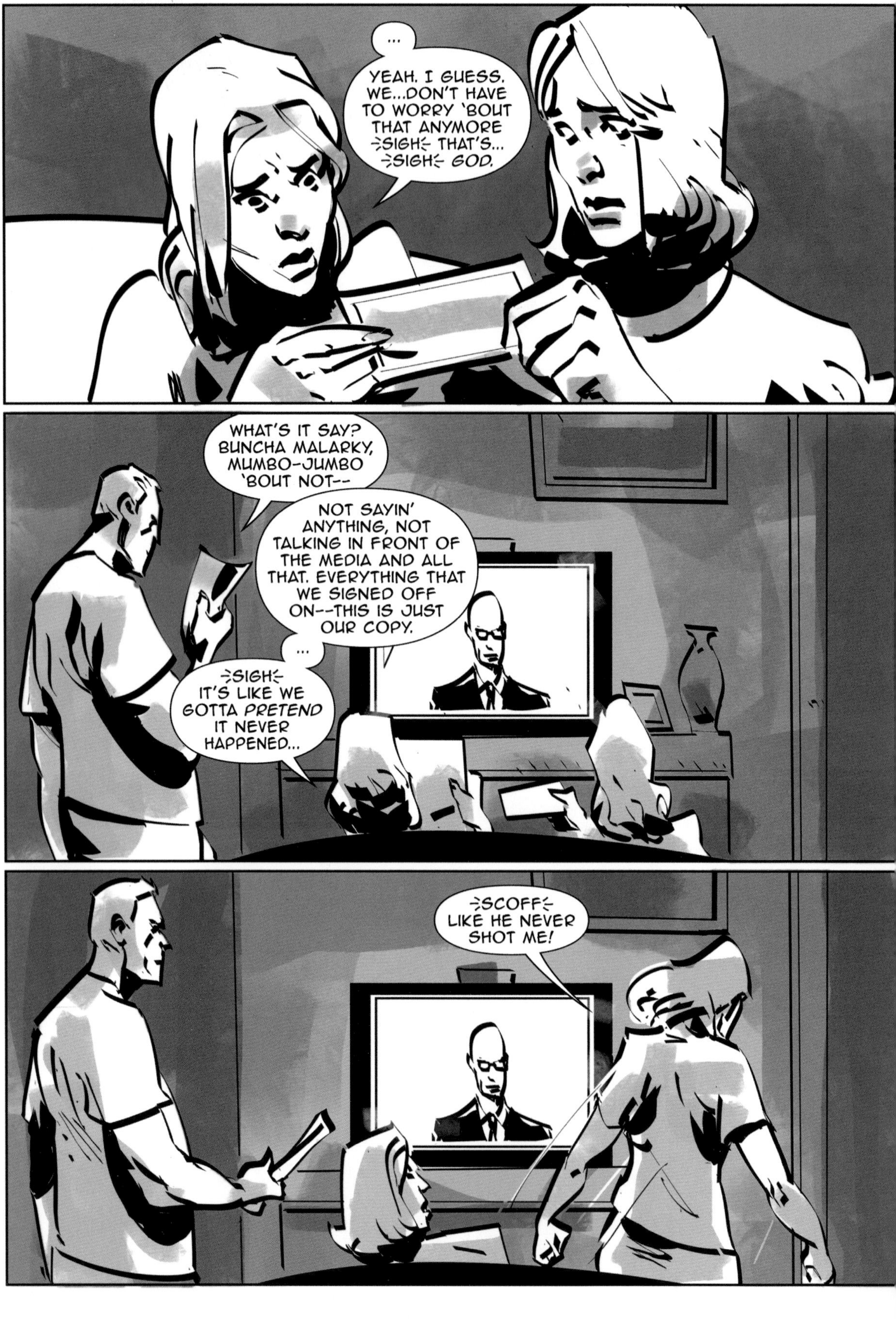
...
YEAH. I GUESS. WE...DON'T HAVE TO WORRY 'BOUT THAT ANYMORE ⁘SIGH⁘ THAT'S... ⁘SIGH⁘ *GOD.*
WHAT'S IT SAY? BUNCHA MALARKY, MUMBO-JUMBO 'BOUT NOT--
NOT SAYIN' ANYTHING, NOT TALKING IN FRONT OF THE MEDIA AND ALL THAT. EVERYTHING THAT WE SIGNED OFF ON--THIS IS JUST OUR COPY.
...
⁘SIGH⁘ IT'S LIKE WE GOTTA *PRETEND* IT NEVER HAPPENED...
⁘SCOFF⁘ LIKE HE NEVER SHOT ME!

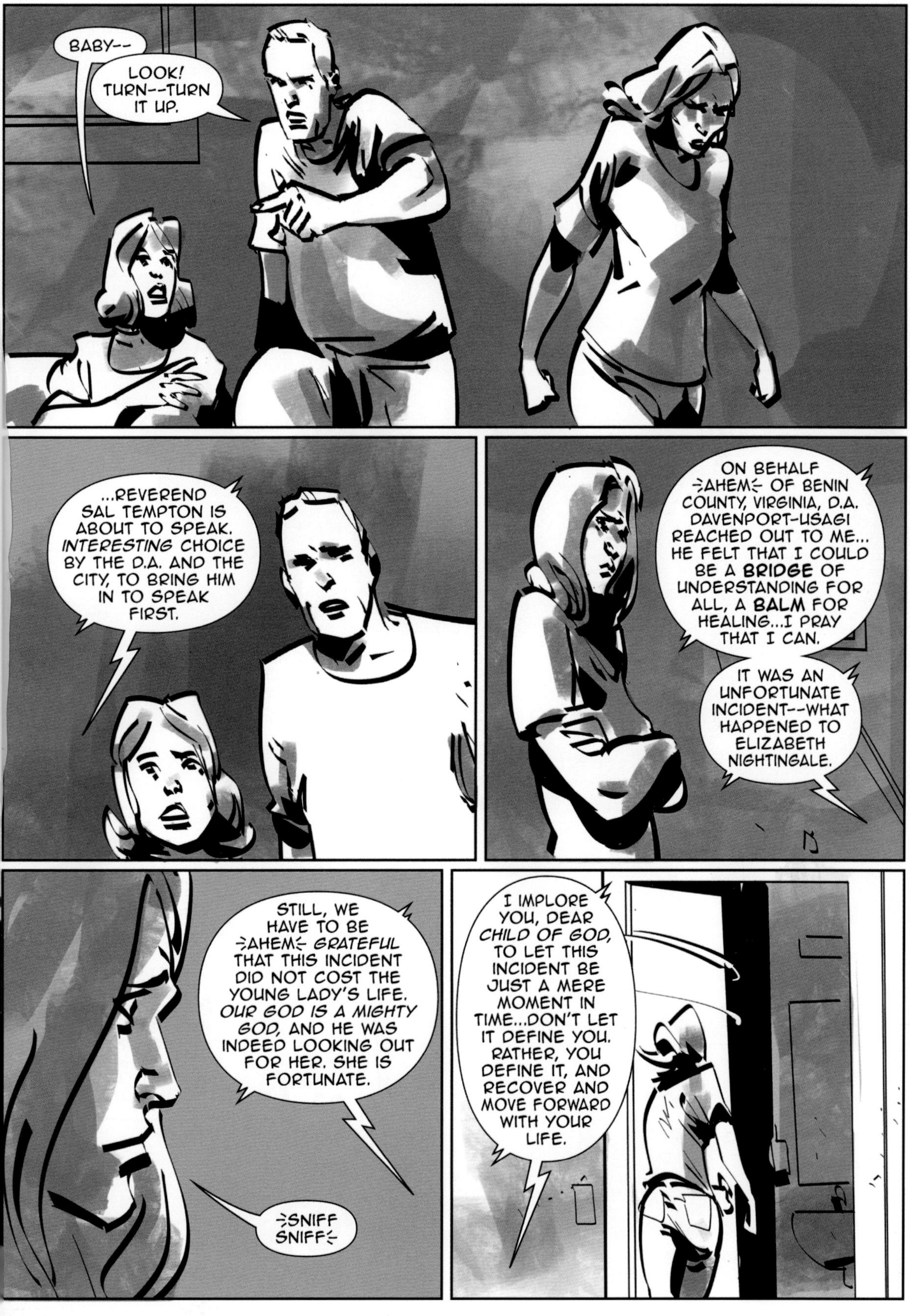
BABY--
LOOK! TURN--TURN IT UP.
...REVEREND SAL TEMPTON IS ABOUT TO SPEAK. *INTERESTING* CHOICE BY THE D.A. AND THE CITY, TO BRING HIM IN TO SPEAK FIRST.
ON BEHALF ⇒AHEM⇐ OF BENIN COUNTY, VIRGINIA, D.A. DAVENPORT-USAGI REACHED OUT TO ME... HE FELT THAT I COULD BE A **BRIDGE** OF UNDERSTANDING FOR ALL, A **BALM** FOR HEALING...I PRAY THAT I CAN.
IT WAS AN UNFORTUNATE INCIDENT--WHAT HAPPENED TO ELIZABETH NIGHTINGALE.
STILL, WE HAVE TO BE ⇒AHEM⇐ *GRATEFUL* THAT THIS INCIDENT DID NOT COST THE YOUNG LADY'S LIFE. *OUR GOD IS A MIGHTY GOD*, AND HE WAS INDEED LOOKING OUT FOR HER. SHE IS FORTUNATE.
⇒SNIFF SNIFF⇐
I IMPLORE YOU, DEAR *CHILD OF GOD*, TO LET THIS INCIDENT BE JUST A MERE MOMENT IN TIME...DON'T LET IT DEFINE YOU. RATHER, YOU DEFINE IT, AND RECOVER AND MOVE FORWARD WITH YOUR LIFE.

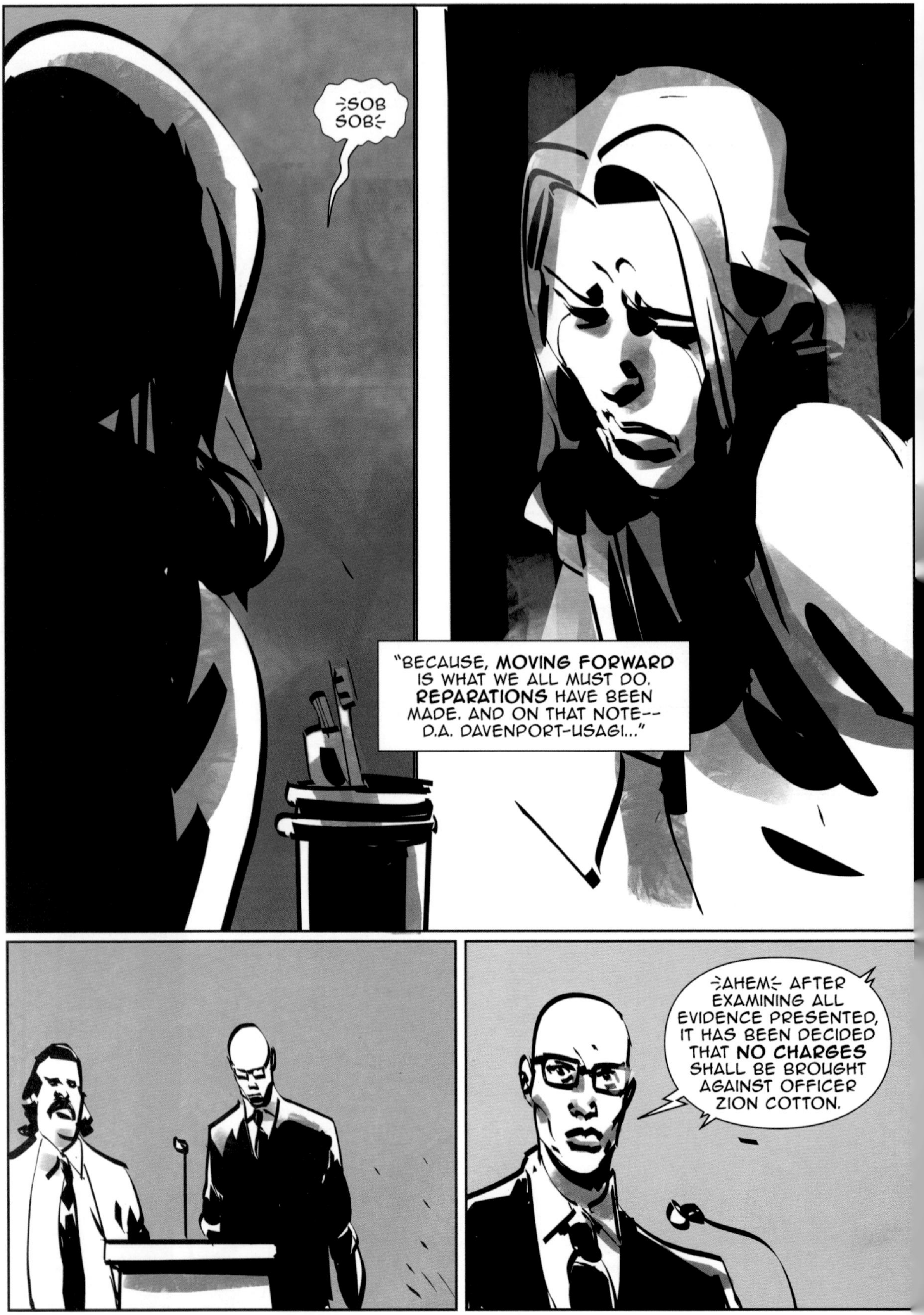

=SOB SOB=
"BECAUSE, MOVING FORWARD IS WHAT WE ALL MUST DO. REPARATIONS HAVE BEEN MADE. AND ON THAT NOTE-- D.A. DAVENPORT-USAGI..."
=AHEM= AFTER EXAMINING ALL EVIDENCE PRESENTED, IT HAS BEEN DECIDED THAT NO CHARGES SHALL BE BROUGHT AGAINST OFFICER ZION COTTON.

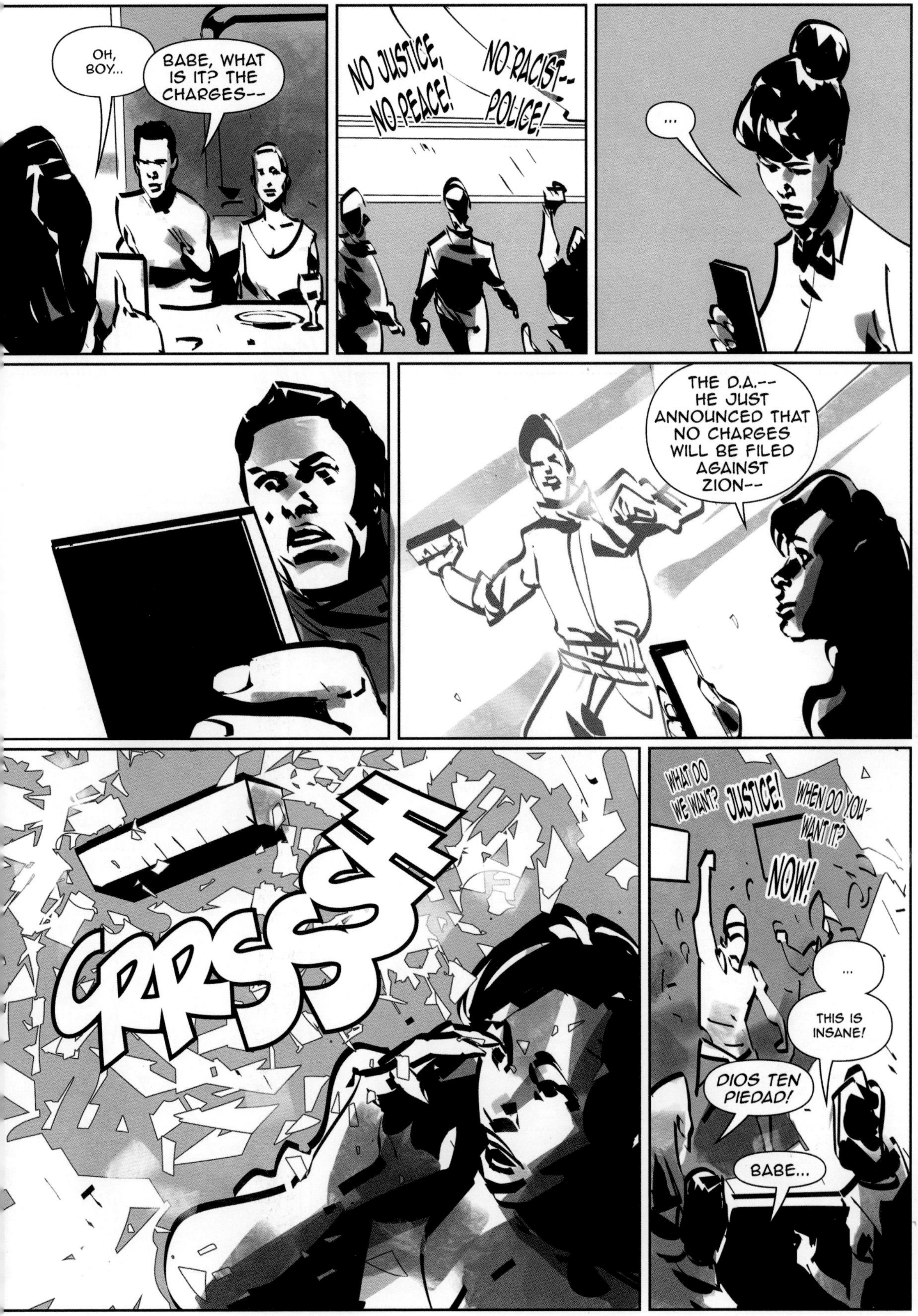
OH, BOY...
BABE, WHAT IS IT? THE CHARGES--
NO JUSTICE, NO PEACE!
NO RACIST-- POLICE!
...
THE D.A.-- HE JUST ANNOUNCED THAT NO CHARGES WILL BE FILED AGAINST ZION--
CRRSSH
WHAT DO WE WANT? JUSTICE!
WHEN DO YOU WANT IT?
NOW!
...
THIS IS INSANE!
DIOS TEN PIEDAD!
BABE...

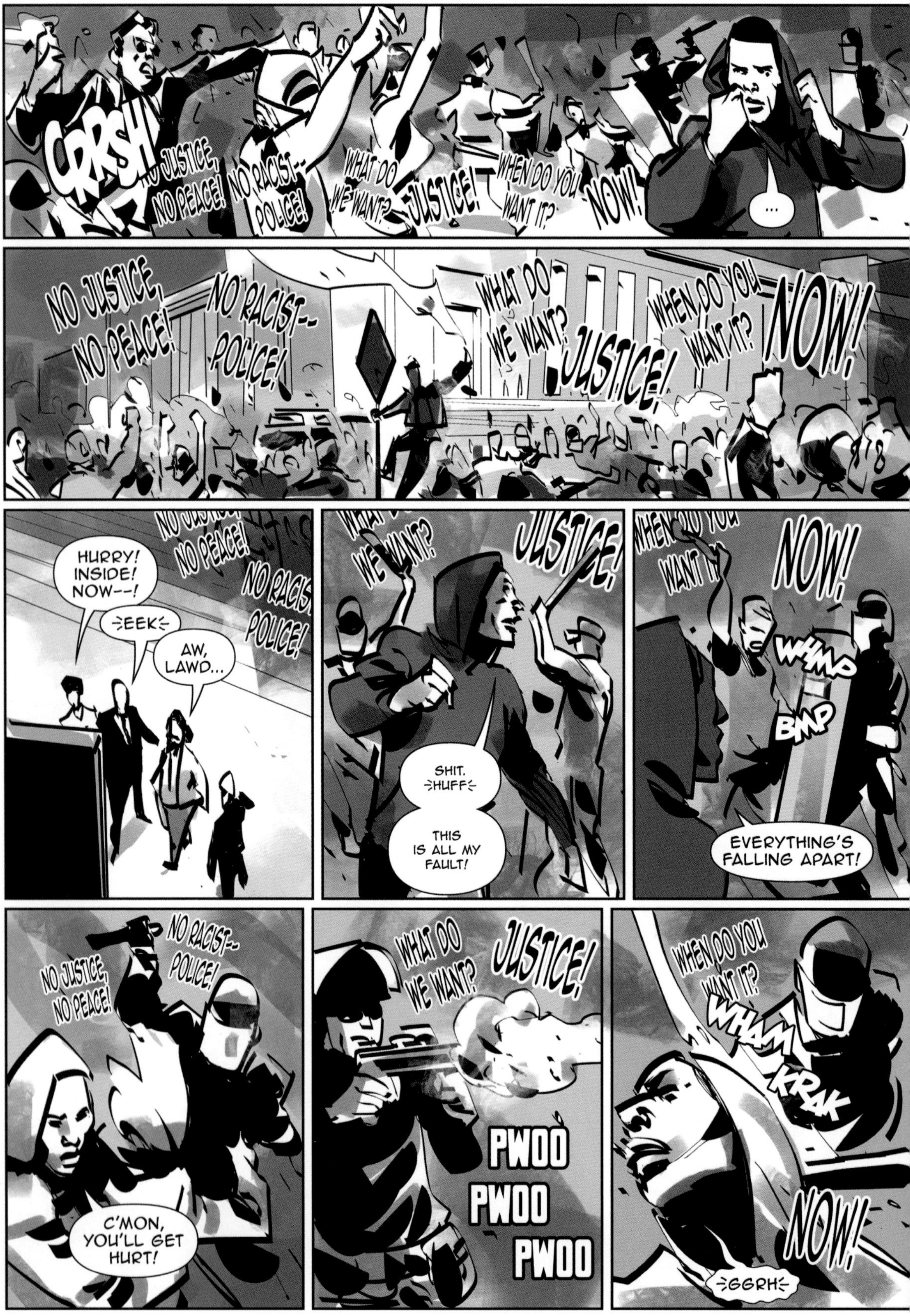
CRRSH!
NO JUSTICE, NO PEACE!
NO RACIST--
POLICE!
WHAT DO WE WANT?
JUSTICE!
WHEN DO YOU WANT IT?
NOW!
...
NO JUSTICE, NO PEACE!
NO RACIST--
POLICE!
WHAT DO WE WANT?
JUSTICE!
WHEN DO YOU WANT IT?
NOW!
NO PEACE!
NO RACIST
POLICE!
HURRY! INSIDE! NOW--!
EEK
AW, LAWD...
WE WANT?
JUSTICE!
SHIT. HUFF
THIS IS ALL MY FAULT!
WANT IT?
NOW!
WHMP
BMP
EVERYTHING'S FALLING APART!
NO JUSTICE, NO PEACE!
NO RACIST--
POLICE!
C'MON, YOU'LL GET HURT!
WHAT DO WE WANT?
JUSTICE!
PWOO
PWOO
PWOO
WHEN DO YOU WANT IT?
WHAM
KRAK
NOW!
GGRH

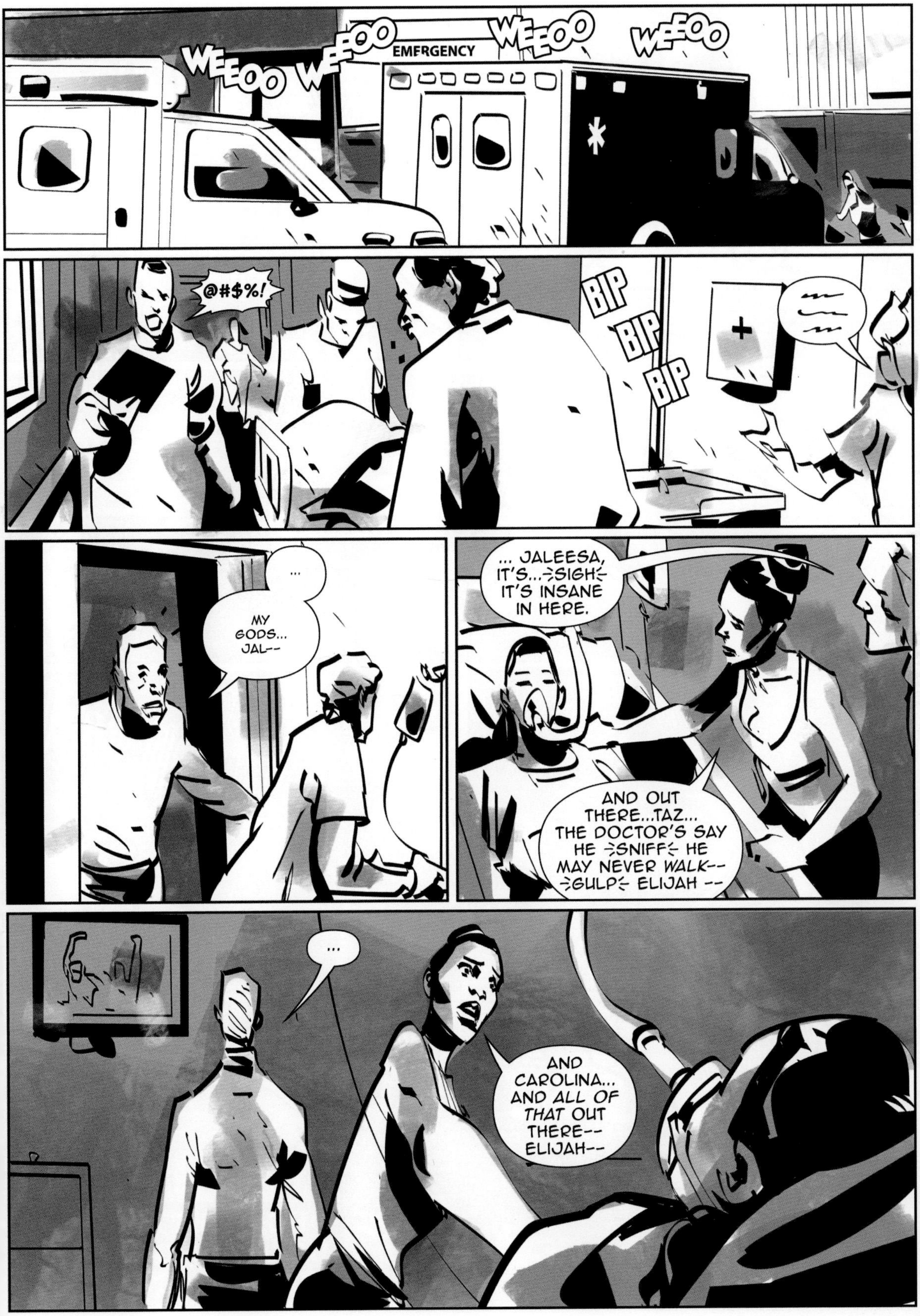
WEEOO WEEOO
EMERGENCY
WEEOO
WEEOO
@#$%!
BIP BIP BIP
...
MY GODS... JAL--
... JALEESA, IT'S... SIGH IT'S INSANE IN HERE.
AND OUT THERE...TAZ... THE DOCTOR'S SAY HE SNIFF HE MAY NEVER WALK-- GULP ELIJAH --
...
AND CAROLINA... AND ALL OF THAT OUT THERE-- ELIJAH--

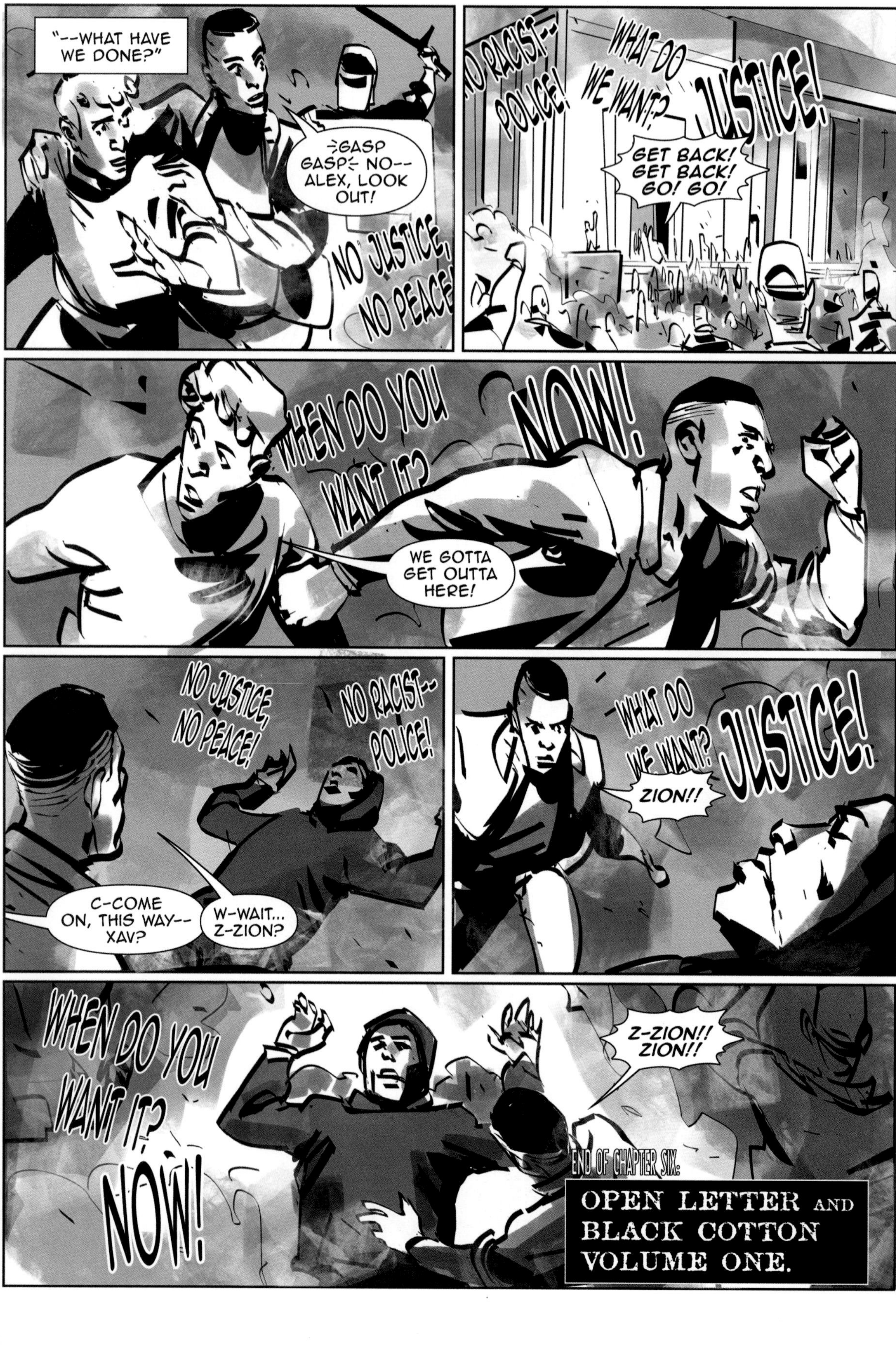
"--WHAT HAVE WE DONE?"
GASP GASP NO-- ALEX, LOOK OUT!
NO JUSTICE, NO PEACE!
NO RACIST-- POLICE!
WHAT DO WE WANT?
JUSTICE!
GET BACK! GET BACK! GO! GO!
WHEN DO YOU WANT IT?
NOW!
WE GOTTA GET OUTTA HERE!
NO JUSTICE, NO PEACE!
NO RACIST-- POLICE!
C-COME ON, THIS WAY-- XAV?
W-WAIT... Z-ZION?
WHAT DO WE WANT?
JUSTICE!
ZION!!
WHEN DO YOU WANT IT?
NOW!
Z-ZION!! ZION!!
END OF CHAPTER SIX:
OPEN LETTER AND BLACK COTTON VOLUME ONE.

**LAST SHOT/
OPEN LETTER**

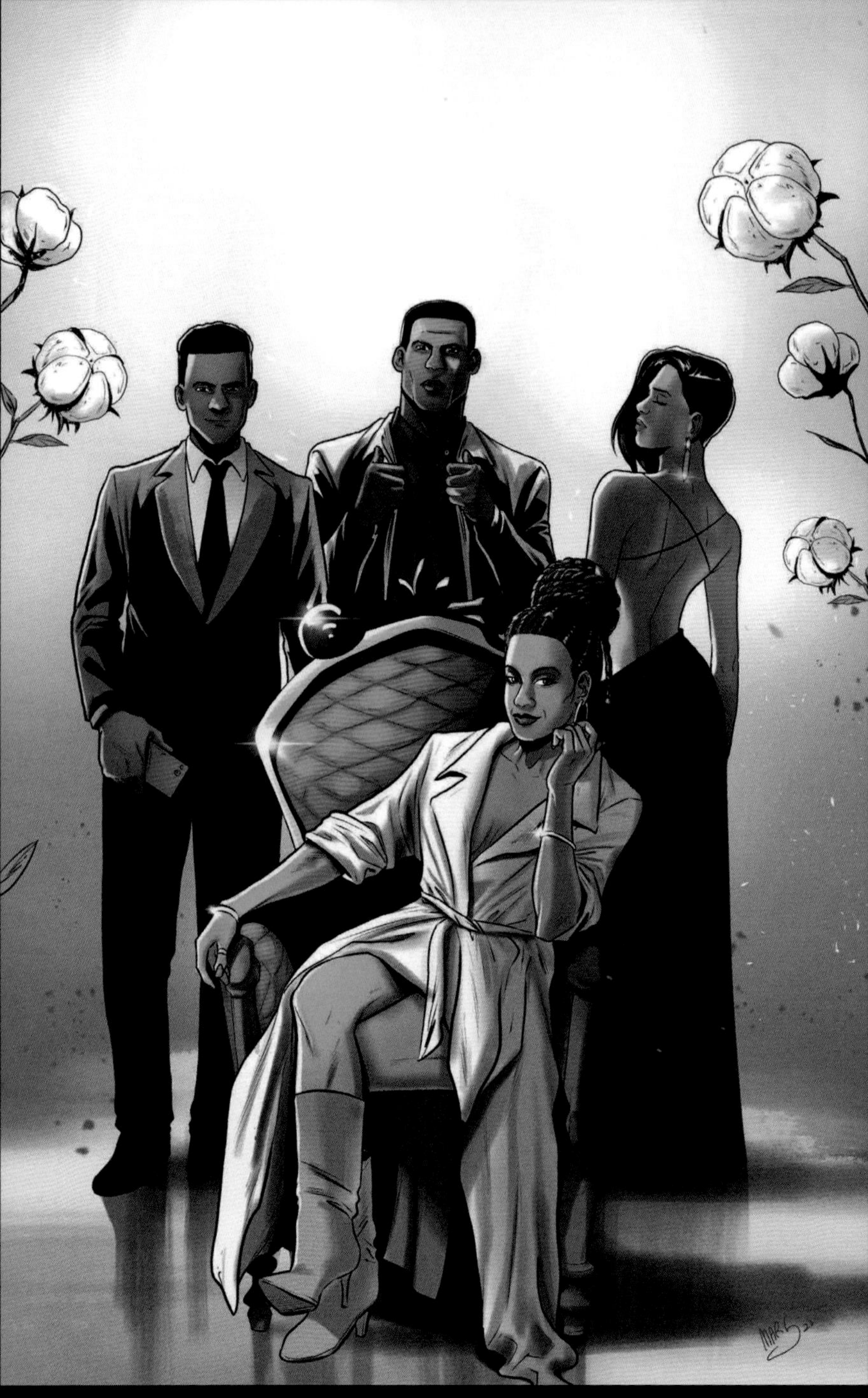

"White Cotton"
by Marcelo Santana

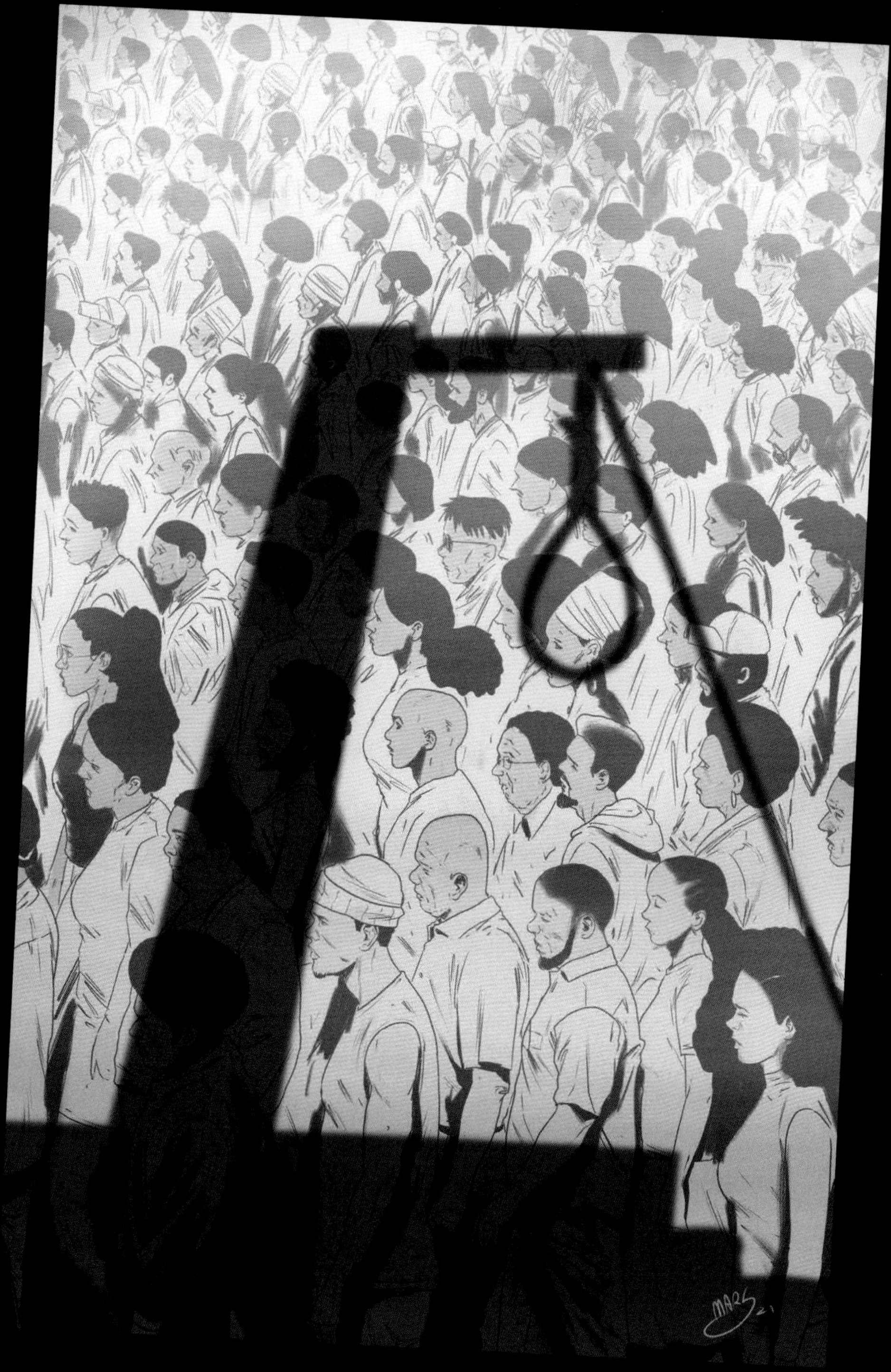
MARS 21

"The Forgotten Ones"
by Marcelo Santana

Sketch of "Qia"
by Marcelo Santana

Black Cotton #5
(cover mockup)
by Marco Perugini and
Jerpa Nilsson

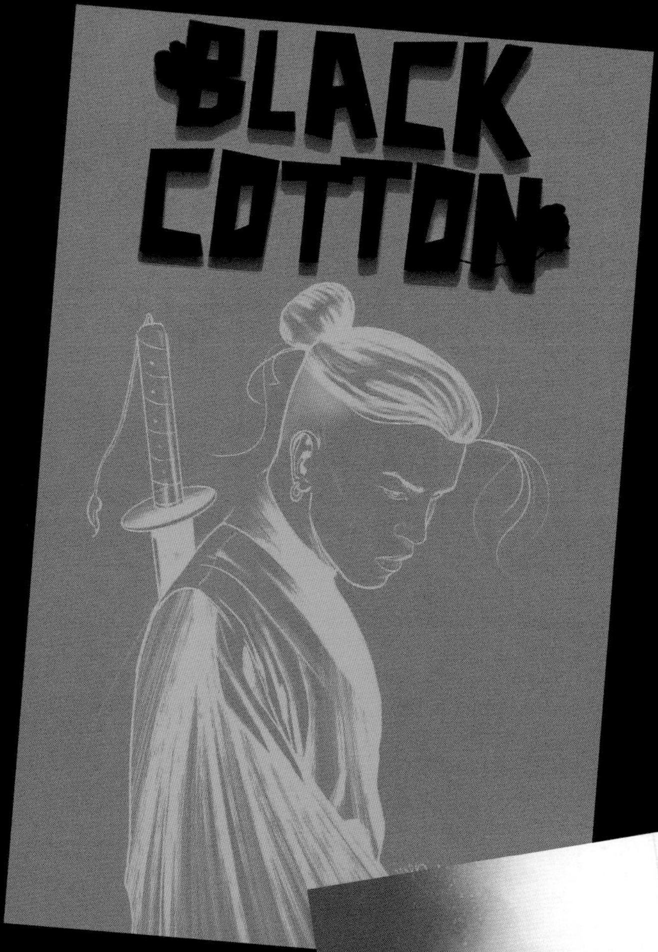
BLACK COTTON

Black Cotton #6
(special negative cover)
by Marcelo Santana

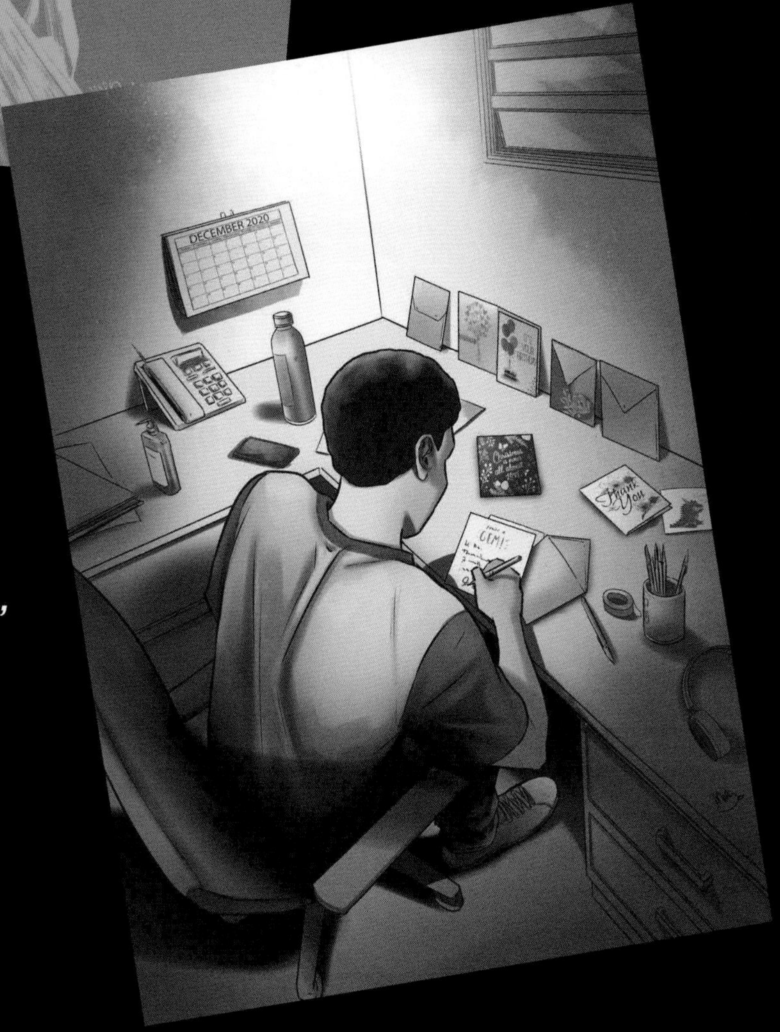
DECEMBER 2020
Thank You

"It's Important"
by Marcelo Santana

It only
seems fitting that we
end this first arc of the series in a
moment of reflection. However, I don't want
to necessarily talk about the *inner* workings of
myself or Patrick in creating this story, nor the brilliance of
Marco Perugini in bringing it to life, or the verve by which the
entirety of our team worked to make this book and series a *thing*.
Those things I think can be seen within the existence of the book
itself, a kind of testament of its own accord. Rather, I would like to take
a few moments to reflect on the impact that *Black Cotton* has had on
me as a *person*.

Black Cotton. The story has challenged me far beyond the last words typed
on the page of the last issue of this arc. Every conversation that Patrick and I
have had, every discourse and/or diatribe between podcasters and reviewers
and ourselves, it's played over in my mind and is heartily ingrained inside
me. And what this all comes down to for me is something that W.E.B. Dubois
wrote so many years ago -- the notion of double-consciousness.

"[T]he Negro is sort of a seventh son, born with a veil, and gifted with
second-sight in this American world, —a world which yields him no true
self-consciousness, but only lets him see himself through the revelation
of the other world. It is a peculiar sensation, this double-consciousness,
this sense of always looking at one's self through the eyes of others, of
measuring one's soul by the tape of a world that looks on in amused
contempt and pity. One ever feels his two-ness, —an American, a
Negro; two souls, two thoughts, two unreconciled strivings;
two warring ideals in one dark body, whose dogged
strength alone keeps it from being torn asunder."

I am left with *this*. Still feeling this. Knowing that my ancestors felt
this, that W.E.B. DuBois felt this and that is why he wrote it, and
it is why (I will only speak for myself) that I co-wrote *Black
Cotton*. As a black man, I still feel *this* and know *this*
well. *Black Cotton* is the manifestation of this double-
consciouness that W.E.B. DuBois wrote about and
coined. It is the *story-manifold* version of it, and each
and every comic page with its panels and dialogue echoes
the truest meaning of double-consciousness.

But it's more than that too. Because the world seems bigger now, but that is only because we have
found ways to capture its vastness and it's variety, and now double-consciousness doesn't just apply to the
"Negro" but it still applies to the many, every single person that feels outside of themselves, looking back in through a societal lens
that's been cast by a group of sometimes nameless and faceless oppressors. My double-consciousness as a black man is equal to
anyone else's -- name it: gender, race, ethnicity, nationality, etc. And that is the truth of *me* and the world we live in, thus my world
view...

We have not gotten better. Humanity has not improved. The seeds of discord and the rot of us is still very much present. What
has gotten better is our ability and willingness to expose it and challenge it. This is the hope. And this is what *Black Cotton* also
encompasses. *Black Cotton* exposes all of us for who we are and challenges us past our perceptions and world views, which teem
with an intrinsic indoctrination that makes up our identity in the most subtle ways. *Black Cotton* is a mirror, and I've used this mirror
to see myself over and over again, and I am still doing so. My reflection and my thoughts as we close this first arc are firmly on *me*
and *who* I am. The only way for me to fully and truly know and understand who I am is to continuously look at myself, my thoughts,
and what's in my mind, where my emotions are, what I am attached to and why... a lot of *why* and a lot of *how*. I guess that's
introspection. But it's become a constant, and what I have found is that it puts me in the *present* more. I am concerned with the *me*
that exists now and how that *me* sees and deals with the world.

So --

BLACK COTTON

Brian Hawkins

Before I get
into my thoughts and reflections,
I must first take this moment and opportunity to
say Thank you to some very special people who are
near and dear to my heart. My Queen, My Equal, My Wife Tara,
you have been my biggest supporter and greatest critic. I truly thank
you, Love for allowing me to shoot for the stars. My Mom and Dad, the
ones who sacrificed so much to raise me, the best that they could, protected
me from the spoils of this world. That is all you can ask for from your parents.
Thank you to my brother Luke Wright because without him Brian and I would not
have met, and *Black Cotton* may still be residing within the realm of thoughts, wishes,
and hopes. The *Black Cotton* team, words could never express the true pleasure it is
to work with such an amazing cast of talented people. Lastly, I would like to thank Scout
Comics and all of the wonderful people who have purchased *Black Cotton*, spoke about
Black Cotton, interviewed us, and wrote reviews on us. It was greatly appreciated and will
never be forgotten.

"Reflection is one of the most underused yet powerful tools for success." - Richard Carlson

As I take this time that has been graciously allotted to me to reflect back on this journey, I am taking
this moment to pause and have serious thoughts about how *Black Cotton* came to existence,
especially now. I guess the real question is why not now? *Black Cotton* has been brewing in
the atmosphere for years but everything has its timing. The world had to arrive to a place
where it could receive and actively listen to the type of message contained within the pages
of *Black Cotton*. Everything we have been witnessing unfolding all around this Nation over
the past four years has allowed this window of opportunity to form for us to bring *Black
Cotton* to you. Many times, I have viewed situations where an individual's perception
is the only perception they are willing to see or consider. Hell, I have done it many times
myself. I too am a work in progress. In the creation of *Black Cotton*, we felt it was
important to give people a safe space to identify perceptions they have and an
opportunity to do some self-reflection without the eyes of others upon them. That
moment is monumental to progression, growth within, and future change.

During this process, I have been introduced to literature I never knew about but
probably should have. I was listening to the *Willie Lynch
Letter & The Making of a Slave* the other day, and it was
an eye-opener for me. It is definitely a hard piece of literature
to hear but one of those pieces of work that provides insight
to the psychological foundation many parts of this land was
built with. That understanding can open eye and possibly create
a new psychological foundation built with empathy. What would
the future look like if empathy was the first action people chose to
deploy before dialog occurs? Just a question.

In closing, I leave you with these words from one of the realest men I
have watched over the years and hope one day to meet him in person; Dave
Chappelle. He stated, "The hardest thing to do is to be true to yourself, especially when
everybody is watching." Throughout this entire *Black Cotton* process, from its creation
to the moment we proofread the last issue of the first story arc, we have tried to keep true to
this very statement with all eyes on us. I cannot tell you how many in-depth conversations Brian and I
have had over these last twenty-four months. Meaningful conversations that have challenged our thoughts,
perceptions, and on several occassions made us take a deeper look at many of the troubling societal issues
erupting not only within America but across this globe. One thing I truly admire about Dave Chapelle is how he
continues to push the line in the content he presents in his comedian stand-ups. He got off the bus and walked. My
dream is that *Black Cotton* will continue to be a thought-provoking work of art that ushers its readers into a meaningful
dialogue with many other people from different walks of life. I hope it starts a chain reaction of individuals not halted by fear
to go against the grain or simply step out on faith to do something that has been on their heart for years. The hardest step is
not the first step, but the thought process in your mind getting you that point where you say YES! That moment right there is
also where your greatest reward lies because it is in that moment that you will replay over and over in amazement in your mind
throughout the entire journey. So, get off the bus and walk. Be a part of the change that you seek... in your environment, in this world,
in your life.

BLACK COTTON

Patrick D. Foreman

Meet the Team

Multi-talented creator and writer. A 25-year retired Marine Corps Master Sergeant. Hails from a small town, Hamburg, Arkansas, but raised in Virginia Beach, Virginia. Chief Operations Officer for the nationally known magazines: *Returning Citizens* and *Positude*. An award-winning gospel songwriter; recipient of the 2020 Independent Music Awards CCM/Gospel Song Winner for his song, "He's Able" featuring legendary vocalist David Scott.

He believes in order for true change to occur people have to be a part of the change that they seek. This is clearly seen in his style of writing and the societal relevant topics he chooses to address.

Patrick D. Foreman

Brian Hawkins is a freelance writer of comic books, novels, and scripts. Additionally, he is an editor for Mad Cave Studios, a freelance writer for BlackBox Comics and Zenescope Entertainment, and the author of two children's chapter books for North Star Editions Publishing. He also has a creator-owned comic book series, *Black Cotton*, with Scout Comics, a self-published horror comic book series titled, *The Lunatic*, *The Lover*, *& The Poet*, and a self-published web-comic titled, *Separate But Equal* on Webtoons. But most importantly, he is a knower of self, enjoys reading and binging on television shows with his wife, and splitting time between playing *LOL Dolls* with his two daughters and watching his son play video games. Find out more about Brian and what he's working on at www.brianhawkinswrites.com.

Brian Hawkins

Marco Perugini works and lives in Italy. He's worked fifteen years professionally in communications for D&G, Nokia, IBM, Iveco, Fox, and special effects and 2D animation for Italian television. He has published the series *Morgan Lost* (Sergio Bonelli Editore), the series *Samuel Stern* (Bugs Comics), various works with *Heavy Metal Magazine*, and the graphic novel *Cuddles* written by Jed McPherson.

Marco Perugini

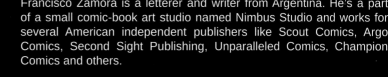

Francisco Zamora is a letterer and writer from Argentina. He's a part of a small comic-book art studio named Nimbus Studio and works for several American independent publishers like Scout Comics, Argo Comics, Second Sight Publishing, Unparalleled Comics, Champion Comics and others.

Francisco Zamora

Marcelo Henrique Santana has a degree in communication and is a lover of different artistic techniques. He studied drawing at some arts institutes in Brazil, and today he works for independent publishers and carries out personal projects, in addition to working as a designer in his spare time. With great skill, Marcelo seeks to position himself in the art and comics industry and at the same time pass his apprenticeships on.

Marcelo Henrique Santana

Jerpa Nilsson is the founder and lead designer of Logical Kaos Design. He is just an everyday Swede. The hand is his symbol because it feels more logical and representative of him that a regular profile pic. He began working a lot with Brian Hawkins and now works on Black Cotton. He has no formal education in the field of work, nor does he draw or sees himself as an actual artist, but since he does work in digital graphics and design, he's decided to be okay with the mantle of Graphic Designer and will continue to do his best to make all projects he's working on come alive to the best of his ability. Reach him at: LogicalKaosDesign@gmail.com.

Jerpa Nilsson

Erica Schultz is an editor and writer best known for her work on Daredevil for Marvel Comics and her participation in DC Comics' first Talent Development Workshop. She was the in-person writing instructor at The Kubert School, and is a freelance editor with Mad Cave Studios.

Erica Shultz

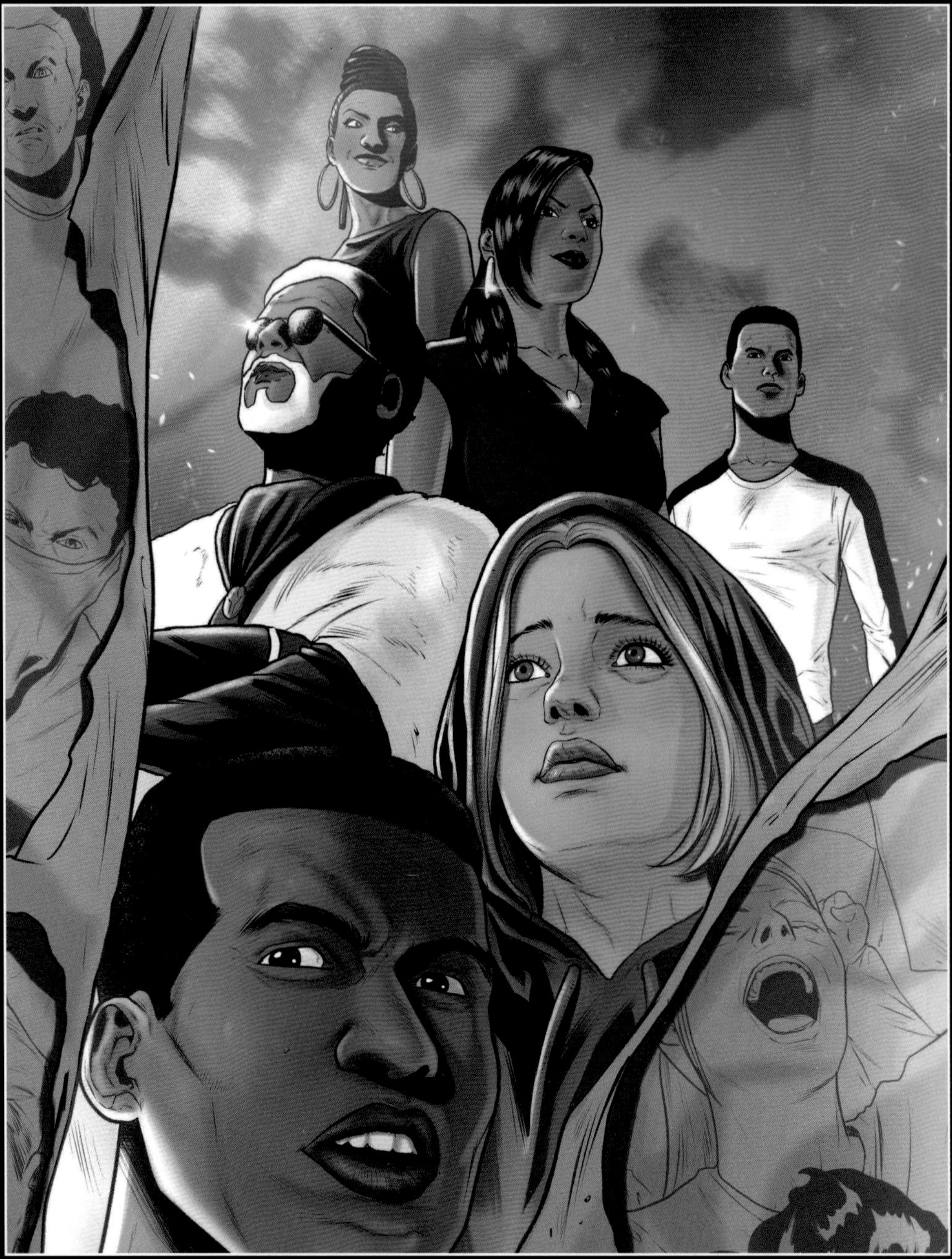

Can't get enough? Follow the struggle at

BlackCottonComic.com